D1456325

THE JOINT VENTURE PROCESS IN INTERNATIONAL BUSINESS:

India and Pakistan

THE JOINT VENTURE PROCESS IN INTERNATIONAL BUSINESS:
India and Pakistan

JAMES W. C. TOMLINSON

The M.I.T. Press
Cambridge, Massachusetts, and London, England

To Mary, who made it all possible, and Julie, who permitted it

CONTENTS

Appendixes

LIST OF TABLES

LIST OF FIGURES

PREFACE

Arguments for and against joint ventures range to extremes which are virtually ideological in their intensity of cathexis and lack of factual supporting evidence. On the one hand, there is the *simpliste* school for which any potential interference with absolute freedom to conduct a multinational enterprise is abhorrent and must at any cost be avoided. On the other hand, there are the *philanthropists* or developmental idealists for whom the sheer beauty of the concept of international cooperation appears at times to be a sufficient end in itself.

There is, of course, a third school—the *strategic pragmatists*—for whom this book is written. For this group, ownership is merely one dimension in the appraisal matrix of the international investor; it is not a sacred artifact. If the market is worth penetrating or developing, if the location of operations is significant to international integration, if the level of return to the investor is right, then "one must be there," and structure is strictly a subsidiary issue, in which case, analysis of tactical possibilities for exploiting an opportunity should presumably include joint operations as one of a number of structural alternatives. This in turn implies that, without necessarily joining the second school mentioned, joint ventures should be considered for overseas operations in any case. The argument becomes stronger in practice, though no more significant in terms of overall strategic concepts, if such ventures are formally prescribed by host authorities.

In order to get away from subjective or quasi-ideological bases for consideration, it seems desirable to analyze in detail some of the measurable dimensions in the joint venture process. It is patently untrue that "if you can't measure something, you can't talk about it." Nonetheless, measurement does provide a more relevant and reliable basis for analysis and opinion. A major objective of this study is to set up at least a framework for a model of the decisions or dimensions involved in establishing and operating joint ventures in international business.

A detailed account of the research and the format of the study appears in Chapter 1 and the related appendixes. To simplify the problems associated with the potential variability in the subjects and their environments, the research strategy adopted was to examine in depth a subset of the total population of joint ventures. The study, therefore, interprets data collected in interviews with senior executives of fifty British corporations involved in joint ventures in India or Pakistan.

The research for this study was carried out while I was the recipient of a Ford Foundation Fellowship. Many of the costs of the research were covered by an International Program research grant from the Alfred P. Sloan School of Management and the School of Economics of the Massachusetts Institute of Technology. A grant from the McKinsey Foundation financed the final analysis and preparation of the manuscript. Without the assistance of these institutions, most of the work would not have been possible.

None of the work would have been feasible without the cooperation and assistance of the many executives who gave generously of their time and interest—in return for which, the anonymity of their firms seems but poor reward. Thanks are due to the staff of India House and the Board of Trade in London for their help whenever needed. I have also been most grateful for the conscientious efforts of Linda Miller to reduce and redraft a conglomeration of notes into manuscript form.

Finally, but far from least, I am indebted to all of the colleagues, advisers, and others who have commented on various parts of the study. This debt is deepest for the guidance and advice given by Richard Robinson, Charles Myers, and Everett Hagen. While clearly absolving them of any responsibility for findings and conclusions, I feel the virtues of the book reflect their comprehensive criticisms and encouragement.

Manchester, England   J. W. C. Tomlinson
May 1969

THE JOINT VENTURE PROCESS
IN INTERNATIONAL BUSINESS:
India and Pakistan

1 BACKGROUND AND PROCEDURE OF THE STUDY

Trends in world trade over the last two decades may, perhaps, be misleading as indicators of future investment opportunities. For example, there has been a disproportionate growth, in terms of value, in the trade between advanced nations as compared with that between industrially less-developed ones. Markets in developed countries have grown more rapidly overall and are sustained by much higher levels of per capita income. As a result, the opportunities for return on investment have been more visible and secure in these markets. These facts have tended to obscure the future potential of the presently under-developed markets as locations for investment.

In the long run, the underdeveloped markets may well be some of the most attractive ones of the future if, or when, these countries achieve a Rostovian "take-off,"[1] or pass over the type of national "watershed" suggested by Fforde.[2] They are likely, however, to be markets which will increasingly have to be permeated through local manufacturing operations, in order to conform to the host nations' needs and aspirations. Whatever may be the arguments in favor of free trade on the basis of comparative advantage in factor endowments or comparative costs, these are probably not the arguments which will prevail upon a country urgently bent on its own national development.

The standard case appears to be that foreign exchange problems of developing nations increase as they develop, at least up to some stage of quasi-equilibrium. These problems may arise in two ways—the needs of industrial development call for increased imports, or the terms of trade work against the export of commodities for which demand is price-inelastic. Unfortunately for the aspirations of such nations, these commodities may be the basis of any initial comparative advantage.

In theoretical terms, it may be possible to fund these needs by means of foreign exchange loans.[3] Past experience appears to suggest,

[1] W. W. Rostow, *The Stages of Economic Growth: A Non-Communist Manifesto*, Cambridge University Press, London, 1960.
[2] J. S. Fforde, *An International Trade in Managerial Skills*, Blackwells, Oxford, 1957, p. 4.
[3] Max F. Millikan and W. W. Rostow, *A Proposal: Key to an Effective Foreign Policy*, Harper, New York, 1957.

1

however, that servicing costs rise faster than diffusion of the benefits from such loans, resulting in diminishing returns to the borrowers.[4] Foreign private direct investment provides an alternative method of satisfying such developmental needs, but the foreign exchange cost to the host country may be even greater in the long run. The Indian Government, for example, has calculated that the ratio of the cost of foreign investment to that of foreign exchange loans is something on the order of 5:1.6, in terms of long-term refunding commitments on the part of a capital-importing nation.[5]

Diffusion of benefits, however, is usually more efficient in the case of foreign direct investment. Thus, the same government has made the strategic decision to try to attract such investment under terms which will stimulate diffusion as much and as rapidly as possible. The argument has been that the technological and training benefits associated with import-substituting as well as the more obviously desirable export-promoting foreign investment are sufficient to justify these efforts.

The tactics, therefore, have been to raise barriers against imports, for example, through tariffs and quotas in India, or through quotas in Pakistan. This has been the rationalization, in economic terms, for a phenomenon which may actually be strongly motivated by nationalistic sentiments in favor of "conspicuous production."[6] From the point of view of foreign investors, these factors have also dictated the situation in which local operations have to take the form of association with domestic capital and interests.[7]

In the short run, the markets in countries of this type are markets for established formulations, processes, equipment, and techniques. Many of these corporate assets are constantly being forced into quasi-obsolescence by the pressures of a rapid rate of competitive technological development in the industrially advanced nations themselves. Markets in the less-developed countries provide a longer potentially productive life for such assets. In many cases, it may be a quieter and more profitable life as the foreign investment sinks peacefully to rest behind a host nation's protective tariff barrier.

[4] Matthew J. Kust, "U.S. Aid to India—How Much is Enough?" *The New Republic,* December 15, 1958.
[5] The difference is accounted for chiefly by capital appreciation of the foreign investment.
[6] This argument is discussed briefly in Charles P. Kindleberger, *International Economics,* Third Edition, Irwin, New York, 1963, pp. 465–468 and 571.
[7] See, for example: Government of India, *Policy Statement on Foreign Capital,* 6th April 1949; Government of India, *Industrial Policy Resolution,* 30th April 1956; Government of India, *Press Note,* 8th May 1961; Government of Pakistan, *Industrial Policy Statements,* 1948, 1958.

This *simpliste* argument may, of course, hide some of the problems. For example, Baranson has described and stressed the problems involved in modifying products for the Indian market.[8] There are likely to be differences in methods of operation, and in needs for some modification in product design, from those which are most appropriate and up-to-date in a market like the United States. The preoccupation with the problems of "gearing down" design, production layout, and production methods in this type of investment, which was described by Baranson for the Cummins case, reflects similar objections put forward by U.S. firms interviewed in an earlier study by Richard Robinson.[9]

The problems may be exaggerated. Baranson also stresses the fact that specifications in a country like India call for reliability, rather than for the most advanced performance in absolute terms. Reliability is often the characteristic of established models that have had a fairly long production life. Tooling, designs, and records of "bugs" which arose at various stages from start-up onward are usually well recorded and available. Under these circumstances, redesign for a less-developed market becomes simpler than the Cummins experience in India appears to imply. This, at least, was the experience of the British firms in the present study, operating in the same country and including a manufacturer of diesel engines which had been in India and Pakistan since Partition.

Appraisal of opportunities of this type presents an interesting set of problems in decision making under uncertainty. There is the clearly discernible relative attraction in the short run of alternative investments in currently developed countries. Coupled with this are the apparent risks, both internal and external to any operation, of investing in a host environment that is likely to be politically vulnerable, socially unstable, and economically unviable.

Against these factors are the tangible ones of highly profitable results from successful past investments in the less-developed nations, true for the general case,[10] and true even for the particular case of India, whose efforts to keep such returns within reasonable proportions have received considerable publicity.[11] Coupled with this attraction are threats of discrimination, in absolute quota or relative tariff terms,

---

[8] Jack Baranson, *Manufacturing Problems in India,* Syracuse University Press, Syracuse, New York, 1967.

[9] Richard D. Robinson, *International Business Policy,* Holt, Rinehart and Winston, New York, 1964, pp. 177–184.

[10] John Fayerweather, *Management of International Operations,* McGraw-Hill, New York, 1960.

[11] *Reserve Bank of India Bulletin,* May 1958, "Returns on Foreign Investments in India," pp. 536–537.

against present and future importers in such nations. The attraction is, perhaps, enhanced by the less tangible, but impressive, potential of these markets if development efforts succeed. They are markets, moreover, where dominant positions are likely to be vested, politically as well as economically, in the firstcomers.

The whole matrix of uncertainty is compounded by the difficulty of obtaining accurate or reliable information, through which the degree of risk along various dimensions of the decision can be evaluated. Even local investors and entrepreneurs cannot always assess these risks with any great accuracy.[12] The problem certainly creates major difficulties in the foreign investment decisions of companies in the developed countries.[13]

Economic advantages to capital-exporting countries are perhaps not proved. In two recent reports, Reddaway suggests that the continuing return benefit to the British economy from overseas investment is only between £4 and £6 annually, per £100 invested. This is on the basis of some conservative assumptions, especially in connection with the effects of reinvestment and capital appreciation.[14] Depending upon which particular axe is to be ground, present values of expected future return flows or, alternatively, point-in-time impact of outflows, can be calculated in such a manner as to suggest vastly different effects upon the balance of payments. Witness, in this connection, the conflicting evidence of U.S. Treasury advisers and business groups in the hearings on the 1963 Revenue Act restrictions on returns from direct investment abroad. The intuitive answer in this conflict of opinion is summarized by Kindleberger, "However, the fact that the investment is undertaken only if the expectation of a higher than normal profit exists suggests that the intermediate as well as long-run effects of direct investment on the balance of payments is likely to be favorable."[15]

While the economic advantages may be in dispute, the political repercussions of overseas investment in less-developed countries are a different matter. Their importance has been recognized specifically in the relatively favorable position of such investments, as compared with those in Europe, under the 1968 restrictions of the U.S. Government on

[12] See, for example: Albert O. Hirschman, *The Strategy of Economic Development,* Yale University Press, New Haven, 1958, p. 120.

[13] Henry G. Aubrey, "Investment Decisions in Under-developed Countries," in *Capital Formation and Economic Growth,* National Bureau of Economic Research, Princeton, 1955.

[14] W. B. Reddaway, *Effects of U.K. Direct Investment Overseas, An Interim Report,* and *Effects of U.K. Direct Investment Overseas, Final Report,* University of Cambridge, Department of Applied Economics, Occasional Papers 12 and 15, Cambridge University Press, London, 1967, 1968.

[15] Kindleberger, *International Economics,* p. 413.

capital exports. Only the relatively desperate foreign exchange straits of the United Kingdom over the past few years have forced the British Government to legislate against overseas investment as a whole.

The theme here appears to be that the economic development of underdeveloped nations is more than just a social, moral, or political responsibility of the advanced countries. To some unidentifiable extent, it is likely, in the long run, to be an important feature of their own continuing growth. It may be that such mutual advantage can best be achieved "by means of international, socially-responsible business enterprise that is solidly built upon international cooperation, mutuality of interest and enlightened management. . . . It seems inevitable that international economic integration, satisfactory investment climates and constitutional governments will follow."[16]

Joint Ventures

Combinations of business interests, motivated either by complementary attributes or by defensive considerations such as the sharing of business and nonbusiness risks, are nothing new. Even before World War I, the large European trading houses and, to a lesser extent, some American firms like United Fruit were involved in operations in the less-developed countries, in association with other interests as well as individually.

There were, however, three significant features of these older joint ventures which differed from the later developments after World War II. The earlier associations were almost entirely concerned with trade, mining, or plantation agriculture, in one form or another. They usually existed between partners from the same parent country, or from different advanced nations, in most cases, fellow colonial powers. When local interests were allowed to participate, their role was almost invariably subordinate to that of the foreign partner.

Two of the most important changes since 1945 in the nature and organization of international business operations have been the geographical diversification of manufacturing and the increased participation of local nationals in joint ventures. Participation, moreover, is carried out under terms which give local partners relatively equal authority. These changes have resulted from a combination of factors: one, the arrival of a major political and economic counterbalance to the power of the "traditionally" advanced nations; the other, the growth of a more permissive political morality, based upon changing social and cultural values, on the part of these nations. Both factors have led to the relaxation of colonial authority.

[16] Robinson, *International Business Policy,* p. 222.

In their turn, the ex-colonies have assumed sovereign responsibility and enhanced independent political status. As a result, they have been better able to insist upon the regulation of foreign activities and investments to conform to what they consider to be in their own best interests. The linking factor has been the attempt to bridge the gap between the needs and ambitions of these new nations and the technological and financial resources of the advanced countries.

According to a study by Friedmann and Kalmanoff, "There appears to be a somewhat greater trend towards joint ventures [as a proportion of investment abroad] in West Germany and the United Kingdom than in the United States, though not to the same degree as in the cases of Italy and Japan."[17] These authors also found that many U.S. firms were becoming convinced that the advantages of joint ventures abroad were sufficient to outweigh the difficulties which might be created. This appeared to be particularly true of firms which were already involved in joint ventures, or had been in the past, even when such operations had turned out badly.

Similarly, the personnel who had been in closest touch with the problems and the disadvantages of this type of operation, the international executives, were the staunchest supporters of joint ventures with local interests from the less-developed countries. This finding turned out to be strongly supported by the results of the present study. To some extent, it was enhanced. British executives, with a longer experience in this type of operation than most of their American counterparts, in an earlier pilot study, were even more favorably inclined toward such ventures in India and Pakistan.[18]

An attractive explanation, at the abstract level, of the growth of joint ventures in the proportion of foreign investment in the underdeveloped nations comes from a theory put forward by Hymer.[19] This theory would seem to argue that such growth arises through changes in the balance of power in a situation of bilateral monopoly. It is a stronger argument if such monopoly is considered to be a reflection of political as well as economic positions, motivated in many cases more strongly by the former than by the latter.

There is not much evidence from the past that what might be called the "cycle of bilateral monopoly" was actually completed, so long as

[17] Wolfgang G. Friedmann and George Kalmanoff, *Joint International Business Ventures,* Columbia University Press, New York, 1961, p. 80.
[18] Study, in 1965, of some U.S. joint ventures in India, Pakistan, and Iran by the author of the present study (unpublished).
[19] Stephen Hymer, *The International Operations of National Firms, A Study of Direct Foreign Investment,* unpublished Ph.D. Dissertation in Economics, M.I.T., 1960.

the country in which the investment took place was in a position of political dependence. The case of the Indian textile industry argues in fact to the contrary.[20] Such a dependent position meant that the country was unable to exploit any improvement in its economic or technical position vis-à-vis investors from abroad. Even where comparative advantage shifted, with such economic and technological development, to the dependent nation, the latter's political subordination meant that vested interests in other countries could prevent it from assuming the benefits associated, in theory, with such a shift.

At the level of corporate policy and decision making, it is not clear that the bilateral monopoly thesis provides a completely satisfactory explanation. It may be that executives do not recognize the real reasons for which they make certain investment decisions. It may also be that they seek to rationalize some decisions in terms of an explanation of corporate requirements, rather than accepting the significance of external constraints upon freedom of choice (although the readiness of most executives to offer pungent comments upon the effects of host country restrictions on foreign investors would appear to belie such an argument).

If it is assumed, however, that responsible executives are sensitive to their own criteria and do not need to disguise them, it should then be possible to test for the significance of a situation of bilateral monopoly as a constraint upon the investment decision. In particular, it should be possible to find out whether executives appear to recognize positive benefits to their own firms as the prime incentive for going into a joint venture, rather than the negative position of being forced (a) into such an operation and (b) into their choice of associate. Both of these aspects of compulsion could be expected to be features of varying importance in a situation dominated by bilateral monopolistic advantage.

To summarize briefly the points raised in this section, there may be an increasing acceptance of the preferability per se of joint ventures, even over fully owned subsidiaries, for operations in less-developed countries. This acceptance on the part of investors in the advanced nations, even the United States, is only partly dictated by external factors, such as legislation enacted in many "new" nations, or shifts in the relative powers of bilateral monopolists. These issues are examined and discussed further in later chapters.

[20] See Wilfred Malenbaum, *Prospects for Indian Development,* Free Press of Glencoe, New York, 1962, pp. 157–159; also, very much earlier, James Mill and Horace H. Wilson, *The History of British India,* Jones & Madden, London, 1844, Vol. 1, pp. 538–539.

A Definition

The definition of a joint venture used in the present study is

The commitment, for more than a very short duration, of funds, facilities, and services by two or more legally separate interests, to an enterprise for their mutual benefit.[21]

The two most important implications of this definition are that

a. There must be some definite commitment with the accompanying risk, but this is a wider concept than participation based purely upon sharing of equity.

b. There is no clearly specified qualifying period of duration. Thus, projects embodying a definite contract period are included when the latter is long enough to create the need for continuing, if short-term, relationships and interplay between the partners.

There are four main subsets belonging to the set "joint ventures," as the latter is defined here. These are

1. *National Joint Ventures,* between two or more interests from the same country. An example would be Burmah-Shell Oil Storage and Distributing Company of India Ltd.

2. *Foreign International Joint Ventures,* in which the partners are of different nationalities, but excluding that of the host country; for example, as in the Electric Lamp Manufacturers Ltd. consortium which operates in several countries, and which includes A.E.I. and G.E.C. (now merged), together with Crompton Parkinson of the United Kingdom and Philips of the Netherlands.

3. *International Joint Ventures,* in which some part of the commitment is by local nationals, excluding host government interests. This is perhaps the most interesting and certainly the most common form of joint ventures discussed in the literature.

4. *Mixed International Joint Ventures or Mixed Ventures,* in which at least some part of the commitment is by the host government, while another is by foreigners. Oil India Ltd., a mixed venture between the Burmah Oil Company and the Government of India is an example of the "purest" form of this type of operation.

Within each of these major subsets there are considerable variations, according to the number of partners from each of the three main categories (foreign, local private and local, or "host" government) and their relative commitments. Out of the sample of joint ventures examined in the present study, two are national and nine are mixed. In one of the latter, the foreign commitment is in the form of a large-scale, long-term service contract, involving the continuing presence of up to 70 foreign

[21] Cf. definitions in Robinson, *International Business Policy,* p. 147 (footnote); and in Friedmann and Kalmanoff, *Joint International Business Ventures,* p. 6.

technicians and advisers. The remainder of the sample are all in subset 3. In view of the small size of the sample, the group is treated as homogeneous in the statistical analysis, differences being examined only at the descriptive level.

Setting Up a Model

One of the original objectives of this study was to discover whether or not it is possible to establish a series of variables that would help to predict the criteria through which associates would be selected for particular joint ventures. These variables consist of characteristics of the parent companies, the joint ventures, and the background situation in which the decision was made. They are grouped into categories, or sectors, each of which can be examined against a further group of selection criteria described by investors as actually constituting the basis for selection.

If significant relationships and predictive capabilities among these sets of variables can be established, they can in turn possibly be associated with certain organizational and structural characteristics of a joint venture. Finally, some elements of evaluation are examined. Internally, these take the form of methods used by parent companies to evaluate the performance of associated joint ventures. Externally, evaluation is considered in terms of measures and criteria set out as part of the framework to describe the success of the joint ventures under study.

Given that the groups of variables prove to be significantly associated and that they can be used to predict at least the direction of variation amongst each other, the framework of an operational model will be established. It should then be possible to enter the heuristic at certain defined points that will describe the likely constitution of the remainder. Similarly, if certain stages or variables are to be manipulated, it should be possible to predict the effects upon other parts of the model. It should then be possible to suggest policy recommendations for similar firms considering investing and operating under similar conditions.

Such a model is intended to provide a tool for internationally operating firms. As a result, the study is chiefly oriented toward the point of view of such firms. At the same time, if the model is valid, it should also be capable of serving as a guide to enlightened regulation of foreign investment by host country planning authorities.[22] In the latter

[22] For some comments on the lack of dexterity of such governments in regulating foreign investment, see Malenbaum, *Prospects for Indian Development,* pp. 251–254 and 258; Matthew J. Kust, *Foreign Enterprise in India,* University of North Carolina Press, Chapel Hill, 1964, pp. 141–142; see also the *Economic Times,* Bombay, 27 April 1963, and 21 May 1963.

role it would be useful in improving the accuracy of intramatrical relationships and resulting predictions of the effects of varying some of the inputs or dimensions to national development matrices. This role is not, however, central to the study and is not considered in any detail.

In order to limit the range of dimensions along which the model can vary, the first sample of foreign parent firms[23] is restricted to those of one nationality. In this case, these are British companies. This is not meant to imply that there is necessarily a universal similarity between firms of different nationalities which operate internationally. It is merely that, at this stage, it was desirable to build in as much homogeneity as possible along this dimension for the first exploration and testing of a complex model. Significant as cross-cultural differences between parent firms might be, for example, they could be tested at a later stage, either by extension of the original tests and model, or through comparison between models set up in the same way.

For a similar reason, the effects of environmental variations resulting from differences in host countries are reduced by limiting the milieu of the study. While there is a growing interest in the subject, there is still a lack of systematic reporting[24] of the actual operations of overseas joint ventures. There is even less covering these operations in less-developed countries.[25] It appears, therefore, that an analysis of joint ventures in such a country, or in a subset of such countries, has

[23] Except where indicated otherwise, or where obviously different in context, the term "foreign" is used throughout to mean "of a nationality other than that of the host country." In the same way, "local" means "local to the host country."

[24] One should make exception here for the studies of: Michael Kidron, *Foreign Investments in India,* Oxford University Press, London, 1965; Karen K. Bivens and Enid B. Lovell, *Joint Ventures with Foreign Partners, International Survey of Business Opinion and Experience,* National Industrial Conference Board, New York, 1966; Friedmann and Kalmanoff, *Joint International Business Ventures.*

[25] The terms "less-developed" and "underdeveloped" are generally used as synonyms, together with "developing," in various classifications which compare achieved with potential performance against national economic indicators. The last term seems misleading, since the most rapidly developing nations, in economic terms, are very often the advanced nations. In practically all discussions of the underdevelopment of national resources, the crux of the problem turns out to be the backwardness of the people. It is perhaps more realistic, therefore, to place the emphasis squarely on this "backwardness," as Myint has suggested, and to talk of the "backward" nations. (Hla Myint, "An Interpretation of Economic Backwardness," *Oxford Economic Papers,* June, 1954.) This would fit in well with one of the most useful measures of relative advancement or backwardness in this area, namely the Index of Human Resource Development suggested by Harbison and Myers. (Frederick Harbison and Charles A. Myers, *Education, Manpower, and Economic Growth,* McGraw-Hill, New York, 1964.) The main problem in such a course of action is probably the implicitly derogatory connotation of the term itself. Hence, it is perhaps more tactful to stand by the euphemisms—"less-," or "underdeveloped"—while strictly meaning "backward" in terms of their level of economic development.

additional value in increasing the available information about an area of growing interest and importance to business firms.

Another of the original objectives of this study was to examine joint ventures of British companies in a group of countries: India, Ceylon, Pakistan, Burma, and Iran. Although the major company to grow out of operations in Burma was in fact studied, this firm is no longer an investor in Burma. At the same time, the political and economic regimes in that country were felt to be too disparate from the others. Iran, too, was only loosely comparable with the southwestern Asian nations. Neither of these two countries, nor Ceylon, had a very large population of joint ventures from which to choose. All three were therefore rejected from the study.

India and Pakistan were felt to be sufficiently alike to treat as one host environment. To some extent, their national politics and alignments and their respective endowments of natural resources appear to refute the argument of similarity. They have, however, a common history, similar social and economic problems, comparable legal systems and business organisations (although there are considerable differences in scale) plus a common business language. In spite of different political structures, their postures toward foreign business interests and, to a lesser extent their patterns of development have been much the same in effect.

This argument was directly supported in discussion by the respondents from British companies who were interviewed. Indirectly, too, in the pattern of their responses to questions about the effects of host government policies upon the joint ventures in which their firms were associated, they appeared to find only marginal differences in operating in the two countries. It was interesting to compare this reaction with those of a smaller group of U.S. managers of international operations who were interviewed as part of the earlier pilot study. (See footnote 18.) The latter group seemed to be far more impressed by official statements made by host country authorities than were the British executives.

One case which stood out in this respect concerned an Indian joint venture set up by the British subsidiary of a U.S. firm. This was a joint capital investment by the U.S. and U.K. companies (as far as the foreign share in equity was concerned) in which the Indian activities were actually the prime responsibility of the U.K. arm. Discussing the relative merits of India and Pakistan as locations for investment, some of the U.S. executives in this particular company paraphrased and extended a quotation by President Ayub, "You can do business in India—You can make a profit in Pakistan."

A British director of the same firm, who had worked in India for many years before and after Partition, agreed that high profits had been the order of the day in Pakistan's early years.[26] He also pointed out, however, that

a. Similar profits were not unheard of as part of Indian operations.

b. The Pakistan Government had tightened up considerably on the monopolistic profits which had previously been encouraged in order to generate reinvestment.

This executive stated further that: "We (as a company) do not know of any decisions made by the Indian Government that have not been reasonable."

Procedure of the Study

In deciding upon the structure of the actual research needed to obtain the information required in this study, and upon the overall significance of the findings, certain prior assumptions were made. An accurate definition of the population of British joint ventures in India or Pakistan was not available from any of the anticipated sources.[27] *The Directory of Free World Enterprises and Collaborations in India* lists some 850 British firms that are involved in "Collaboration" agreements in India,[28] but the vast majority of these cases are simple licensing or technical assistance contracts. In many cases, they involve only the provision of instructions and drawings, with little or no supervision, policing, or continuing contact.[29] No comparable information appears to exist in published form for Pakistan.

Because a clear definition of the population of British joint ventures in these two countries was lacking, it was decided that the best way to obtain a significant body of data on these operations was to build a sample that was largely self-generating. Its significance would be represented by the importance of the companies concerned, measured in two main ways: first, the importance of the U.K. parent firms in their home environment, chiefly as expressed by their size; second, the importance of the joint ventures as a proportion of the total British

[26] See also Gustav F. Papanek, *Pakistan's Development, Social Goals and Private Incentives,* Harvard University Press, Cambridge, Mass., 1967, pp. 32–40.

[27] These had included The Board of Trade Offices and Library in London, the Offices of the High Commissioners for India or for Pakistan, the Library at India House in London, the Indian Investment Centre, the Library at the Office of the High Commissioner for Pakistan.

[28] *Directory of Free World Enterprises and Collaborations in India,* 1st ed., Champaksons, New Delhi, 1966 (Author unspecified), pp. 141–184.

[29] This statement is based upon the comments made in discussion and correspondence with actual respondents and many of the other British firms listed in *The Directory,* as being involved in collaborations in India.

and other foreign private direct investment in their respective host countries.

Generating the Sample

The London Stock Exchange compiles an annual list of the largest British companies, based upon the size of quoted equity market capitalization. Part of this list was published in the *Financial Times* as "Britain's Top 200 Companies."[30] An initial sorting of these 200 companies was carried out by means of a cross-examination, using the list of firms published in *The Directory* mentioned earlier, or through preliminary correspondence with many of the firms listed in the 200. This resulted in an approximate breakdown of the "Top 200" as shown in Table 1.1.

Table 1.1
Breakdown of Britain's Top 200 Companies

Classification of Companies	Number	Comments
Banking, insurance, investment trusts, or finance	58	Rejected as likely to have had Indian interests nationalized, or to be unable to operate in India because of local legislation
Retailing, wholesaling, brewing, associated activities	23	Rejected as unlikely to be able to operate in India
Shipping, motion pictures, radio, television, or associated activities	11	Rejected as being outside the main scope of interest of the study
Companies with no investments in India or Pakistan (although some had licensing agreements with local firms)	43	Rejected as unsuitable
Companies operating in India or Pakistan through branches or 100% subsidiaries, rather than joint ventures	26	Rejected as unsuitable
Companies unable to cooperate	9	At least 4 of these were later found to be unsuitable
Companies which did not reply to requests for information	3	
Suitable firms, prepared to discuss their joint ventures in India or Pakistan	27	Interviewed

[30] The *Financial Times,* London, 19 May 1967.

Further correspondence, based upon firms listed in *The Directory,* in Kidron's *Foreign Investments in India,* or in an incomplete list provided by the office of the High Commissioner for Pakistan, resulted in the addition to the sample of 23 more British companies. Six of these, in terms of size, would have been in the top 50, and one in the top 200, companies in the United Kingdom, according to a comparison with the criteria of the London Stock Exchange. Out of these seven, three were large private companies that did not publish statements and were not quoted in the stock market. The other four were British subsidiaries of other foreign companies (Dutch, U.S., and two Canadian).

In each of the last four cases, the U.K. subsidiary was said to have been fully responsible for investment and policy decisions and for setting up an operational liaison in connection with Indian interests. The same reasons were also accepted in adding to the list five firms which had been taken over by members of the "top 200." Finally, eleven smaller firms which were prepared to cooperate were added, making a total of fifty in the original sample.

Because of the possible sensitivity of some of the information and the volume of data required, it was decided that each of these fifty companies should be interviewed. As a check on the validity of this argument, a questionnaire was sent out with a detailed covering letter, to another 61 firms involved in "Collaborations" in India. Out of this control group, only 2 companies provided the information requested.[31]

Interviews with companies in the main sample were carried out over a four-month period from May through August 1967. By the end of this time, information had been obtained from 49 parent firms, three of the original sample having been eliminated as unsuitable, as the result of interviews. The information covered 71 joint ventures, of which 58 were in India and 13 were in Pakistan.

Value of the British Stake

The *Reserve Bank of India Bulletin* periodically lists the total values of outstanding foreign investments in India. As the basis for these figures, private investments are grouped in two categories. Branches and foreign-controlled rupee companies are classed as "direct." All others are included under "portfolio." The Reserve Bank's definition of control may perhaps be open to debate. It appears to include joint-stock companies other than subsidiaries, in which 40 % or more of the ordinary

---

[31] Of the remaining 59, 15 companies were unsuitable, 24 companies were unable to cooperate, 16 companies did not reply (7 of these were later discovered to be involved in joint ventures in India), and 4 companies agreed to cooperate but failed to do so.

shares are held in one country abroad, or 50 % or more are held in two countries, unless managerial control appears in the official view to be in the hands of the local partner.[32]

This is a definition which assumes that foreign technical and financial strengths are likely to dominate over a simple equity position. When the local shareholding is widespread, there is considerable justification for this argument, which is equally valid in an advanced nation. The definition is perhaps out-of-date in India for cases in which 51 % to 60 % of the equity is held by a local partner. In any case, 40 % is a purely arbitrary figure.

Of the British firms in the present sample, some seemed to dominate and control associated joint ventures in which their own share of equity was well under 40 %. At the same time, one firm involved in two joint ventures, holding 60 % of the voting equity in one, and 49 % in the other, found control completely different in the two cases. This was true to the extent that the executives of the British parent company found considerable satisfaction in the fact that the local operation which they formally controlled was doing better than the other—controlled by the local partner.

At the other extreme, respondents from several firms felt that the countervailing powers of the local government were such that they could not apply a majority advantage with the same rigor that they could in Europe. If a local minority partner opposed a proposal, they had to be persuaded, rather than voted down, in case they elicited host government support for their objections.

In spite of these possible difficulties in interpretation, the Reserve Bank's figures provide the most comprehensive estimate available for foreign investment in India. They have therefore been used to test the representative significance of the joint ventures examined in this study. The value of the British stake in the 58 Indian joint ventures was estimated to be Rs. 243.7 Crores at the end of the 1966 financial year. (These calculations appear in Appendix B.1.) This figure excluded an additional Rs. 26.3 Crores in long-term loans, made to the joint ventures (JVs) by the U.K. partners. About Rs. 19 Crores out of the stake above was owned by British firms holding less than 40 % of the equity in 15 associated joint ventures, leaving about Rs. 225 Crores which appeared to correspond to the Reserve Bank's category, "Direct Foreign Private Investment."

[32] Taken from Reserve Bank of India, *Survey of India's Foreign Liabilities and Assets*, Bombay, 1957.

The significance of the sample of 58 Indian joint ventures, in terms of the value of the British stake as a proportion of foreign investment in India, could therefore be evaluated in several ways as follows:[33]

a. Total UK Stake/Total UK Direct Investment in India (in 43 JVs) Rs. Crores—225/495 = 45%

b. Total UK Stake/Total UK Private Portfolio Investment in India (in 15 JVs) Rs. Crores—19/72 = 26%

c. Total UK Stake/Total UK Private Investment in India (in 58 JVs) Rs. Crores—244/567 = 43%

d. Total UK Stake/Total Foreign Direct Investment in India (in 43 JVs) Rs. Crores—225/671 = 34%

e. Total UK Stake/Total Foreign Private Portfolio Investment in India (in 15 JVs) Rs. Crores—19/172 = 11%

f. Total UK Stake/Total Foreign Private Investment in India (in 58 JVs) Rs. Crores—244/843 = 29%

If the total Indian interests of these British firms were to be considered as a proportion of foreign and U.K. investment in India, these figures would underestimate the importance of this group of investors. Twenty of these firms had investments in India, other than those in the joint ventures examined in this study. At least eight of these other interests were much larger than the joint ventures in question.

A similar understatement also applies to the case of the significance by value of the 13 Pakistani joint ventures in the sample. A rough estimate of foreign private direct investment in Pakistan suggested a figure of Rs. 109 Crores by the end of 1966. (This calculation was based upon Papanek's figures,[34] and appears in Appendix B.3). The total U.K. stake in the 13 U.K.-Pakistani joint ventures of the study was calculated to be Rs. 33 Crores at the same time. The value of this stake as a proportion of foreign direct investment in Pakistan could therefore be estimated to be

g. Total UK Stake/Total Foreign Private Direct Investment in Pakistan (in 13 JVs) Rs. Crores—33/109 = 30%

No published information was found on which the representative significance of this stake could be assessed as a proportion of total U.K. private direct investment in Pakistan. On the basis of a visual comparison with the figures for the Indian sample, it may be reasonable to make a very tentative projection of about 40% to 45% for this relationship.

---

[33] Comparisons are with the estimates shown in Appendix B.2, of the magnitude of such investment, based on Reserve Bank of India figures.

[34] Papanek, *Pakistan's Development, Social Goals and Private Incentives.*

Some Assumptions

The first major assumption is that the experiences in India and Pakistan of the companies in this sample provide a significant representation of the overall experiences of British firms involved in joint ventures in these two countries. If this is true, then the responses of these firms can be taken as typical. Their decisions and attitudes can therefore be used to describe or predict past, current, or future behavior of British companies. Subject to allowance for environmental variations in the United Kingdom and in the host countries, these can be extended to the general case. This argument is based upon

1. The status of the sample of British parent firms in their home country.
2. The significance of the firms' investments in these joint ventures as a proportion of British and other foreign investment in these two host countries.

A second series of assumptions is concerned with the nature of respondents and the validity of the information which they provide. It seems reasonable to expect that responsible senior executives will be able to offer evidence which provides an accurate representation of their companies' corporate responses and attitudes. This is probably true if such executives

a. Have a genuine knowledge of, and involvement in, the parent firm's policy and decision making at the highest levels.
b. Have been concerned with the actual decision process and operations associated with a specific joint venture under discussion.

Out of the 49 British parent companies in the final sample, respondents are classified as follows:[35]

22 at parent company director level (including chief executives).

23 at divisional director or general manager level.

 1 senior functional manager, responsible for liaison with a joint venture.

 3 deputies of the directors with whom interviews had been arranged.

(The latter having been taken ill, or called abroad at short notice). Of the first 45 above, all but three were currently, or had been in the past, involved in the operations of the joint ventures discussed.

It is more difficult to control for the further assumption that the evidence of such respondents is not biased by their personal value judgments. Logical consistency over a range of answers could be, and was, checked, but this was only limited validation, since bias could

[35] Classified by the senior man for cases in which groups of respondents were involved.

presumably provide a series of consistently inaccurate answers. In cases where interviews were carried out with groups of respondents, personal bias was perhaps balanced out to some extent.

However, it was felt that extending the study to include dual or multiple responses from each firm would probably have been inefficient. This was argued on the grounds that there would be a potentially decreasing marginal return against additional research costs—even if all companies had been prepared to cooperate in such cross-checking. The last assumption is therefore accepted, with the "fail-safe" corollary that, at the least, the responses represent the attitudes and judgments of a sample of influential executives. These executives were, moreover, in a position of high authority over the subjects of interest to the study.

The prior assumption is also made, that these executives would be prepared to provide accurate and comprehensive answers to an impartial but external questioner. It seems likely, however, that this would depend upon two additional factors: first, a guarantee that the information would remain anonymous; second, direct interviewing would be a more promising approach than that of simply asking executives to complete questionnaires. This seems likely to be true for several reasons.

Through the direct contact, respondents could evaluate for themselves the researcher's potential integrity in dealing with sensitive details. It was also expected that many busy senior executives would have an antipathy toward completing questionnaires. This would probably be associated with a subjective conviction that the information required could be provided more rapidly in discussion with an interviewer. Parallel to these arguments was the fact that it would also be possible to ensure correct understanding and interpretation of the questions and answers.

While the requirement of anonymity may really have been no more than a minor gateway, many of the respondents referred to it in discussion and correspondence. Several stated explicitly they would not have provided such frank answers without this guarantee.

In general, the preference for direct interviewing appeared to be justified. This was particularly noticeable in a comparison of the refusal and nonresponse rates between the groups of firms actually interviewed and the control group, which merely received a questionnaire.

Further descriptions of the organization of the research and the methods of analysis appear in Appendix A.1. This covers in particular the interviewing of the sample of respondents, organization and analysis of data and secondary research. The actual questionnaire format which was used as the basis for data collection is shown in Appendix A.2.

A Brief Outline of the Presentation

The variables and the methods of classification used are described as they appear in the course of the text. Forward references are provided in cases when a particular measure has not already been described. The analysis in the study concentrates upon activities, relationships, and decisions arising after there was some commitment to invest in the host country.

In its final form, the analysis is structured in terms of eight groups of variables as follows:
1. Size and profitability of British parent firms.
2. The nature of the business involved.
3. Attitude toward control on the part of the British parent firms.
4. Variables describing various features of the background to the two chief decisions of major interest in the study.
5. Reasons for deciding to go into a joint venture.
6. Reasons for selecting a specific associate.
7. Structural characteristics of the joint ventures.
8. Internal and external evaluation criteria.

These variables will be discussed in the following chapters. The last chapter summarizes some of the implications for investors and management and the general conclusions arising out of the study. Finally, Appendix E includes a list of topics that are considered worthy of further research.

2 THE JOINT VENTURE DECISION

Two decisions are central to this study. One is the actual decision to go into a joint venture; the second involves the selection of associates. These two issues are not necessarily the most important considerations in this type of foreign investment situation, but they are of greatest interest in the present context. Of particular importance in general terms would have been the original decision to invest abroad and, more specifically, to invest in India or Pakistan. Before discussion of the joint venture decision itself, it is helpful to look at some of the background and reasons given by this group of respondents for their firms' investments in these host countries.

Attitudes toward Foreign Investment — India and Pakistan

It could be argued with considerable justification that any decision to invest in Pakistan or India, especially in the latter, is in effect a decision to invest in a joint venture.[1] Starting from the first days of Independence in 1947, both countries showed concern over the possible substitution of economic for political imperialism. Coupled with this concern were the dual decisions to seek to develop states based upon socialist philosophies of distribution and responsibilities. These philosophies were more apparent in the public statements of Nehru and the Indian Congress party leaders, but they also appeared to be part and parcel of the early orientation of Pakistani leaders under Jinnah. Both nations immediately issued statements of industrial policy which firmly circumscribed the freedom of foreign investors.

The *Indian Policy Resolution* published in 1948 stated, "the major interest in ownership and effective control should *always* be in Indian hands."[2] The *Industrial Policy Statement* issued by the Government of Pakistan in the same year decreed that foreign investment would be permitted, provided it "claims no special privileges, and that opportunities for indigenous capital are provided and monopolies avoided."[3]

[1] Matthew J. Kust, *Foreign Enterprise in India,* University of North Carolina Press, Chapel Hill, 1964, pp. 142–149.
[2] Government of India, *Industrial Policy Resolution,* 6 April 1948, par. 10.
[3] Government of Pakistan, *Industrial Policy Statement,* 1948.

20

In interpretation, this meant that Pakistani nationals should have the chance to subscribe to at least 30% of the equity in all companies, and at least 50% in those on a special list of industries.[4]

The difference in the levels of freedom permitted to foreign investors reflected the relative initial endowments of the two new nations after Partition. Pakistan was left with a shortage of administrators, entrepreneurs, industrial plant, and resources. It was not, therefore, in a position to impose the same restrictions upon desperately needed foreign investment as was India, which had benefited from the major share of the above factors and had greater foreign exchange reserves.

India's fluctuating flirtations with foreign private investment have been well recorded, in particular in Kidron's comprehensively annotated account.[5] Pakistan's attitudes are not as thoroughly documented, but have been described, in less detail, by Papanek.[6] Of chief interest here is the fact that by the second half of the 1950s both nations were in severe foreign exchange difficulties and therefore predisposed to lower the entry fees to foreign investors.

In the Pakistan Government's *Industrial Policy Statement* of 1958, the new Ayub regime formally reduced the insistence upon local equity participation to the extent that it merely "expected that the required local expenditure would be met from local equity capital." The only reservations made were for:

a. Oil refining, where "substantial participation of Pakistani capital in equity" was required,

b. Trade and banking, which were distinguished from industry, and in which Pakistani interests were expected to have control, in both equity and practical terms,

c. A special list of activities reserved for the Pakistan government: atomic energy, rail and air transport, telecommunications, arms and ammunition.[7]

India appeared to regret the effects of the tone of the 1948 Resolution almost immediately and was endeavoring to make the appropriate noises toward foreign investors even by 1949.[8] It was not until 1961,

---

[4] The list included cement, coal, cotton, spinning and weaving, fish canning and fish oils, electric power generation (excluding hydroelectric), heavy chemicals and dyestuffs, minerals, glass and ceramics, preserved and prepared foods, shipbuilding, power alcohol, tanning leather, and sugar. (*Ibid.*)

[5] Michael Kidron, *Foreign Investments in India,* Oxford University Press, London, 1965, "Part II—Indian and Foreign Capital," pp. 65–177.

[6] Gustav F. Papanek, *Pakistan's Development, Social Goals and Private Incentives,* Harvard University Press, Cambridge, Mass., 1967, ch. 2.

[7] Government of Pakistan, *Industrial Policy Statement,* 1958.

[8] Prime Minister of India, *Policy Statement to Parliament on Foreign Capital,* 6 April 1949.

however, that a formal welcome appears to have been placed on record in the standing orders related to foreign investment. A list of industries in which the investment of foreign private capital in joint ventures would be considered was published in an official Press Note in that year. (This list appears in Appendix D).

Together with the list was the comment,

> The fields in which foreign capital is ordinarily not needed have also been listed. This list includes banking, trading, and commercial activities, insurance, and plantations . . . , the industries listed in Schedule A of the IPS of 1956. In special circumstances however, exceptions may be made where, after full consideration, this is found to be in the public interest . . . . While Indian majority holding would be generally welcome, the ratio of foreign to Indian capital that is to be permitted in any case has necessarily to be judged on merits.[9]

For India, therefore, the investment decision has usually been a joint venture decision. Both Kust and Kidron have described cases where fully owned subsidiaries have been permitted,[10] but these were few and involved companies such as I.B.M. which had highly desirable benefits to offer, including advanced technology and foreign-exchange-earning potential through exports, as well as import substitution. In Pakistan, the situation was not so clear-cut. Joint ventures constituted an option which was strongly desired by the host government, but not so strongly insisted upon as in the Indian case.

A Trend in Attitudes toward Foreign Investment

In both India and Pakistan, there has been a relaxation over time in the terms of entry for foreign investors. This has been manifested chiefly in changing policies toward composition and control, combined with an increasingly pragmatic interpretation of such policies "on the merits" of specific cases. The evidence appears to suggest there may be a trend in the development of the situation in these two nations which could form a guide to long-term policies with respect to this type of investment in less-developed countries. Generally, such a guide would be relevant both to the formulation of investment strategies on the part of internationally operating companies and to the development of optimum policies toward foreign capital by host nations.

Such a trend in the investment environment can be said to pass through four main stages:

1. A new nation fears the dangers of economic imperialism by investors
    from developed nations. At the same time, there is a reaction from

[9] Government of India, *Press Note*, 8 May 1961.
[10] Kust, *Foreign Enterprise in India*, pp. 146–150; Kidron, *Foreign Investments in India*, Table 16 facing p. 286, also pp. 188–223.

previous domination, even exploitation, by an elite group which may have been a foreign colonial power or a now-displaced local elite. This leads to deliberate fostering of a different pattern of distribution of benefits and responsibilities, either along socialist or egalitarian lines or else in favor of a different section of the society. During this stage, foreign private direct investment may be suspect, and therefore restricted, on two grounds. First, it is private, in an environment which may be exploring the possibilities of state intervention, at the very least, because of the needs of a new regime to establish centralized control over the society and its economy. Second, it is foreign and powerful in both economic and political terms—a dual threat to newly won sovereignty.[11] This could be described as a stage of *Unilateral Antagonism*.

2. As and when the nation becomes increasingly concerned over the primary problem of stimulating its own economic development, certain patterns emerge. Foreign exchange may become a scarce resource as development calls for vastly increased imports, so that both foreign capital and technology are needed to overcome bottlenecks in development. Alternatively, in the general case, foreign exchange may be available through the revenues obtained from foreign-owned extractive enclaves.[12] However, much of the wider range of technological resources necessary for economic development over a broader front are available, or can be exploited, only as a corporate asset of foreign investors.[13] In either case, the conditions of entry for such technology and capital are likely to be relaxed, while still being fairly rigidly constrained. At this stage, both foreign investors and capital-importing governments may have considerable doubt over the mutuality of their interests. It is a stage of *Mutual Suspicion*.

3. If the foreign investment is successfully absorbed and perceived social benefits to the host country exceed social costs, and as the

[11] These ideas owe a certain amount to those discussed in Max F. Millikan and Donald L. M. Blackmer, eds., *The Emerging Nations: Their Growth and United States Policy*, Little, Brown, Boston, 1961, which are, in turn, indebted to those of W. W. Rostow, E. E. Hagen, D. Lerner, and P. N. Rosenstein-Rodan, among others.

[12] See J. V. Levin, *The Export Economies, Their Patterns of Development in Historical Perspective*, Harvard University Press, Cambridge, Mass., 1960, especially ch. 1.

[13] J. S. Fforde, *An International Trade in Managerial Skills*, Blackwells, Oxford, 1957, ch. 3; Nurkse has also described the problems arising from the special case of enclave development and the lack of diffusion of benefits through the nonenclave sectors of underdeveloped economies, in Ragnar Nurkse, "Some International Aspects of the Problem of Economic Development," *The American Economic Review*, May 1952, Vol. 42, No. 2, pp. 571–583.

needs of development create their own self-generating momentum,[14] this relaxation continues. Stability and responsible behavior by the local government may stimulate a congruent reaction on the part of further foreign investors. This is apparently the stage which may have been reached by India and Pakistan, even though there may be doubts about the internal political stability in both countries.[15] One could describe it as a stage of *Joint Acceptance*.

4. Where the trend will end is not clear. It seems reasonable to assume, however, that satisfactory past experience with foreign private investment, future needs for its continuance, and growing economic and political maturity may all contribute to the logical extension of the relaxation mentioned. Foreign investors may be permitted entry in any form of operation which they desire. Insofar as local collaboration and participation are felt to be desirable or even necessary, they may well be promoted through discriminatory fiscal and financial incentives, rather than through legislative prohibitions. So far as foreign investment in the host country is concerned, this would be a stage of *Sophisticated Integration*.

Reasons for Investing in India and Pakistan

Motivation toward overseas investment can be described in terms of economic, financial, or psychological primacy.[16] Economic abstraction would suggest an ultimate explanation that investment occurs where the net discounted return to capital is greatest. If this arises overseas, then that is where investment will be located. Similarly, a financial interpretation would depend upon reinvestment of surplus funds outside a market where saturation limits potential levels of return, combined possibly with arguments based upon advantages resulting from portfolio diversification.

According to the complex of disciplinary approaches subsumed under organization theory, investment can be interpreted as maximizing or, more accurately perhaps, "satisficing"[17] utilities related to the aspirations, needs, or goals of individuals, groups, or social systems.

---

[14] This term may be original; the ideas have been discussed in W. W. Rostow, *The Stages of Economic Growth: A Non-Communist Manifesto,* Cambridge University Press, London, 1960.

[15] See Dilip Mukerjee, "India in Transition, Politics of Manoeuvre," *Foreign Affairs,* April 1968, Vol. 46, No. 3, pp. 519–530.

[16] The theories in this field are comprehensively discussed in Yair Aharoni, *The Foreign Investment Decision Process,* Division of Research, Graduate School of Business Administration, Harvard University, Boston, 1966, especially ch. 10.

[17] See James G. March and Herbert A. Simon, *Organizations,* Wiley, New York, 1958, ch. 1, one of the best summaries of theories of organizations.

One could presumably also consider motivation in terms of the political dimension of maximizing national and international security.

These are dimensions and depths of interpretation which are undoubtedly important and probably valid in explaining particular aspects of motivation toward foreign investment. At a second level of primacy, however, they can in turn be incorporated in specific response phenomena in the form of stated business objectives. In the present study, executives were asked to interpret the reasons for their companies' investments in India and Pakistan in terms of such objectives. Basic underlying motives were not examined as such in detail.

At this level, the domain of possible reasons for investing abroad is well-established in the literature of the field.[18] These reasons were divided into eight major headings, and British respondents were presented with a multiple-choice question embodying nine alternatives (a final catchall category having been added). These were:

1. Developing a new market, including geographical diversification of the company's operations.
2. Future protection for existing markets.
3. Overcoming specific tariff barriers.
4. Matching the investment or operations of competitors in a given area.
5. Capitalizing upon specialized corporate assets, especially patents, licenses, and equipment.
6. Lower cost conditions, in particular, labor costs in manufacture and transportation costs.
7. The need to obtain raw materials, facilities, or resources.
8. Incentives offered by the host government, its attitudes toward foreign private investors, and political stability.
9. Other reasons (the only responses received in this category involved subjective preference for the host country on the part of the decision maker).

Executives were also asked to order up to four of these alternatives in terms of their significance to the decision made by their firms. The results are shown in Table 2.1.[19] Probably the most interesting part of this table is the final column—in other words, the omissions. Lower cost conditions were not considered to have been significant in 70 cases, nor

---

[18] See, for example, Aharoni, *The Foreign Investment Decision Process.*

[19] Because of the preponderance of first-choice responses in two categories, this variable was not tested against most others in the framework of the study. Even over four rounds, only four reasons appeared to stand out. Because of the similarity in effect between efforts to protect markets and efforts to overcome tariff barriers, it would perhaps be more accurate to consider these as three reasons. Two of these three were related to what could effectively be considered as the null hypothesis of market considerations.

Table 2.1
Reasons Cited by British Parent Companies for Their
Investment in India or Pakistan

Reason	Order in Which Reason Was Cited				Total Responses	Possible Number of Cases in Which the Response Was Not Cited
	1	2	3	4	(Out of 71)	
					Number of Cases	
New market/geographical diversification	36	11	3	—	50	21
Protecting existing market	30	9	5	—	44	27
Overcoming tariff barriers	1	14	6	4	25	46
Matching competitors	—	4	1	3	8	63
Using patents/licenses/ equipment	—	10	11	1	22	49
Lower cost conditions	—	1	—	—	1	70
To obtain materials/ facilities/resources	1	4	7	1	13	58
Host govt. incentives/ political stability	2	2	4	1	9	62
Other reasons	1	1	1	2	5	66
Total responses	71	56	38	12	177	

host government incentives in 62. The need to match competitors was not recognized, or at least not admitted as a motivation, in 63 cases. Although it was referred to in connection with 22 joint ventures, the exploiting of patents and equipment was never said to be a primary reason for investment. All of these were objectives which had been described as being of basic importance in the decision matrices of investors, according to the theories of foreign investment mentioned previously. The evidence here suggests that, while they may have been of importance, there was some doubt as to their primacy. For these companies, primacy seemed to have been reserved for market development and protection.

The Joint Venture Decision

If a decision to invest in a given country has been made and this can be distinguished from the decision to go into a joint venture, why should a corporation adopt the latter form of investment? The possible answers to this question can be arranged in seven categories which cover the range of major reasons likely to have affected the decisions of British companies investing in India or Pakistan. These categories are listed here, with a summary of actual reasons given in Table 2.2.

Table 2.2
Reasons Cited by British Firms for Choosing the Joint Venture Form of Investment in India or Pakistan

Reason	Order in Which Reason Was Cited			Total Responses (out of 71)	Weighted Score*	Possible No. of Cases in Which This Response Not Made
	1	2	3			
	Number of Cases					
Explicit host govt. pressures	19	4	—	23	65	48
Implicit host govt. pressures	11	7	12	30	59	41
Spreading the risk	6	18	3	27	57	44
Need for local facilities/resources	27	18	6	51	123	20
Associate's project	6	3	3	12	27	59
Local identity	2	10	12	24	38	47
Other reasons	—	—	—	—	—	71
Total responses	71	60	36	167		

* To obtain a basis for overall comparison of the relative importance of each of the reasons, executives were asked to put in order as many reasons as had been directly relevant to the decisions of their corporations. A rough weighting scale was then applied to the ordered responses. Each time a reason was cited by a respondent as first in significance, it was multiplied by 3, as second it was multiplied by 2, and as third, by 1. These weighted values were then summed over each category to give a total weighted score for that reason. The chief effect of these calculations was to emphasize the importance of explicit pressures by the host government.

1. *Explicit pressures* by the host government. More specifically, a definite ruling by an agency of the government that a given project would have to take the form of a joint venture.
2. *Implicit pressures* by the host government. This covered cases in which a British firm would have preferred to invest through a fully owned subsidiary or branch, but did not do so, either because of the suspicion that such a procedure would not be permitted or for fear that discriminatory action might be taken against an investment of this type.
3. The *desire to spread the risk* of the venture. Two possibilities were included in this category. First was the desire to share "normal"

business risks; second was a policy of sharing the risk created through the unpredictability of the environment, in particular along the dimensions of national political and economic uncertainty.

4. The *need for local facilities and resources* which could best be obtained through association with a local interest. In particular, these covered knowledge of local custom and practice and legal intricacies, influence with local authorities, capital and physical resources, technical and administrative personnel, access to a reasonably competent labor force, marketing facilities.

5. *Associate's project.* The opportunity to participate in an attractive project which was already under the control of local interests, and where competition was prescribed or not considered feasible.

6. *Local identity.* Better access to the benefits accruing to a locally identified operation or one involving local participation. These included access to local government or institutional sources of capital, preferential treatment in terms of taxation, tariff protection, or import quotas.

7. *Other reasons.* In some cases, foreign investors have been said to enter into joint ventures for reasons which do not fit neatly into any of the previous six categories. In an earlier study of the experiences of a small group of U.S. companies involved in joint ventures in southwest Asia and Iran,[20] two reasons were described which were unusual in that sample. The first involved Kaiser Industries in connection with its interest in Hindustan Aluminium. This U.S. parent corporation's policy was to take a minority position in joint operations in less-developed countries, preferably between 25% and 30% of the voting equity. This strategy was based upon two reasons. One, it provided a tangible gesture to host countries that Kaiser was seriously concerned over its contribution to national development but was not seeking a dominating position. It was hoped that such a practice would make a foreign investor secure in these host countries because of the local goodwill generated. Two, Kaiser *was* seriously concerned about national development in these countries, as part of the corporate philosophy dictated by its founder. "The desire to contribute by establishing a new industry" was also described as an important motivation for overseas investment in a study by Harry Robinson.[21]

---

[20] Unpublished study of U.S. joint ventures in India, Pakistan, and Iran carried out in 1965 by the author of this study.

[21] Harry J. Robinson, *The Motivation and Flow of Private Foreign Investments,* Stanford Research Institute, International Development Center, Menlo Park, California, 1961, p. 1.

The second "other reason" was put forward by the Sun Oil Company. Joint ventures with suitable and reliable partners, as in the case of its own participation in one of the Iranian oil consortia, enabled a company to spread its corporate capital over a wider range of interests and markets. Such ventures provided a useful option for a corporation pursuing a strategy of rapid international growth and coverage.

Both of these special considerations appeared to be reasonable, if rare, and provision was made for their possible occurrence. In fact, neither appeared to have appealed to British firms as a specific primary justification for joint venture investment in India or Pakistan—even though some of the relationships of the U.K. oil companies in consortia in these two countries were similar to those of the Sun Oil group in Iran.

Whatever ranking system was used, whether by first-choice responses, raw totals over three rounds, or weighted overall scores, the most important single reason appears to be the need for local facilities or resources.[22] In view of the official insistence upon local participation in any operations in India and the preference for such participation in Pakistan, it was expected that foreign investors would feel these pressures almost universally. In over 22% of these cases, they do not appear to be of any significance, while in over 57% they are clearly of subsidiary importance in influencing the decision to go into a joint venture.

Of secondary importance are the issues of spreading the risk and of obtaining the benefits of local identity. The former is of primary importance in only 9% of the joint ventures under study, while in 60% of these cases it does not appear to be considered at all. This is rather surprising in view of the importance often ascribed to risk-avoidance schedules in the literature on overseas investment policies and decisions.[23] Local identity appears to be even less of an attraction. It was only mentioned as a primary reason in two cases. It was not even considered in 45 out of 71 joint venture projects. Again, this was described in theory as an important motivation toward joint ventures.[24]

One explanation of these apparent contradictions is probably the special nature of the relationships between British interests and these two host countries. Such an explanation is certainly supported by

---

[22] This order was altered only when both reasons associated with types of host government pressures were combined into a joint score, in which case this became the most important motivation, but only marginally more so than facilities and resources.

[23] See Wolfgang G. Friedmann and George Kalmanoff, *Joint International Business Ventures*, Columbia University Press, New York, 1961, p. 137; also Aharoni, *The Foreign Investment Decision Process*, pp. 35–39.

[24] Friedmann and Kalmanoff, *Joint International Business Ventures*, pp. 138–139.

comments made in discussion. It is also supported by the large proportion of U.K. firms in the sample which had long experience in the
Indian market and which employed executives at higher levels who had
lived and worked in India for many years. Only in eleven of these cases
was nobody in the British parent company familiar with Indian or
Pakistani conditions prior to the consideration of a joint venture. In
over 60% of the sample, this familiarity arose because one or more
individuals had been previously stationed in these nations, either in the
employ of the British company reported in the sample or for some other
reason (i.e., employment in the Indian Civil Service, the armed forces,
or with another company).

These companies and executives considered that they themselves
already possessed something of a local national identity and status.
They knew the countries and their markets well and were themselves
well known. Thus not only was much of the uncertainty of the local
investment environment reduced but the environment was even felt to
be familiar. To the extent that risk, in foreign investment terms, was a
compound of business risk and perceived environmental uncertainty,
these particular host countries were probably not considered very high
risk areas on either count by these respondents—at least, not at the
time when the investments were made.

In order to analyze some of the relationships between the reasons
given for going into joint ventures and other characteristics of the
ventures themselves, the seven categories described could be combined
into four. Explicit and implicit pressures and the spreading of risk stand
as in the original classification. All other reasons are included under the
convenience of local facilities and resources. At a slightly broader level
of definition, this category could be interpreted as including facilities
and resources embodied in an existing local operation or, alternatively,
the advantages implied in local identity. The actual measure used to
represent the motivation of British parent firms is the first and most
important reason cited for going into a specific joint venture.

Variations over Time

Four important age bands can be established for classifying joint
ventures in India and Pakistan along the time dimension. The year of
Independence for both countries, 1947, would be an obvious cutting
point. The year 1958, in which foreign exchange reserves virtually ran
out, was described as a turning point in India by Kidron.[25] It was also
the year in which the Ayub regime came into effective operation in

[25] Kidron, *Foreign Investments in India,* pp. 120, 127, 140–143.

Pakistan. Another year of foreign exchange crisis was 1962. This was also the year of the Third Plan in India, when in an important general election many members of the state capitalist wing lost their seats.[26] Finally, it was the time of the Sino-Indian conflict, which jolted India somewhat in its neutralist stance.

Using these cutting dates, the British joint ventures in this study are grouped according to the year in which the joint venture was set up:

a. Pre-Independence (1947): 6 cases
b. 1948 to 1957: 20 cases
c. 1958 to 1962: 25 cases
d. After 1962: 18 cases

There is a definite progression over time in the relationship between the age of joint ventures and reasons why they were established.[27] This has been plotted as a U-shaped curve in Figure 2.1, and seems to lend itself to a predictable interpretation in the light of the historical development of these two host economies.

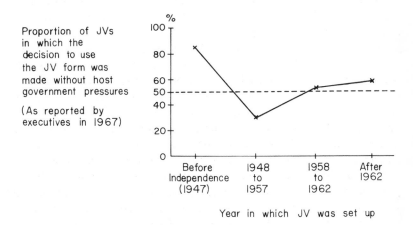

Figure 2.1
Relationship between Age and Pressure to Go into a Joint Venture

Before Independence and Partition, there was little Indian Government pressure on foreign investors to enter into local joint ventures rather than into fully owned subsidiaries or branches. Because of this, the chief motivation for such investors to set up joint ventures was either

---

[26] *Ibid.*, p. 152.
[27] Significant at the marginal 0.081 level. Throughout the text, in all cases where significance levels are described without further explanation, these refer to the chi-square statistic.

the desire to spread the risk in investment or the convenience of certain local resources or facilities. However, British firms appear to have envisaged little risk in connection with investments in India before 1947, and no companies mentioned such risks as a reason for going into a joint venture. Five out of six joint ventures in the earliest group were set up as such because of the convenience of local facilities or resources. The sixth was originally established prior to World War II, but did not go into operation in its present form until after 1947, by which time there was Government of India pressure to take in a local associate.

In the first years after Independence, two factors militated against anything but joint ventures so far as the authorities in these two host countries were concerned. First was the economic nationalism of the two newly independent states. Second was the relatively healthy condition of foreign exchange reserves, which made it possible for local industrialists to import, as required, materials, components, and, to some extent, technology. Only four of the twenty joint ventures in this subgroup were set up in Pakistan, where the national political and economic viability as a locus for investment still appeared to be very much in doubt at that time.[28]

The changed conditions after Independence meant that some U.K. firms began to see India and Pakistan as a possibly risky environment. The desire to spread the risk of investment was mentioned as a primary consideration in 15% of the joint ventures set up in this second period. Another 20% were established because of the British parent company's need for local resources and facilities. Of the joint ventures set up in the first ten years after Independence, 65% were said to have been formed as such primarily because of explicit host government pressures.

By the 1958 to 1962 stage, both nations were in foreign exchange difficulties. In both there was said to be some relaxation of explicit pressures upon foreign investors. At the least these pressures were not felt to be quite as significant as they had been earlier in the decision matrices of this group of British firms. Only 48% of the joint ventures which they established during this period were said to have been forced upon them by such pressures. Risk sharing was still a consideration, but of rather less importance overall, and accounted for only 12% of

[28] The disturbances in early 1969 probably again reduced the attraction of Pakistan as a location for overseas investment after a decade of stability and growth. At mid-1969 it appears likely that reassumption of control by a military junta under President Yahya Khan will lead to a renewal of stability, at least in the short to medium term. The character of the convulsions which arose in the jockeying for position and advantage after Ayub's original decision to retire seems to make it doubtful whether Pakistan can afford anything but an autocracy until its economic development can sustain the luxury of its own democratic processes.

cases. Of the joint ventures set up in this period, 40% were stimulated by the foreign partner's need for local facilities or resources.

Since 1962, the impression of risk appears to have subsided to pre-Independence levels. None of the joint ventures in the last age-band were set up primarily in order to spread the risk of investment. Host government pressures also continued to relax. They were a major consideration in only 44% of the last group of joint ventures, and in the majority of these cases the pressures were implicit rather than explicit. During these years, motivation became positive rather than compulsory, in the sense that 56% of the joint ventures in this last group were the result of a U.K. firm's need for local facilities or resources. An additional factor contributing to this change over the last few years was the British Government's tightening up on overseas investment by U.K. nationals. As a result, local capital became an increasingly attractive and important resource for British firms investing abroad.

Size of Project

There is a positive correlation between size of British parent firms and that of associated joint ventures. There also appears to be a tendency for larger parents to feel forced into a joint operation while smaller firms seek local facilities or resources. By transposition, therefore, smaller joint ventures should have been set up to take advantage of local facilities and large ventures should have been forced upon their foreign parents.

Actually, the relationships are not quite as clear-cut as this. Project size is defined in terms of the capital represented by voting stock or equity, a measure which shows a high positive correlation over the range of common data entries, with joint venture size as measured in assets or total capital employed.[29] The joint ventures can be grouped into four categories along this dimension of size.[30] The relationship with the joint venture decision is shown in Table 2.3.[31]

The relationships predicted would have shown a trend in the concentration of cases along a diagonal running from southwest to northeast in Table 2.3. The lower end of the diagonal actually corresponds with the results laid out in the table. Over 53% of each of the two smaller groups

[29] Respectively, $r = .913$ and $r = .874$, both significant at 1% level for size of N.
[30] *Voting Equity Capital in $ Millions*   *Category*   *Number of JVs*
       1.0 and under   Very small   26
       1.1 to 5.0   Small   24
       5.1 to 10.0   Medium   11
       Over 10.0   Large   9
[31] Relationship significant at the 0.042 level for chi-square.

Table 2.3
Size of Project and Reasons for Going into Joint Ventures

Reason for Going into Joint Venture	Size of Joint Venture				
	Very Small	Small	Medium	Large	Total
	No. of Cases and Cell % Based on Column Sum				
	No.	%	No.	%	No.	%	No.	%	No.
Explicit host govt. pressure	6	23	5	21	6	55	2	22	19
Implicit host govt. pressure	6	23	3	13	1	9	1	11	11
Spreading the risk	—	—	3	13	3	27	—	—	6
Need for local facilities/ resources	14	54	13	53	1	9	6	67	34
Total and % based on row sum	26	37	24	34	11	16	9	13	70

of joint ventures were set up because of the reason predicted, while 80 % of the cases in which this reason was cited as the primary consideration involved smaller joint ventures. At the other end of the diagonal, however, the trend is not quite so clear. Although 55 % of the medium-sized joint ventures were set up following explicit pressure, two thirds of the largest were established by British firms seeking local facilities or resources. At the same time, two thirds of the joint ventures set up because of host government pressures were in the two smaller categories.

Selection of Associates

If the reasons which caused foreign companies to invest through the joint venture form were known, it would be reasonable to expect that this information would assist in the prediction of the choice of a specific type of associate. When a joint venture was set up because of explicit pressures by the host government, it would be quite likely that the choice of an associate would also tend to be forced upon the foreign partner. To a lesser extent, this might also be true when the pressure was implicit.

In either of these two cases, the pressure could have been direct, or it could have been exerted in an indirect manner. An indirect manner, for example, would exist if the host government granted an exclusive license to a particular local firm when the latter made strong enough representations for this advantage and when it was sufficiently competent to justify preference. This double-force situation could be expected to apply also where mixed ventures were established, especially in areas of activity preempted by the local government.

There is also the consideration that implicit pressures tend to be associated with the element of fear—fear on the part of foreign investors that discriminatory action may be taken against them unless they go into a joint venture. If this were true, they would also be likely to feel the need for local status so as to reduce their unfavorable "visibility," and they would tend to choose an associate accordingly. Status in a local partner would likely be an attraction for a foreign company particularly concerned over the potential risk in a proposed investment. An alternative strategy for minimizing risk would possibly be to reduce the area of uncertainty which constitutes part of the risk in foreign investment by choosing an associate, wherever possible, who is already known.

Finally, it seems evident that if a joint venture was originally sought because of the foreign investor's need for local facilities or resources, then a particular associate would be selected for the same reason. How do these assumptions fit the facts? For the case of India and Pakistan, the relationship between the reasons for which British corporations went into a joint venture and the primary motive cited in the selection of specific associates[32] is shown in Table 2.4.

Table 2.4
Criteria for Selecting Associates and Reasons for
Going into a Joint Venture

Reason for Going into Joint Venture	Reasons for Selecting a Specific Associate								
	Forced Choice		Associate's Contribution of Resources /Facilities		Favorable Past Association		Associate's Status, etc.		Total
	Number of Cases and Cell % Based on Row Sum								
	No.	%	No.	%	No.	%	No.	%	No.
Explicit host govt. pressure	8	42	3	16	4	21	4	21	19
Implicit host govt. pressure	1	9	2	19	4	36	4	36	11
Spreading the risk	—	—	2	33	3	50	1	17	6
Need for local facilities/ resources	3	9	17	49	9	25	6	17	35
Totals	12	17	24	34	20	28	15	21	71

[32] Significant at the 0.035 level.

Most of the assumptions are reasonably accurate. Over 70 % of the cases in which an associate was selected for the contribution of facilities and resources were joint ventures sought for the same reason. The figures in Table 2.4 appear to suggest that in less than 50 % of the cases when facilities or resources stimulated a joint venture did they also lead to the selection of a given associate. However, in another 25 % of these cases, they led to the choice of an associate ostensibly because of favorable past association. While such association was cited by this subgroup of British parent companies as the main reason for selecting a particular partner, in most cases the past association had originally arisen because a local licensee or distributor had available certain facilities or resources which were later needed for a joint local operation.

Although the relationship between the forced-choice categories in the two decisions was not as marked as might be expected, British firms felt they had no choice of partner in 42 % of the joint ventures explicitly forced upon them. This relationship held true chiefly for mixed ventures. In other cases when a joint venture was compulsory, the compulsion did not appear to extend to the selection of associates.

This last situation also applied to joint ventures set up because of implicit pressures, only one of which involved a forced choice of part-ner. Implicit pressures leading to joint ventures were connected with the selection of associates because of their status in only 36 % of cases. Another 36 % of the joint ventures caused by this type of pressure involved partners chosen on the grounds of favorable past association. Again there was the possibility which could not be adequately distin-guished, that some of these past associates were also capable of provid-ing the status desired.

The number of times that risk reduction was a primary motivation for entering into a joint venture was very small. In 50 % of such cases a partner had been chosen because of favorable past association. This would have been consistent with the alternative strategy described earlier for minimizing foreign investment risks. Local status did not appear to have been an important attribute in the eyes of risk-conscious British companies. However, in this respect, the subsample size was probably too small to indicate whether or not this result was significant.

Bilateral Monopoly

Reasons given by foreign companies for their involvement in joint ventures abroad are, in part, a reflection of the effects of bilateral

monopoly.[33] The general line of argument in this subset of monopolistic competition is roughly as follows. Terms under which foreign
private direct investment occurs are in effect the product of bargaining
between a potential foreign investor and the host government. The
results of such bargaining depend upon the relative advantages held by
each side in terms of the attraction to the other party of what is offered.
Essentially this is a confrontation between a monopolist and a monop-
sonist. Its nature alters over time as the learning processes of both sides
and the redistribution of endowments cause changes in relative
advantage.

In theory, this advantage tends to turn toward the host government.
Initially, many administer badly endowed, underdeveloped nations. At
this stage, the advantage lies with foreign investors who are in a position
to offer much-needed technological know-how, capital (especially
foreign exchange), and often international marketing facilities. To the
extent that these factors are not available elsewhere, their owners are
theoretically able to dictate the conditions of entry. Specifically, they
would not be expected to feel forced into collaboration with local
interests except on their own terms.

As soon as foreign investment is committed, the balance of advantage
begins to shift because of the financial and organizational costs of
disengagement for the foreign company. Gradually the extent and the
degree of commitment tend to increase, while markets and local
economic and technological know-how develop. One should perhaps
exclude here the case of export-oriented industrial enclaves. These may
remain insulated from the economy of the host country, importing
capital, technology, even on occasion labor, but more commonly using
labor and natural resources and selling their products abroad.[34] It is
precisely against this enclave type of operation that modern less-
developed nation governments are most concerned to exert what
powers they possess, as the international oil and copper companies are
discovering.

As local development occurs, the foreign-owned factors can be
substituted so that their significance and peculiar advantages decrease.
Kindleberger summarizes the situation as a non-zero-sum game: "the
solution to which is indeterminate . . . both parties can win, both parties
can lose, or one may win more than the other loses. As in other non-
zero-sum games—love, war or raising children—the balance of advan-

---

[33] See Stephen Hymer, *The International Operations of National Firms, A Study of Direct Foreign Investment,* unpublished Ph.D. Dissertation in Economics, M.I.T., 1960.
[34] Levin, *The Export Economies*; Nurkse, "Some International Aspects of the Problem of Economic Development."

tage will shift with time and circumstances."[35] Henceforth, the local
government is in a stronger position to insist that a greater share of the
benefits should accrue to the host country. In particular, it is better able
to enforce local participation, with the result that more foreign investors
are likely to be forced into joint ventures.

To what extent do the reasons given for setting up the British joint
ventures in India and Pakistan fit in with this general argument? There
is obviously some support for the theory of bilateral monopoly in that
U.K. parent firms were forced, either explicitly or implicitly, into 42%
of these joint ventures by host government pressures. At the same time,
in view of the formally stated policies of these governments concerning
local participation, such pressures would be expected in a preponderance
of cases. In fact, joint ventures were sought by British firms in 58% of
the cases for positive reasons which were apparently of their own
volition. For these cases, bilateral monopolistic advantages did not
constitute an issue and did not dictate the course of the investment
decision.

Variations in the nature of the motivation toward joint ventures
according to the time when they were set up seem to indicate that their
creation could be partially explained in terms of bilateral monopoly.
At the times when host governments appear to have been strongly
concerned over local participation, the majority of joint ventures are
said to have been set up because of governmental pressures. When this
concern appears to decrease, so does the proportion of compulsory
joint ventures. On the other hand, there seems to be a U-shaped trend
in the relationship between the proportion of joint ventures undertaken
for voluntary reasons and the date when they were set up (as shown in
Figure 2.1). This was not consistent with the kind of trend in this relationship to be expected under conditions of bilateral monopoly. Under
such conditions, this particular curve should show a decrease in the
proportion of voluntary joint ventures over time, as the relative
advantage of host countries increased and that of foreign investors
declined.

Two alternative reasons may help to explain this apparent incon-
sistency. In keeping with the basic premises of the theory, it could be
argued that the eventful shift in advantage had not yet arrived. Because
of the increase in foreign exchange problems caused by the development
of these economies, their relative advantage could actually be said to

---

[35] Charles P. Kindleberger, "Public Policy and the International Corporation," Statement submitted to *Hearings on "Foreign Trade and the Anti-Trust Laws"* of the Sub-
committee on Antitrust and Monopoly of The Committee on the Judiciary, United
States Senate, April 27, 1966.

have declined. Combined with this might be the suggestion that changes in the endogenous requirements of foreign investors led them to seek joint ventures in increasing proportions for their own reasons.[36] This interpretation is not entirely satisfactory. At best it implies that the theory should be refined in terms of the changes suggested over time.

Without denying the possible validity of the argument, however, an alternative explanation is favored here. This is based upon what was described earlier as the third stage in the trend of host government attitudes toward foreign investors. It would suggest that favorable past experience, economic development, and increasing economic and political sophistication tend to cause increased substitution of the carrot for the big stick on the part of governments of developing nations. The existence of these factors in turn contributes to an increase in the tendency of foreign investors to seek joint ventures in such countries for positive reasons.

If conditions of bilateral monopoly are in fact important determinants of decisions to go into joint ventures, it is also important to define the situations in which such conditions are likely to arise. Presumably it would be reasonable to expect that these conditions should tend to increase directly in importance with the significance of the proposed new investment to the host economy. This significance could be measured fairly simply, for example, along dimensions such as:

1. The size of the investment relative to the host economy—in absolute terms, the larger the project, the more likely it would be that countervailing powers of host governments are aroused.
2. The nature of the business involved—the less advanced the technology incorporated in the project, the more likely that a foreign investor would be forced into a joint venture.

In terms of the variables and relationships related to the joint venture decision described, the larger the size of the basic capital investment in a joint venture, the greater the likelihood should be that the British parent company would report that it was forced into this form of investment. The results which appear in Table 2.3 do not agree very closely with this hypothesis. Most of the compulsory joint ventures were in the smaller groups, while most of the large joint ventures were set up to obtain local resources or facilities. This did not indicate there was

---

[36] See, for example, the discussion in Chapter 3 or in Borrmann (W. A. Borrmann, "The Problem of Expatriate Personnel and their Selection in International Enterprises," *Management International Review,* Vol. 8, No. 4/5, 1968, pp. 37–48) on shortages of managers for overseas operations.

necessarily any greater intrinsic bargaining power associated with the larger projects. Size of joint venture was significantly and positively correlated with parent size, and larger parent firms tended to feel forced into joint ventures.

There was little support for the bilateral monopoly thesis from these results. They seem to suggest that if size is an important determinant, then it is the size of the foreign investor rather than that of the joint venture which is significant. This, in turn, implies that the actual operation of conditions like those of bilateral monopoly may be basically stimulated by fears of economic imperialism—dominance of the host economy by large and powerful foreign corporations.

To the extent that certain industries may have more to offer an underdeveloped nation on technological grounds, pressures to enter into a joint venture should vary according to the nature of business. In the light of the comments in Chapter 5, such pressures should be felt more by firms in the engineering and electricals groups, less by chemicals, vehicles, and possibly metals group companies.

There were few striking variations and tendencies in the actual relationship between nature of business of joint ventures in India or Pakistan and the reasons cited by British firms for setting them up.

Table 2.5
Variations by Nature of Business in Reasons for Going into Joint Ventures

Nature of JV Business	Reasons for Going into Joint Venture								
	Host Govt. Pressure Explicit		Host Govt. Pressure Implicit		Spreading the Risk		Convenience of Local Facilities/ Resources		Total
	Number of Cases and Cell % Based on Row Sum*								
	No.	%	No.	%	No.	%	No.	%	No.
Oil	6	50	1	8	—	—	5	42	12
Chemicals	4	24		18	1	6	9	53	17
Engineering	—		2	22	2	22	5	56	9
Electricals	6	43	—		2	14	6	43	14
Vehicles	2	22	3	33	—		4	44	9
Metals	—		—		1	17	5	83	6
Tobacco and food	1	25	2	50	—		1	25	4
Totals	19	27	11	15.5	6	8.5	35	49	71

* Percentages do not all add up to 100% because of rounding.

Despite the low level of significance of this relationship,[37] the evidence shown in Table 2.5 does not conform to the kind of pattern suggested by the bilateral monopoly argument, except for ventures in the metals group and perhaps marginally for the tobacco and food joint ventures. The figures for the engineering joint ventures are actually the reverse of what might be expected in line with this argument.

A possible explanation for this apparent lack of difference, according to the nature of business involved, in the experiences of these foreign parent firms has been indirectly suggested by Kidron. He states that, whatever the industry, all foreign investors in India were technically the leaders in their fields.[38] This is probably true, but in fact they did not always bring their more advanced products and processes into the country with them. When they did, they sometimes got into considerable difficulty as compared with corporations which "geared down" their technological transplants more appropriately.[39] Compare, for example, the experiences in India of Cummins[40] and Perkins[41] in diesel engine projects. In spite of the Government of India's expressed desires, many of the U.K. firms in the present study, for example, had been interested in extending the profitable life of patents, processes, and equipment which were well-established or even semiobsolescent in developed markets.

On the whole, the evidence in this study does not refute the thesis that conditions of bilateral monopoly determine the terms of foreign investment. Nor does it support such a thesis very clearly. Certain modifications and additions to the theory or the way in which it is expressed are perhaps implied. On the side of host governments, the extent to which they assert any theoretical monopsonistic advantage is likely to be governed by the level of their fear of economic imperialism and their degree of commitment to political and economic nationalism. So far as foreign investors are concerned, conditions of bilateral monopoly do not seem to create an issue for many companies, particularly not for smaller firms and those which seek local facilities and resources. Finally, increased sophistication of host governments and

[37] Only remotely significant at the 0.148 level. This significance was not improved when the second and third reasons detailed in Table 2.2 were incorporated in a weighted overall "reason" for the joint venture decision and then tested against the nature of business.

[38] Kidron, *Foreign Investments in India*, p. 244.

[39] Jack Baranson, "Transfer of Technical Knowledge by International Corporations to Developing Economies," *American Economic Review*, Vol. LVI, 2 May 1966.

[40] See Jack Baranson, *Manufacturing Problem in India, the Cummins Diesel Experience*, Syracuse University Press, Syracuse, New York, 1967.

[41] H. A. R. Powell, "Why Operate Overseas," in *Planning and Managing an Overseas Business*, British Institute of Management, London, 1966.

changing corporate investment policies are perhaps likely to make interpretation in terms of bilateral monopolistic advantage largely irrelevant, or at best incomplete.

3 THE SELECTION OF ASSOCIATES

> Regardless of the type of business, all investors, whether foreign or local, take a partner into a joint venture for the purpose of gaining from that partner some skill or resource that they lack . . . it might be that the presence of the local partner is justified simply because . . . restrictions in the host country are based on the assumption that 100% foreign ownership is undesirable.[1]

One of the major weaknesses of much of the existing published information on joint ventures is lack of definition of the manner in which associates are selected. There seem to be two chief approaches to defining and grouping the reasons for such selection.

In the first, possible motives for going into a joint venture are simply transposed into those for selecting a specific associate. These possibilities are listed in generalized terms. A relevant case is cited, and the reason is then added to the list as validated. This leads eventually to categorization, which is of little value and is patently uncontradictable. Although such a method of classification is obviously comprehensive in general terms, it can be questioned on the grounds of the validity, for a specific case, of the basic transposition. The evidence in the present study indicates that the two reasons and the two decisions are not necessarily identical. A basic justification for a joint venture is not always the reason given for selecting a specific associate. This in turn suggests that the two decisions should be distinguished, if it is acknowledged that in practice they are often strongly related.

A second method of classification is even more general in nature than the first but has greater potential usefulness. In this method, motives are initially examined in psychological terms and classified as generalized or specific.[2] Under the first subgroup come factors which can roughly be summarized as sociopsychological or sociocultural compatibilities. Specific motives are then discussed in terms of political or economic

---

[1] Karen K. Bivens and Enid B. Lovell, *Joint Ventures with Foreign Partners, International Survey of Business Opinion and Experience,* National Industrial Conference Board, New York, 1966, p. 15.
[2] See, for example, Wolfgang G. Friedmann and George Kalmanoff, *Joint International Business Ventures,* Columbia University Press, New York, 1961, pp. 125 ff.

factors. This approach has considerable promise but so far is lacking in execution chiefly because

a. Compatibilities are not adequately classified. They have not been examined in sufficient depth, nor are measures suggested whereby their useful application can be tested.

b. Discussion of the specific motives tends to descend to the level of generality criticized in the first method of classification. It also shows the same lack of distinction between motivation toward a joint venture and reasons for selecting a particular associate.

c. The relationships between compatibilities and specifics, particularly their relative primacy and interdependence, have not been adequately explored.

These are strong criticisms and may be unfair. Studies of joint ventures involve the examination and discussion of effects along a number of different dimensions. They cover several associated decision processes. There is also considerable temptation to add to descriptive knowledge, in the form of case, country, area, or market information, at possibly disproportionate length. The selection of associates involves only one of these decisions. However, it is internationally considered by executives experienced in overseas investment to be a decision of major importance. The following comments are typical of many others made during the course of this study and an earlier series of discussions with U.S. executives.

Good partners are the most important factor in joint ventures, once the supply of necessary raw materials is arranged. [Metal processing]

Local partners are always all-important, localization demands are universal and local selling is very difficult for foreigners. [Vehicle producer]

Our partners are vital to this operation—they provide the senior man and significant political and commercial know-how. [Vehicle components]

Absolutely vital. Local conditions and government's attitude demand local associates. [Tobacco]

Vital, they run the operation most effectively as well as being politically necessary. [Electrical equipment]

Our local partners are vital. Without them, this joint venture would have failed. In general, the importance depends upon why they are chosen, their attitude, approach and qualifications in each case. [Chemicals][3]

[3] These comments were made in answer to a group of questions asking executives to comment on their corporation's joint venture associates. (Nature of business of the respondent is shown in brackets.)

In 1965, a vice president of Foremost International made a very similar summing-up in an earlier interview:

Local partners are always the key to success in joint ventures abroad. One has to select a foreign (i.e., local) partner rather in the same way as a bride. The normal financial and personnel checks cover some of the ground, but the final assessment is always dependent upon subjective considerations.[4]

The validity of these comments appears to be supported by the relationship between associates' contributions and the profitability of joint ventures discussed in Chapter 7. There was therefore a strong argument for research which would provide an adequate system for categorizing selection criteria and predicting the results. One of the first major steps was to attempt to distinguish the selection of associates from motivation toward a joint venture and to interpret some of the dimensions associated with this selection. This is one of the objectives of the present study.[5]

Separability of the Selection of Associates

Three major decisions can be distinguished in connection with joint ventures:
1. The decision to invest, in particular, to invest in a given host country.
2. The decision to invest through the joint venture form.
3. The decision to associate with a specific partner.
It seems reasonable to assume that as a general rule these decisions tend to arise in the sequence listed and that if they are interdependent, dependence would arise in the reverse order. Ordering of both the time and the dependence could theoretically be altered. Thus in a given instance the joint venture decision, even the original decision to invest, might depend upon an original contact with, or stimulus by, a compatible potential associate. In order to determine the actual importance of such a reversal, one can examine the way in which the initial contact between partners occurs and the identity of the initiator. In general, reversal should tend to be associated with cases in which the foreign investor is not the initiator. For the case of British joint ventures in

---

[4] Unpublished study of the U.S. joint ventures in India, Pakistan, and Iran by present author in 1965. (Appendixes).

[5] The analysis of motivation was carried out only at the level of stated business objectives for each decision. At the same time, classification was defined so that interpretation could be based upon measurable differences, rather than purely upon cumulative conjecture. Further research is obviously needed in order to refine the measures and classifications used. However, such research in depth into sociocultural and psychological aspects of motivation would form the basis for a major study in its own right.

India and Pakistan, the location of the original initiative is shown in
Table 3.1.

Table 3.1
Initiator of First Approach to Set Up a Joint Venture

Origin of Approach (Initiator)	Number of JVs	% of Sample
British parent company or its representative	41	58
Associate or its representative	27	38
Third party	3	4
Totals	71	100

The first approach with a proposal to set up a joint venture was made
by the associate, rather than the British parent, in 38% of these cases
and by a third party in a further 4%. Theoretically, the reversal of
dependence and occurrence of decisions mentioned could have
happened in any of these thirty cases. However, when executives were
asked how the initial contact with, or consideration of, the chosen
associate had originated, a different picture emerged.

As shown in Table 3.2, on thirteen occasions the British partner had
been approached after it had expressed an interest in establishing a

Table 3.2
Origin of Initial Contact with Chosen Associate

Method/Origin of Initial Contact	Number of JVs	% of Sample
U.K. firm was known to be interested and was approached by the associate	13	18
Associate was known to be interested and was approached by the U.K. firm	14	20
"Cold canvass"—U.K. firm contacted by associate	11	15.5
"Cold canvass"—associate contacted by U.K. firm	17	24
Partners put in touch by a private third party	1	1.5
Partners put in touch by host government	3	4
Initial contact made at personal level	6	8.5
Partners already JV associates	6	8.5
Totals	71	100

joint operation. Three more were set up after the host government put a
British firm known to be interested in a joint venture in touch with a
partner. In another, the same function was performed by a private

intermediary. In two more, an existing joint venture partner suggested a further investment in a new operation to the British parent.[6] Only in eleven cases (16%) was a "cold canvass" of a U.K. firm carried out (i.e., when it was not already known to be interested in investment). Even in these eleven, it is not possible to state that the U.K. parent had not already considered the possibility of a joint venture.

The evidence indicates, therefore, that the assumptions concerning the three decisions were valid. More specifically:

a. The selection of associates constituted a separable decision in the majority of cases.

b. In temporal sequence, the selection decision tended to occur after a foreign investor had decided at least to consider a local investment, possibly in the form of a joint venture.

c. Investment and joint venture decisions very rarely originated primarily from the appearance of a potential partner with an attractive proposition.

At the same time, however, the evidence does not necessarily detract from the possibility that there could be some underlying interdependence between the three decisions. It merely indicates a justification for separate analysis of the selection of joint venture associates. This selection decision is not significantly related to attitudes toward control or to the ranking of, or attitudes toward, specific types of associate. The absence of such relationships appears to indicate a pragmatic approach on the part of British firms to investment in joint ventures. Although these companies had certain clear preferences with respect to different types of associates and in their attitudes to control, the decision to go into a joint venture and the selection of a specific associate were decided on the merits of the particular case.

Selection of Specific Associates

From the point of view of a foreign investor, one can group the possible reasons for which a specific associate may be selected into six categories:

1. *Forced:* Cases in which the choice is effectively forced upon the foreign investor either because of explicit host government direction or indirectly because the associate preempts an exclusive license.

2. *Facilities:* Convenience to the foreign partner of local facilities under the control of the associate. Among these would be a site or

---

[6] These two cases were not placed in a special category. They were included in the six cases in Table 3.2 in which initial contact arose through an existing joint venture between the same two partners.

plant, marketing or distributive facilities, or a strong market position; cases in which the associate was already in the same line of business as that of the proposed joint venture.

3. *Resources:* Convenience of local sources of managerial and technical personnel, materials, components, or local capital which can be contributed by the associate.

4. *Status:* Status and capability of the associate in dealing with local authorities and public relations. This subset would also include status defined in terms of general financial and business soundness and standing.

5. *Past:* Favorable past association with the associate when the latter had been an agent, licensee, major customer, or partner in a previous joint venture. The category includes special cases in which there might have been strong personal contacts between individuals in the foreign and local parent companies, possibly even individuals common to both.

6. *Identity:* Cases in which a partner would be chosen chiefly to obtain local identity, often through association with a potential "sleeping partner."

How important are such selection criteria in choosing a partner in a less-developed country like India or Pakistan? British executives were asked to order one or more of these reasons according to their importance in the selection of a particular associate. Their answers were again weighted (in the same manner as were reasons given for going into a joint venture) to provide an overall basis for comparison as presented in Table 3.3.

Table 3.3
Reasons Cited by British Parent Companies for Their
Selection of a Specific Joint Venture Associate

Reason	Order in Which Reason Was Cited			Total Responses	Weighted Score	Possible No. of Cases in Which This Response Was Not Made
	First	Second	Third	(Out of 71)		
	Number of Cases					
Forced	12	4	2	18	46	53
Facilities	11	19	12	42	83	29
Resources	13	13	17	43	82	28
Status	11	15	19	45	82	26
Past	20	14	3	37	91	34
Identity	4	4	3	11	23	60
Totals	71	69	56	196		

The criterion cited most frequently as the prime reason for selection was favorable past association. Out of the other five reasons, four were approximately equal in importance as primary motives. Although the forced-choice situation, when it arose, was usually felt to be a basic justification for choosing a particular partner, it was described as a subsidiary reason in an unexpectedly high proportion of the cases in which it was actually cited ($33\frac{1}{3}\%$). There is an explanation for this reaction. Some of these British firms considered the limitation upon the choice of partner to be less important to the selection decision than other, more positive, contributions which an associate was able to offer.

Weighting of the responses in Table 3.3 appears to emphasize two factors. It decreases the overall importance of past association, and it increases slightly that of status. The first appears to suggest that if a sufficiently favorable past association existed, this in itself would tend to lead a foreign parent company to consider such associates at an early stage in the selection of partners for a proposed joint venture. They were less likely to be considered if the past association was not a sufficient cause in itself for their selection.

Status, on the other hand, appears to be more of a secondary consideration. In absolute terms, it was the reason mentioned most frequently out of the original six groups. Most of these references occurred in the second and third round of responses, however, which implies that other motives were of greater significance in the selection of a given associate. A similar argument also applies to the question of local identity. This potential contribution by an associate ranks lowest in importance on both the raw and weighted scores. In the special case of India and Pakistan, local identity was not considered a significant issue by British investors.

Local Managerial Resources

A curious contradiction appears to arise in connection with managerial and technical resources. Whenever foreign investment in less-developed nations has been discussed by capital-exporting or capital-importing governments, by foreign or local businessmen, or by academics, one thing has generally been agreed: one clear benefit to the host nation arising out of foreign investment lies in the provision of competent management and more sophisticated technical skills,[7] both of which are recognized to be in short supply in less-developed nations.[8]

[7] Thus for the Indian case see, for example, Ashok Kapoor, "Foreign Collaborations in India," *The Oriental Economist,* Vol. 36, No. 693, July 1968, pp. 31–32.
[8] The extent of this shortage is comprehensively defined in Frederick Harbison and Charles A. Myers, *Education, Manpower and Economic Growth,* McGraw-Hill, New York, 1964.

There has been little argument with this thesis. Thus the effort to make the most of the corporation's own technical and managerial resources has been accepted as a reasonable and commonplace justification for overseas investment by international firms.

Yet half of the British firms in this sample considered that the most important reason for selecting a specific associate was the latter's provision of managerial skills.[9] This seeming difference between practice and theory[10] is due mainly to the fact that the relevant time dimension was not defined. What these host nations needed was not the provision of technicians and managers as such but rather provision and diffusion of technical and managerial skills. The evidence for such an argument is shown in the demands of the Indian and Pakistani governments for "localization" of personnel or removal of expatriates at all levels as soon as possible after investment[11] (sometimes sooner, or so the comments of this group of executives would suggest).

A host nation philosophy of this nature could not be expected to lead to the most effective allocation of domestic resources in all cases, because of the opportunity costs of the employment in joint ventures of skilled local nationals. Several British executives commented explicitly that the high levels of local taxation prevented their firms from using experienced expatriates; this hindered the rapid growth of their local operations. It can be argued strongly that competent local personnel might well be better employed in activities for which foreign personnel could not be obtained, in order to try to achieve a more rapid overall rate of national economic development.

It is difficult to evaluate the relative opportunity costs of this type of transformation in resource allocation.[12] In India and Pakistan the policies of the host governments seem to favor the theory of behavior which suggests that learning is most rapid if effective responsibility is assumed early. More specifically, this would also be consistent with the

[9] A similar finding was reported in Friedmann and Kalmanoff, *Joint International Business Ventures,* pp. 136–138.

[10] In the "resources" category of Table 3.3, no responses were received which stated that materials or components were a reason. There were four responses citing capital on the first round, two on the second, and three on the third. The remainder of the figures included in this category were related to the desirability of local managerial and technical contributions. Forty-three responses in this category, less the nine just described, left thirty-four, which is approximately 48% of the total sample of joint ventures.

[11] The Indian case is discussed in Michael Kidron, *Foreign Investments in India,* Oxford University Press, London, 1965, pp. 294–296.

[12] See, for example, Hollis B. Chenery, "Comparative Advantage and Development Policy," *The American Economic Review,* Vol. 51, No. 1, March 1961, pp. 25–41.

theory that the fastest way to stimulate local skills is to develop them in conjunction and contact with foreign expertise.[13]

These are rational interpretations, however. In many cases one suspects that demands for localization of personnel may actually be little more than the reflection of political nationalism or short-term balance of payment arguments concerning the foreign exchange expense of employing highly paid foreigners. In its broadest sense, this whole topic would open up a wide debate. Presumably this would become a debate related to the merits of issues such as balanced versus unbalanced growth strategies for promoting economic development.[14] As such, it would be beyond the scope of the present study.

Whatever the merits of the demands for "localization," they caused problems which had to be met by these British corporations. As a result, the corporations looked for local partners with competent administrative staffs who appeared capable of the peculiar technical expertise necessary. In some cases it was primarily the shortcomings of the British parent company more than any pressures for "localization" which led them to seek a local associate which could provide the necessary managers.[15] These were the firms, seven or more, which were generally short of management and even had difficulties in their home operations. Naturally management was the resource they sought first in a partner.

With respect to the availability of local managers, India is in an unusual position. Historically, what skills existed have been widely diffused through free market mechanisms in order to overcome the shortage of competent administrators. The most important of these mechanisms were initially the Managing Agency Agreements. When these became the objects of political odium and restriction, they were

---

[13] J. S. Fforde, *An International Trade in Managerial Skills,* Blackwells, Oxford, 1957, ch. 3.

[14] On one hand, Albert O. Hirschman (*The Strategy of Economic Development,* Yale University Press, New Haven, 1958) is the chief protagonist of unbalanced growth. On the other hand are several arguments, including those of Ragnar Nurkse (*Problems of Capital Formation in Underdeveloped Countries,* Oxford University Press, New York, 1953), Harvey Liebenstein (*Economic Backwardness and Economic Growth,* John Wiley and Sons, New York, 1957), W. A. Lewis (*The Theory of Economic Growth,* Irwin, Homewood, Illinois, 1955), and P. N. Rosenstein-Rodan ("Problems of Industrialization of Eastern and Southeastern Europe," *The Economic Journal,* Vol. 53, No. 210, June/September 1943; also by the same author, "Notes on the Theory of the Big Push," a paper submitted to the Rio Roundtable of the International Economic Association, 1957 [mimeographed]) among others.

[15] This problem is not limited to British companies but is increasingly important for German and U.S. firms as their needs for overseas managers grow along with their overseas operations. See, for example, Werner A. Borrman's study ("The Problem of Expatriate Personnel and Their Selection in International Enterprises," *Management International Review,* Vol. 8, No. 4/5, 1968, p. 39.)

replaced by systems of interlocking directorships, or Secretaries and Treasurers Agreements, very often entered into by the same local interests as those of the managing agencies.[16]

Another device adopted by entrepreneurs to retain their industrial empires, even in the teeth of the Companies Act, has been the conversion of Managing Agency rights into those of Secretaries and Treasurers. During 1st April 1956 through 15th August 1960, the date after which no person could be managing agent of more than ten companies, the Central Government approved as many as 137 cases of conversion of existing managing agents into Secretaries and Treasurers, out of a total of 181 cases of appointment of Secretaries and Treasurers.... Further, because no limit has been placed on the number of companies that can be managed by a firm as Secretaries and Treasurers, many Industrial Houses in India, ... today control larger numbers of companies in their capacity as Secretaries and Treasurers than as Managing Agents.[17]

This evidence was supported by the report of the Managing Agency Inquiry Committee under Mr. I. G. Patel in 1966 which stated that there was hardly any difference between Managing Agencies and Secretaries and Treasurers.[18]

Even though their social and political merits might be debated, the existence of the agencies has provided a source of local management for joint ventures in India. Most of the agencies had been largely taken over by Indian interests by the time of this study.[19] They could assume

[16] A managing agent could be an individual, a firm, or a body corporate, appointed in the Articles of a company or by contract to manage all the affairs of the company. (See *The Indian Companies Act*, 1956, as amended, Sec. 2[26].) Secretaries and Treasurers were much the same except that:
a. An individual could not hold the office.
b. They could not hold equity or appoint directors in a managed firm.
c. They could be appointed without a contract.
d. They were not limited to holding office in ten companies.
Since May 1969, both these corporate mechanisms have been formally outlawed by the Government of India.
[17] M. L. Kothari, *Industrial Combinations, A Study of Managerial Integration in Indian Industries*, Chaitanya, Allahabad, 1967, p. 48.
[18] Government of India, *Report of the Managing Agency Inquiry Committee,* 3rd May 1966.
[19] The subjects of managing agencies and their effects in terms of monopolies or the combination and concentration of industry form important and interesting parts of any comprehensive discussion of the private sector in the business environment in India. The scope of such a discussion is too wide for the present study. In any case, the issues have been thoroughly covered elsewhere. (For agencies see R. K. Nigam, *Managing Agencies in India* [*First Round: Basic Facts*], Government of India, Ministry of Commerce and Industry, New Delhi, 1958; S. K. Basu, *The Managing Agency System in Prospect and Retrospect,* World Press, Calcutta, 1958; R. K. Hazari, "The Managing Agency System: A Case for its Abolition," *The Economic Weekly,* Bombay, Annual No., February 1964. For monopolies see M. V. Namjoshi, *Monopolies in India, Policy Proposals for a Mixed Economy,* Lalvani, Bombay, 1966. For industry see L. A. Joshi, *The Control of Industry in India, A Study in Aspects of Combination and Concentration,* Vora, Bombay, 1965; Kothari, *Industrial Combinations.* For private sector see R. K. Hazari, *The Structure of the Corporate Private Sector, A Study of Concentration, Ownership and Control,* Asian Publishing House, New York, 1966.)

responsibility for administration even though lacking technical specialists. Several British joint venture parent corporations decided that it was more effective to graft necessary technical skills onto the sounder stock represented by this type of management than on less-sophisticated local alternatives. Some of the executives stated quite firmly that particular joint ventures would not have been possible without the managing agency system. In nine of the joint ventures in this sample, the local partner was a managing agency.

Prior Knowledge of Associates

In cases where a "colonial divorce" has been achieved relatively peacefully, considerable benefits appear to accrue to the previous "guilty parties," or at least to some of their dependents. The situation is perhaps more akin to that of a judicial separation, in which the newly separated protagonists continue to be joined by bonds of mutual benefit. Mutual benefit arises in these cases from the inertia of established custom and practice, particularly the convenience of continuing existing business relationships. It may also arise from a common business training, often from a common business language, even more frequently from the channeling of "alimony" or "separation endowments," in the form of tied public sector grants to ex-colonies or dominions.

The long association of British interests with India and Pakistan and the extent of the prior knowledge of their chosen associates made this group of foreign parent companies unusual in the general context of overseas investment. Such knowledge does not, for example, appear to have been a common attribute among U.S. firms investing abroad in the past.[20] On the other hand, it does bear some relationship to the continued predominance of French interests in the ex-colonies of French West Africa, and even in Algeria, after the latter achieved independence.[21]

The nature and extent of this prior knowledge is likely to have considerable effect upon the selection of associates. For the British corporations of the present study, the relationship is shown in Table 3.4.

Only 15% of the associates chosen had not been known previously by at least one person in the British parent company. In 79% of these joint ventures, the associate either was known by several people or had even been an agent, licensee, customer, or partner of the foreign investor. The extent of this local knowledge was emphasized in the answer to a further question put to respondents regarding the manner in which

[20] Richard D. Robinson, *International Business Policy,* Holt, Rinehart and Winston, New York, 1964, pp. 214–218.
[21] See Russell Warren Howe, "Man and Myth in Political Africa," *Foreign Affairs,* April 1968, Vol. 46, No. 3, p. 589.

Table 3.4
Reasons for Selection and Prior Knowledge of Associates by
British Parent Firms*

	Manner in Which Associate Was Known				
	Known as Previous Associates	Known by People in U.K. Firm			
		Several	One	Nobody	Total
Reason for Selection	Number of Cases and Cell % Based on Column Sum				
	No.	%	No.	%	No.	%	No.	%	No.
Forced-choice	2	8	7	23	—	—	3	27	12
Convenience of facilities/resources	7	28	10	32	2	50	5	46	24
Favorable past association	14	56	5	16	1	25	—	—	20
Status/identity	2	8	9	29	1	25	3	27	15
Totals and % of row sum	25	35	31	44	4	6	11	15	71

* Relationship significant at the 0.026 level. In the relationships between reasons for selecting associates and other variables, the six earlier groups were combined into four categories. The forced-choice and favorable past association classes stood as before. Convenience of facilities and resources were combined into one group of reasons, while status and local identity made up another. The selection criterion used was the primary reason cited by British parent companies for choosing a specific partner.

local interests had been "vetted"[22] prior to their selection. This was an issue which had been described by U.S. investors and potential investors in India or Pakistan as a major difficulty.[23]

It was not perceived as a problem by British companies. In cases when further "vetting" was considered necessary, it was carried out, simply and adequately, through personal and business contacts in the United Kingdom or the host country or through British and local banks. The only U.K. firm in this sample which had initial problems in knowing where to start seeking information was a subsidiary of a U.S. corporation. Even this firm soon resolved these problems through its British contacts.

A strategy often discussed in connection with investment abroad involves a progression from licensing a local manufacturer or agent to buying into the operation if it proves successful and the relationship

[22] As used here, the term represents the procedures involved in checking the financial status, general standing and reputation, and the business competence of a prospective associate.

[23] Unpublished study of U.S. joint ventures in India, Pakistan and Iran by present author.

is satisfactory.[24] This course of action does not appear to have been important as an entry strategy for British corporations in these two countries. Only 28 % of their partners were chosen because of a past association. Only half of the local interests previously associated were selected again for this reason. Nearly 40 % of this last group of interests were reselected because of their local status or the convenience of the facilities or resources which they were able to contribute.

This evidence appears, therefore, to support the argument that past association, if it was favorable, is an important primary reason for continuing the association with a partner. Possibly because of their knowledge of local conditions, however, half of these foreign investors did not appear to consider that favorable past association was sufficient reason in itself to justify the reselection of an existing associate. It was certainly not sufficient on the grounds of the possible uncertainty of the host environment. In this respect, these companies behaved in a manner which would conform to expectations based upon rationality in decision making. Their choice was made on the merits of the case, relatively unclouded by fear of the effects of uncertainty.

Availability of Alternative Associates

A problem commonly discussed in connection with joint ventures in less-developed countries is the lack of suitable local associates for foreign investors.[25] On the one hand is the incompatibility of such potential partners as might exist, in terms of differences in business mores and objectives, technical capabilities, and the disparate sizes of local and foreign interests. Alternatively is the complete absence of any potential local associates. This shortage has been cited particularly as a justification for mixed ventures with a host government.[26]

Such a shortage has not been a significant problem for British investors in India, partly because India is a singularly well-developed underdeveloped environment. Its low per capita income has tended to conceal the existence of a large and varied industrial development.[27] This was almost exactly the comment of a representative from a large vehicle accessory manufacturer: "India is an exceptional less-developed country for joint ventures because of its large source of suitable potential

---

[24] Friedmann and Kalmanoff, *Joint International Business Ventures,* pp. 163–165.
[25] *Ibid.,* pp. 272–274.
[26] Fforde, *An International Trade in Managerial Skills,* p. 88.
[27] The extent of the alternatives arising from this development (itself emphasized by any of the Five-Year Plan Reports) is indicated by the sheer number of local enterprises reported by Joshi or Hazari. (Joshi, *The Control of Industry in India,* pp. 130–228; Hazari, *The Structure of the Corporate Private Sector.*)

partners." As a result, British firms found a reasonable amount of choice in considering associates. Although the two nations were not distinguished along this dimension, this appeared in discussion to be less true for Pakistan.

It is quite possibly true that more potential associates are actually available in less-developed countries than appear to be recognized by many foreign investors and their chroniclers.[28] The question of what might be called the "visibility" of potential local associates is tied in with the kind of difficulty discussed earlier, namely, the experience of potential U.S. investors in India in trying to appraise local interests. Both issues probably stem from a lack of familiarity with conditions in the host country, and the U.S. experience in the past was in marked contrast to the experiences of British firms in the same environment. The availability of associates visible to the latter and the interdependence with the actual selection decision are shown in Table 3.5. One or more alternative associates were available for all but a fifth of these joint ventures, even though they were not seriously considered in 28 % of the

Table 3.5
Availability of Associates for Joint Ventures

Reason for Selecting an Associate	Number of Alternative Associates Available* (excluding the chosen associate)										
	None		None Were Considered		Only One		A Few		Many		Total
	Number of Cases and Cell % Based on Column Sum										
	No.	%	No.	%	No.	%	No.	%	No.	%	No.
Forced choice	6	46	1	5	2	50	2	18	1	4	12
Convenience of facilities/ resources	4	31	8	40	—	—	4	37	8	35	24
Favorable past association	3	23	8	40	1	25	3	27	5	22	20
Status/ identity	—	—	3	15	1	25	2	18	9	39	15
Totals and (% of row sum)	13	(18)	20	(28)	4	(6)	11	(16)	23	(32)	71

* Relationship significant at the 0.030 level.

[28] This conjecture can only be offered as a hypothesis for future study. There is some evidence that the hypothesis is worth testing, even after allowing for the fact that India's level of industrial development may create a situation which is not typical of most other underdeveloped nations.

cases. For 48 % there appear to have been several alternatives—in fact, quite a reasonable choice. Most of the joint ventures in which alternatives were not considered involved the selection of associates because of favorable past association or because of resources or facilities offered by a potential associate. Some of the latter had been peculiar to the specific local partner, thus limiting the foreign investor's freedom to choose, for example, a suitable site for a chemical plant in a preferred location.

The situation has already been discussed in respect to past associates. It was reasonable to expect that, if a previous association was sufficiently favorable, alternative partners might not be considered for a new joint venture (provided that the new operations were within the competence of the existing associates). The fact that alternatives *were* actually considered for 45 % of the joint ventures in which past associates were eventually selected emphasizes two features of these investments. First is that U.K. firms were not committed to their local associates to the extent that they were forced to continue the association in further joint ventures. Second is that these foreign investors did not view the uncertainty of the environment as so threatening that they needed to reduce its area by the cautious strategy of preferring known to unknown "evils."[29]

The availability of alternative local status contributors for this group of joint ventures supported the argument that the shortage of potential associates for foreign investors was not as great as the literature would suggest for less-developed nations as a whole. Local status and local identity were contributions which could be offered by a fairly wide variety of local interests. When status was the primary reason for choosing a specific partner, there was always a choice of associates, even though the alternatives were not always considered. For three quarters of this subgroup of joint ventures, there had actually been several "status-worthy" alternatives.

It would seem to be virtually tautological to predict that foreign investors would state they had been forced into their choice of partners if no others were available for a given joint venture. This situation arose in this study in less than half of the joint ventures for which there had been no alternative partner. In a quarter of this subgroup, the partner was chosen because of a favorable past association. For another third the selection was determined by the associate's contribution of facilities or resources.

[29] Cf. Yair Aharoni, *The Foreign Investment Decision Process*, Division of Research, Graduate School of Business Administration, Harvard University, Boston, 1966, pp. 281–282.

This finding provides further evidence of the positive approach of this group of foreign investors suggested earlier. Even when these companies appeared to have no other choice of partner, this absence of an alternative was not an adequate reason in itself for complying with a forced-choice situation. More important in justifying the selection of a specific associate was the latter's ability to offer a positive contribution to a joint venture.

The "Driving Force" and the Final Decision Maker

For foreign investments in general and overseas joint ventures in particular, one can argue that the responsibilities for originating, promoting, and approving a project are likely to be located with different people. This is really what might be called the "null hypothesis" of rationality.[30] Theoretically this envisages some kind of ideal investment practice in which various types of decision or preparation for decision are variously located within the corporation. Thus, for example, motivation and stimulus for the examination of a joint venture opportunity, including search for and selection of potential associates, may well arise through the efforts or the "driving force" of an interested individual or group. This would be especially true if there were people within the corporation with a special knowledge or experience of a given environment. On the other hand, the results of any appraisal and project preparation would be audited and judgment passed by a superior executive authority within the firm.

It is worth remembering that this is a theoretical concept, and practice has an unfortunate habit of varying from theoretical constructs. The ideal can vary, actual practice can vary from the ideal, or differences in the location of responsibility for the "driving force" and effective decision making may become blurred. As the location of responsibility alters, it is likely to have an effect upon the nature of the criteria used to select associates. If one assumes that executives can distinguish and describe separately the "driving force" and the effective responsibility for the decision (not the board's rubber stamp of approval), one might predict relationships such as the following:
1. Selection of an associate because of favorable past association and both stimulus and final decision by an individual familiar with local conditions (a "familiar individual"). If this were true, it would suggest that the favorability of past association would tend to be

---

[30] Description of rationality as a null hypothesis would appear to be supported by Aharoni's conclusions regarding the foreign investment decision process. (*Ibid.*)

judged on the basis of the personal opinions of such individuals, rather than on possibly more objective grounds.[31]

2. Selection because of an associate's status and both stimulus and decision by a "familiar individual." Here the argument would be that a foreign company's corporate judgment of local status would be determined by that of an individual who was familiar with the local definition of such status.[32]

3. Forced choice of a partner and use of an impersonal decision-making procedure (this could be described roughly as "normal channels" and would approximate a rational ideal). Insofar as the choice was forced, there would probably be less scope for the effects of an individual stimulus or preference.

For the British joint ventures in India and Pakistan, there was a significant relationship between the location of responsibility for the "driving force" or the final decision and the criteria used in the selection of associates.[33] All three variables have been combined in Figure 3.1.[34]

The relationship described in 1 occurred as predicted. In twenty joint ventures, associates were selected on the grounds of past association. The favorability of the association was stressed by an individual familiar with local conditions in 70% of this subset of joint ventures. In 65%, the decision was made by such an individual.

Decision and drive by a "familiar individual" did not appear to be the major factor in the selection of associates on the grounds of status. The prediction in 2 appears to be incorrect. The responsibility for the selection of associate by over half of this group was said to be largely an impersonal matter, carried out through normal channels. Exactly half of these impersonal choices of status-worthy associates were made by U.K. companies in the vehicles group. These firms made their decisions through normal channels in an unusually high proportion of cases, largely because these decisions were externally, rather than internally,

[31] Compare the findings in Raghbir S. Basi, *Determinants of United States Private Direct Investments in Foreign Countries,* Bureau of Economic and Business Research, Printed Series No. 3, Kent State University, Kent, Ohio, 1963.

[32] *Ibid.*

[33] At the 0.019 and 0.027 levels respectively.

[34] In Figure 3.1 the horizontal axes are calibrated in percentages. Each of the four major, vertically divided segments represents the proportion of joint ventures, over the sample as a whole, in which associates had been selected for the reason given. The length of the bars running right or left from the central vertical axis represents the proportion of cases within each major vertical segment in which responsibility was attributed to the category of individuals or groups described at the left-hand margin. Bars running to the left represent proportions in the "driving force" variable, while those to the right represent the location of the final decision.

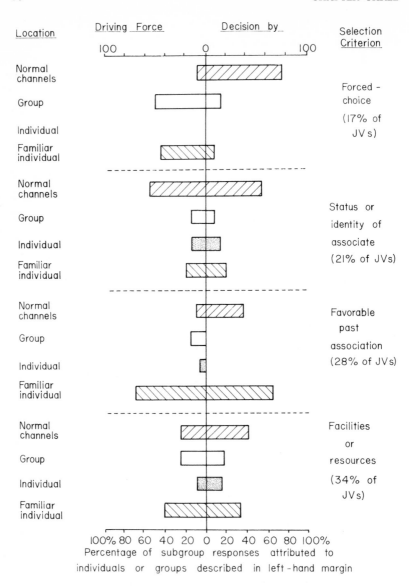

Figure 3.1
Variations in Location of Responsibility for Promotion ("Driving Force")
and Decision According to Reason for Selection of Associate

derived. When these vehicles group ventures are omitted from this category, the results conform rather more closely to the relationship predicted in 2.

For 75% of the cases in which the choice of a partner was forced upon a British company, the decision was made through normal channels. This result agrees with the prediction described in 3. Six out of twelve joint ventures in this subgroup involved oil interests, all of which were decisions through a regular formalized procedure because of the international complexity of the decision matrices. There is a marked difference among the forced-choice joint ventures in the attribution of responsibility for initiating and promoting on the one hand, and for the final decision on the other. A special-interest group was said to have developed the project in 50%, while in a further 47% the "driving force" was an individual familiar with the environment.

The evidence provided by the results for cases when associates were selected for their facilities or resources is less informative. As in the group of forced-choice joint ventures, there was more scope for development and promotion than for decision making by individuals. As a result, there was some difference in the location of responsibility for drive and decision, but this was slight. The difference, coupled with the similar difference in location of responsibility in the forced-choice ventures, seems to be consistent with what has been described as the null hypothesis of rationality.

The overall results include two features which are not so consistent. First, there was virtually no change in the location of responsibility for joint ventures in which an associate's status was the chief criterion for selection. Second, there was little change in the proportionate responsibility of individuals for those joint ventures in which partners were chosen because of favorable past association. This lack of change was, in effect, a deviation from the variation predicted in the null hypothesis. The implication of such deviations from apparent rationality appears to be that forecasts or interpretations based on rational grounds are of less value when status or favorable past association formed the major grounds for appraisal and decision making. Presumably this is because of the scope for irrational and nonrational elements in these two criteria.[35]

Importance and Effectiveness of Associates

If a foreign investor is forced into the selection of an associate, the investor is likely to have a limited confidence in the associate's effective-

[35] Richard D. Robinson, *International Management,* Holt, Rinehart and Winston, New York, 1967, pp. 13, 16.

ness, even after the event. This is due chiefly to the effects of two factors. At the objective level, the evaluation of the compatibility of partners is not likely to be as thorough as when the associate is sought out for more positive reasons. Also, this class of partner would not necessarily offer much in the way of tangible contributions to a joint venture. Typical of this last situation would be the watching, rather than participating, brief of a host government agency acquired as a compulsory partner. At a subjective level, the fact that an association is forced upon the foreign parent may well lead the latter to resent this infliction and therefore to downgrade the value of any contribution actually made.

The situation may in effect be reversed. If a partner is chosen on the basis of desired facilities or resources, then the actual provision of such facilities or resources should constitute an effective contribution to a joint venture. At the same time, since the associate has been chosen deliberately, the foreign parent company should tend to be favorably disposed toward its partner in assessing the latter's effectiveness.

Both of these predictions were accurate so far as the reactions of British investors were concerned. Even after allowing for the overall preponderance of satisfied foreign partners, Figure 3.2 indicates that there was a marked difference in the opinions held concerning associates selected for these two reasons.

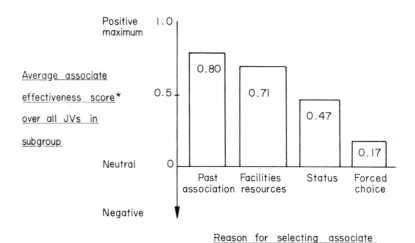

Figure 3.2
Effectiveness of Associates According to Primary Reason for Their Selection

* Appendix C.3 shows how this score was calculated.

These figures suggest that reactions similar to those in the positive situation described also arose in connection with associates chosen on the grounds of favorable past association. Presumably, for these partners effectiveness had already been proved; otherwise they would not have been reselected. The position was not so clear, certainly not so clearly favorable, for associates chosen for reasons of status. There was a slightly sour note in the opinion concerning this last subgroup. Even though they represented only a fifth of all the status-worthy local interests, half of the ineffective associates were in this category. Perhaps there was a slight tendency for status to become somewhat statuesque.

One would expect that reactions represented by the stated importance of associates would vary according to the reasons for their selection in much the same way as opinions describing effectiveness. This was certainly true for the joint ventures in this study as indicated by the figures in Table 3.6. Because of the condition that executives had to

Table 3.6
Importance of Associates According to the Reason for Their Selection

Reason for Selecting an Associate	Stated Importance of Associates								Total
	Important (Specified)		Useful		Necessary (Negative)		Useless		
	Number of Cases and Cell % Based on Column Sum*								
	No.	%	No.	%*	No.	%	No.	%	No.
Forced choice	3	7	3	25	5	50	1	17	12
Convenience of facilities/ resources	16	37	7	58	—	—	1	17	24
Favorable past association	14	33	1	8	3	30	2	33	20
Status/identity	10	23	1	8	2	20	2	33	15
Totals and (% of row sum)*	43	(61)	12	(17)	10	(14)	6	(9)	71

* Percentages do not add up to 100% because of rounding.

make a more explicit judgment in describing the nature of the importance, this second set of results is slightly more sensitive to analysis than those in the measure of stated effectiveness (in effect, the proportion of strongly favorable responses is not quite as overwhelming).

The negative assessment of forced-choice partners is more marked than in the effectiveness measure. Half of the responses in this group described associates as necessary (in a negative sense), or useless. At the other extreme there was a higher proportion of favorable comments on partners chosen for facilities or resources. Over 95% of the latter were considered important in some specified manner, or at least positively useful to the joint operation in which they were involved.

There is a slight apparent deterioration in the overall assessment of partners chosen because of favorable past association. This indicates that as many as one in four of the associates in this group may actually have been selected in order to provide local identity or status, as well as for a favorable existing relationship. Since importance was associated with a more explicitly defined contribution to a joint venture than was effectiveness, associates in this subcategory were perhaps less definably "important" than they were generally "effective."[36]

Selection of Associates and Profitability

One of the most convincing ways of justifying one basis for selecting associates over another would be to show that there was a significant difference in the performance of resulting joint ventures. As a general rule, one might expect that more positive contributions by all members of a partnership would tend to lead to better performance and vice versa. If this were so, then joint ventures in which associates were chosen for the facilities or resources which they could offer, or because they had proved their competence and contribution in a past association, should tend to be more profitable than others.

How valid was this argument, and how convincing was the evidence with respect to the joint ventures of British corporations in India and Pakistan? Details of return on investment were available only for a limited number of cases. Even over a small subsample, there was a clear difference, as shown in Figure 3.3, in the performance of joint ventures, according to the reason given for selecting a specific associate.[37]

The results shown in Figure 3.3 cast some doubt on the value of associates chosen to provide local status or identity to a joint operation. None of the joint ventures in this category were in the highest profitability group. Provision by associates of facilities or resources, or of the advantages which had made a past association favorable, could be considered as tangible and positive benefits to a joint venture. Status in this sense would have been little more than a neutral contribution.

[36] "Effective" was taken by most respondents to be akin to "necessary." The existence of this particular semantic ambiguity was one of the major reasons for including both these evaluation measures in the framework of the study. Overall, the results for the two turned out to be very similar.

[37] Relationship marginally significant at the 0.061 level.

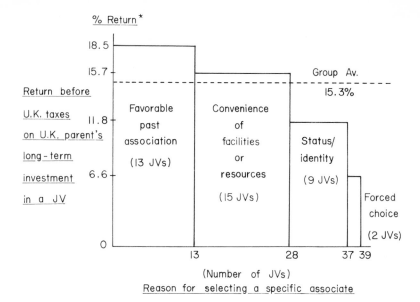

Figure 3.3
Profitability of JVs According to Reason for Selection of Associate

* Weighted average figures were calculated from the actual returns on investment shown by the joint ventures within each group, classed by reason for selection. In general terms the figures for the forced-choice category were probably misleadingly low. One of these joint ventures was a cable-manufacturing company, operating in a local market which had been overlicensed and subject to cutthroat competition in the years immediately preceding the study. The other was a newly set up pharmaceuticals company which had not yet achieved the anticipated level of profitability. Unfortunately, no other detailed returns were available for joint ventures in which the choice of partners had been forced upon the British parent company. No comment upon the profitability of joint ventures in this particular category was felt to be valid.

If this distinction is used, these results again indicate that higher profitability was associated with positive contributions by an associate. Lower returns were associated with less tangible contributions, even if forced-choice cases were ignored (this argument would have suggested that these should have been the least profitable of all). The implication is that more should be sought from a partner than just local status. This was explicitly confirmed by the comment of an executive of a British company in the engineering group, "We would welcome joint ventures as the best way to start in a 'new' country if the local partner had something to offer beyond nationality, which is not enough."

Both of the other groups of joint ventures were able to achieve a rate of return well over the figure of 10% before U.K. taxes. This was described by British executives in discussion as the minimum acceptable level for investment in these host countries. These levels of profitability were also higher than the figures reported in the Reddaway study of 1967.[38] The latter were taken largely from the operations of overseas companies which appeared to be subsidiaries or branches of British firms, rather than joint ventures.

In spite of the limitations of the data and the problems involved in comparisons across differently designed studies, these variations indicate that joint ventures are apparently no less profitable than operations through subsidiaries. To this should probably be added this reservation: provided that local associates are carefully selected for the positive contributions they can offer, rather than for the illusory benefits of local status, or simply because there are no alternatives available. This particular comparison was not a primary objective of the present study. It appears to be an important topic for further research. Corroboration of the implications would have considerable impact upon much of the folklore concerning the structuring and control of overseas investment.

Summary

The selection of associates involves a special decision process, one which is usually initiated by the foreign partner. Existing typologies of reasons for selection are inadequate. Ideally, such a typology should be defined through a specific interdisciplinary research project examining the nature of the motivation involved.

Most associates in this sample were chosen because of favorable past association, or to obtain facilities or resources. Only one in six was felt to have been forced upon the foreign partner. Even when no other partner was available, this was not considered sufficient reason for selection; in a third of such cases, the associate was chosen primarily for some other reason. The status of a local partner was recognized as a

---

[38] A direct comparison between the two studies may not be valid, because of differences in allocation of accounting data. Also because the Reddaway report figures cover India, or the world, while those described here deal with operations in India and Pakistan. After drawing a deep breath, one can plunge in and suggest that a comparable return to the U.K. using the Reddaway figures may be about 12%. This would be estimated as follows: Profits after overseas tax for world-wide operations = 8%; the same figure including capital appreciation = 10.9%. (Both figures from Table XIV.1, p. 124, of the Reddaway report.) The difference of 2.9% was then added to the figure for post-tax profitability to the U.K. group from Indian operations (Table IV.5, p. 43) = 8.6% (8.6% + 2.9% = 11.5%, or about 12%). (W. B. Reddaway, *Effects of U.K. Direct Investment Overseas, An Interim Report,* University of Cambridge, Department of Applied Economics Occasional Papers 12, Cambridge University Press, London, 1967.)

useful additional benefit by most British firms but was usually considered a reason of secondary importance in selection.

Whatever the theoretical optimum division of responsibility for joint ventures is in less-developed nations, half the foreign investors in this sample looked for managerial and technical staff as an important asset in a local associate. This was due partly to exogenous pressures for the "localization" of personnel at all levels by host governments. It was also due to endogenous pressures within some of the foreign companies themselves, for example, an absolute shortage of skilled managers and technical personnel, or a relative shortage of potential overseas staff.

There was an important distinction in the selection of past associates. If the previous association had been highly favorable, it was very often an important primary reason for selection. It was not so important per se as to make its continuation a desirable or necessary end in itself. Only half the associates which had been previously associated were again chosen for this reason. Even in these cases, primacy was probably debatable. Almost by definition, past association involved an associate's contribution of resources or facilities. In general, U.K. investors in these two countries did not view the uncertainty of the environment as so threatening they had to stick to people they knew.

This, in turn, was probably because the operations of British corporations in these countries constituted a special case in overseas investment. They were aware of the range of alternatives available, and they knew how to evaluate the potential. As a result, they generally appeared to have plenty of choice and were not forced into many joint ventures.

One can, however, speculate from this special case. Familiarity with the host environment probably leads to the recognition of rather more potential associates than are sometimes supposed in theory to exist in less-developed nations. This may be especially true if local status or identity of a partner *is* felt to be sufficient recommendation in itself.

Location of responsibility for initiation, promotion, and decisions varied with different reasons for selection. If associates were chosen for their facilities or resources, or if the choice was forced, there was scope for promotion by individuals or interested groups. The decision tended in such cases to be made through formal procedures. This distinction was particularly marked among the forced-choice category, in which most of the foreign parents were large companies concerned over the international integration of their operations.

When previous associates were reselected, both the "driving force" and the final decision maker tended to be an individual or a special interest group familiar with local conditions. This seems to imply that favorability of past association was judged chiefly on the basis of personal recommendation. In general, the greater the scope for judgment on subjective grounds of a potential associate, the more likely it was that a decision would be made by a promoter. Conversely, if this scope was limited, a decision was usually made through a formal procedure, even though an individual or an interested group may have promoted the project within the foreign parent firm.

When associates were felt to have been forced upon the foreign company, they were usually assessed as less effective and important. Past associates were generally given a favorable rating; presumably this had already been predetermined in any case. Contributors of facilities or resources were usually considered to be both effective and important. In these last two groups, evaluation and appraisal before selection was most thorough. There also was little cause for resentment over lack of freedom in choice. There may also have been an unconscious need on the part of respondents to justify the accuracy of their choice, comparable to the freezing of values through decision suggested by Lewin.[39]

There appears to be some doubt as to the validity of local status or identity as reason for selection. Such associates made less positive contribution to joint ventures and were felt to be less effective and important. Joint ventures in which these associates were involved also appear to be less profitable than those in which the contribution of local partners was more tangible—perhaps causing the lower assessment by British firms of the importance or effectiveness of these associates. A possible implication appears to be that, in the best interests of both joint venture and foreign parent, more should be sought from a local associate than just local status or identity.

Although the evidence is far from conclusive, there is some indication that joint ventures may be more profitable vehicles for foreign investment than subsidiaries, at least for investment in India or Pakistan. A final recommendation is made for further research which would specifically test the validity of this last argument.

[39] See Kurt Lewin, "Group Decision and Social Change," in Theodore M. Newcomb and Eugene L. Hartley (eds.), *Readings in Social Psychology,* Holt, Rinehart and Winston, New York, 1947.

4 SIZE AND PROFITABILITY OF THE FOREIGN PARENT COMPANY

Many of the characteristics of a particular joint venture are determined by those of the foreign parent company. Even if a more cautious interpretation of the causes is adopted, there are likely to be certain patterns of association between variables describing characteristics of the two organizations, and between these variables and others related to the manner in which the joint venture relationship was established. These patterns and their consistency or significance can be defined, but this naturally requires some preliminary classification.

Among the most useful dimensions along which firms can be classified are size, profitability, and nature of business. With such classifications, it is possible to analyze the manner in which variations are associated with different characteristics of joint ventures, of the relationship between partners, and of the foreign parent company itself. The effects of differences in the size and profitability of British parent firms are described here in terms of relative size, profitability, and structure of joint ventures, attitudes and decision criteria of the parent companies themselves, and methods used for evaluating performance.

Size in Terms of Assets and Sales

There are many possible methods of classifying corporations according to size and capital structure or gearing,[1] as any manual on financial analysis will testify. Arguments for and against these methods are best left to such manuals. For this study of joint operations, a measure defining resources available to the British firms involved seems to be the most useful basis for distinguishing firms by size. The measure most indicative of the resources available to a foreign parent company is the volume of resources actually used. Thus the figures used to describe firms in terms of their local assets include: value of fixed assets net after

---

[1] As used here, the term "gearing" refers to the debt:equity ratio in capital employed. It varies with the proportion of loan capital. The higher this proportion, the higher, or greater the gearing.

depreciation; investments at book value; and gross value of current assets, loans, and advances.[2]

In order to provide a second measure to assist in describing and explaining relationships between size of the British parent and other variables, size is also defined by the value of sales. The actual figures used in this case are those for consolidated group sales of the U.K. parent companies.[3] The two size measures are similarly correlated with another group of variables describing joint venture characteristics, especially the asset size and gearing of the latter, and the value of the long-term investment in a joint venture by the U.K. parent. Parent company size is also significantly related to

a. attitudes toward control,

b. reasons for going into a joint venture,

c. reasons for selecting a specific associate,

d. certain measures and methods used to evaluate joint ventures.

The size measures are classified in four categories, as shown in Table 4.1.

Table 4.1
Classification of Joint Ventures and U.K. Firms by Total
Assets and Sales of the Foreign Parent Company

Value of Parent Company Assets or Sales (in $ millions)	Category	Number of Cases			
		Size in Assets		Size in Sales	
		U.K. Firms	JVs	U.K. Firms	JVs
Under 51	Small	9	11	5	6
51–100	Medium	9	11	14	17
101–500	Large	17	24	13	17
Over 500	Very Large	14	25	17	31
Totals		49	71	49	71

Size and Gearing of Joint Ventures

On a priori grounds, the size of a U.K. firm would be likely to have some bearing on the size of an associated joint venture. In other words,

[2] As would be expected, this measure showed a high positive correlation with capital employed and with shareholders capital ($r = .993$ and $r = .991$ respectively, both significant at the 1 % level for size of N). In turn, these three measures were each and all similarly correlated with certain other variables. The evidence therefore suggested little reason for preferring either of the other two over total assets. On the other hand, more cases were available for the assets measure from available data sources.

[3] Again, this measure showed a high positive correlation with size in assets, $r = .988$ (significant) at the 1 % level (for size of N).

the size of the British firms should show a positive correlation with the size of joint ventures as measured in terms of total assets. This is in fact the case.[4] It is quite possible that a large foreign parent could be involved in a small joint venture abroad, but it is unlikely or very rare that a larger joint venture would involve a small foreign firm as the chief partner.

From the host country point of view, a large local joint venture would imply a large local matching investment, usually possible only for the government or for a large local interest. To the extent that advanced technology is more likely to be associated with larger firms, at least among firms which invest abroad, any technology required by a large local company which cannot be transmitted through licensing or via Fforde's "individual route"[5] is also more likely to be a corporate asset of a larger foreign company.

On the reverse of the coin, one of the more common reasons given by small to medium-sized firms for rejecting a potential local associate is the relatively large size of the latter. This is said to be associated with the fear of excessive dominance of the proposed joint operation by such an Indian or Pakistani partner. The justification for this fear is not well established. The potential ability to dominate is present, but only one British firm mentioned having actually experienced pressures of this sort. Several others indicated that there had even been a "drawing-off" from close involvement, by a large local partner, to leave the joint venture virtually independent. (Both extremes were cited with reference to experiences with Tata interests, the largest potential partners among nongovernment firms in India. There is certainly no trend in behavior here.)

Larger British companies are expected to be better able to obtain loans abroad for joint ventures with which they are associated.[6] Parent size in assets shows a slight positive correlation with the gearing of joint ventures,[7] but the cause and effect of this relationship, which is shown in Figure 4.1, is likely to be complex. If large U.K. firms tend to associate with large local interests in large joint ventures, then the fact that these joint ventures are better able to attract loan capital than smaller ones may be due to several reasons.

[4] At the 1 % level, $r = .667$ for parent size in assets and $r = .668$ for parent size in sales.

[5] J. S. Fforde, *An International Trade in Managerial Skills,* Blackwells, Oxford, 1957, pp. 26 ff.

[6] George Rosen, *Some Aspects of Industrial Finance in India,* Asia Publishing House, Bombay, 1962, pp. 13–45.

[7] At the 1 % level, when the ratio used to define gearing was total capital employed by a joint venture, divided by shareholders' capital, $r = .349$.

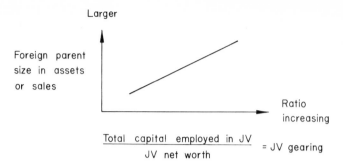

Figure 4.1
Relationship between Size of Foreign Parent Company and
Gearing of Joint Venture

One reason may be the ability of the large, presumably important and credit-worthy local partners to obtain loans through their own standing. Another possible explanation could be the potential significance of a large new joint venture to the national economy. An important new company of this type would probably have the dual status of a virtuous recipient of government-directed loans and a reliable source of return upon private funds. There is some evidence[8] that this last source of capital tends to be most attracted, in the form of both equity and loans, to local companies associated with prestigious foreign firms. To the extent that size is one aspect of prestige, the size of the foreign parents helps to explain a high gearing ratio in joint ventures with which they are associated.

Problems arose in trying to examine the effects of varying the size of the local associate upon the gearing of a joint venture, since sufficient financial information on Indian or Pakistani partners was not available. In several cases, not only was this information unavailable during the study, but it also appeared that some British companies rarely got a chance to look at their partners' books. Since many of these partners are private companies and not under obligation to publish financial details (except for taxation purposes), it may not be possible to obtain this information under any circumstances. Nonetheless, subject to the existence of such a difficulty, this dimension of joint venture organization is one worth examining in more detail in future research.

On the whole, the argument that size of the joint venture is in itself an explanation of the availability of loan capital does not appear to be supported by the evidence. None of the measures of joint venture size

---

[8] For some details of oversubscription of issues by foreign-associated companies in India, up to 1962, see the *Economic Times,* of Bombay, July 10, 1962.

are highly correlated with those of joint venture gearing. More important was the size of the foreign firm's share in the equity of the joint
company. Over a subsample of the local joint operations, there is some
indication that joint ventures' gearing ratios tend to increase with the
size of the British share in the equity of the joint venture.[9]

This is partly due to the fact that an increase in this share is likely to
make the foreign parent more prepared to provide loans itself to the
joint venture. The concern expressed in many of these British firms for
control over a joint venture's operations is consistent with a greater
inclination to provide loan funds to a clearly controlled local company
than to one in which a local partner holds an equity majority. Such an
inducement appears to have some validity according to responses
during discussion. For example, a large vehicle manufacturer was
negotiating a deal with the host government whereby the firm would
make a loan indirectly to a joint venture in which they were involved
in order to enable the latter to carry out a needed expansion project.
The collateral desired by the British partner was government permission
to convert the loan into an equivalent holding of equity in case of
default. Such conversion would have increased the foreign share in
equity to a majority holding, an undesirable concession according to
official Indian Government policy.

Also relevant was the attraction of a joint venture with which a
powerful or well-known foreign firm was associated. The attraction
would presumably be enhanced if the foreign partner clearly had the
ability to dictate operations. Local (or foreign, third party) funds
would therefore be more attracted to a joint venture as its equity
distribution suggested increasing control by a well-known foreign
company.

As a general rule, gearing should also be correlated with the performance of a joint venture, on the grounds that loans would be more
readily available to profitable operations. This idea receives some
support from the results of the study. Gearing ratios showed some
positive correlation with the ratios of profits to sales and profits to
capital employed.[10] (Since, however, this whole relationship was of
post hoc, rather than *propter hoc*, status, it was of less interest for
predictive purposes.) No other joint venture characteristic appeared to
be very strongly related to its gearing. It seemed reasonable, therefore,
to assume that the latter was primarily a function of the characteristics
of the foreign parent company, of its size in particular, measured in
terms of both assets and sales.

[9] At the 5% level, $r = .246$.
[10] At the 1% level, $r = .419$, and at the 5% level, $r = .348$, respectively.

Size, Control, and Reasons for Going into a Joint Venture

Some of the previous studies of joint ventures have suggested that the size of the foreign parent company has an effect upon its attitudes toward control, equity control in particular.[11] "A big international company is more likely to demand—and get—control of a new joint venture, than any other," according to the comment of Kidron on foreign investment in India.[12] A study published by the National Industrial Conference Board (N.I.C.B.) in 1966 reported, "The survey findings indicate that, if the foreign investor is a large internationally aggressive company, with ample resources to expand outside the home market . . . [it] feels in a position to demand majority ownership in a joint venture, and, as a matter of policy, will seek [this] out."[13]

On the whole, the case of British joint ventures in India and Pakistan supports these arguments. More specifically, there is a significant[14] relationship between size of foreign firms and their attitudes toward equity control, as represented in Figure 4.2. Over half the cases in

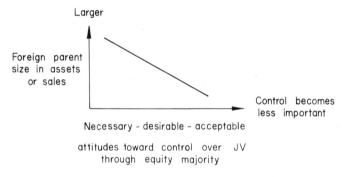

Figure 4.2
Relationship between Size of Foreign Parent and Attitudes toward Control

which majority control is felt to be necessary involve large, or very large, companies. In over 80% of their joint ventures, firms in these two classes felt that such control was necessary or desirable, as compared with less than 50% of the joint ventures of small or medium-sized firms.

[11] The control measures are described in Chapter 5.
[12] Michael Kidron, *Foreign Investment in India,* Oxford University Press, London, 1965, p. 278.
[13] Karen K. Bivens and Enid B. Lovell, *Joint Ventures with Foreign Partners, International Survey of Business Opinion and Experience,* National Industrial Conference Board, New York, 1966, p. 6.
[14] Significant at the 0.020 level for asset size, and the 0.016 level for sales size. The discussion in the last paragraph is based upon the figure for parent size in assets.

Over 60% of the cases in which majority control is described as being no more than acceptable involve small and medium U.K. parents.

This finding may be partly due to a pragmatic recognition of the realities of the situation. Smaller companies would be expected to have a weaker bargaining position, vis-à-vis the host government, in insisting upon a majority share in the equity of a joint venture. If so, attempts at reduction of possible dissonance between ability to achieve and aspirations might result in rationalization of the latter at a lower level.[15] Such an argument would certainly be consistent with the comments of Kidron and the N.I.C.B. study on the other end of the scale.

This relationship may, however, reflect more than just the consequences of a toe-to-toe bargaining conflict. It is quite possible that the differences arise because of a genuinely more relaxed attitude toward control on the part of smaller firms. Such an attitude is not necessarily evidence of a major difference in the managerial philosophies of companies related to their size. Rather, it may be a result of the way in which a joint venture is set up and its original *raison d'être*. When parent size is examined in relation to the chief reason given by U.K. parents for going into a particular joint venture,[16] there appears to be some support for this refinement of the interpretation, as shown in Table 4.2.

Table 4.2
Foreign Parent Size in Assets and Reasons for Going into a Joint Venture

Reasons for Going into a Joint Venture	Foreign Parent Size in Assets								
	Number of Cases and Cell % Based on Column Sum*								
	Small		Medium		Large		V. Large		Total
	No.	%	No.	%	No.	%	No.	%	No.
Explicit host government pressure	1	9	2	18	3	13	13	52	19
Implicit host government pressure	3	27	—	—	5	21	3	12	11
Spreading the risk	—	—	1	9	5	21	—	—	6
Need for local facilities/ resources	7	64	8	73	11	46	9	36	35
Total and (% based on row sum)	11	(16)	11	(16)	24	(34)	25	(35)	71

* Percentages do not all add up to 100 because of rounding.

[15] This appears to be a reasonable application of the ideas in Leon Festinger, *A Theory of Cognitive Dissonance,* Stanford University Press, Stanford, 1957.
[16] This relationship was significant at the 0.007 level for size in assets, and at the 0.009 level for size in sales.

Over 60 % of the very large foreign companies felt that they, in effect, were forced to go into a joint venture in a given case. More than 50 % felt that this pressure was quite explicit. On the other hand, only one out of eleven cases involving small British companies, and two out of eleven cases involving medium-sized British companies, were said to have been forced upon these foreign parents explicitly. Three more small firms felt that fear of such pressures influenced their decision.

The remainder of these smaller companies chose to go into a joint venture in a particular case primarily for other reasons. Usually, this was because they themselves needed certain facilities or resources possessed by potential associates in order to operate satisfactorily in India or in Pakistan. If they were expecting these contributions to be provided by a local partner, they could be expected to recognize the latter's claim to a larger share in the equity of the joint venture.

If one assumes that most foreign investors prefer a majority share in joint venture equity and if one ignores for the moment the arguments for and against such a predilection, is there an easing off in the desire for ownership once the significant figure of 51 % is attained? Does this desire vary with the size of the foreign investor? In order to find an answer to these questions, parent size in sales was examined in relation to the attitudes of these investors to a holding of 75 % or more of the joint venture equity.[17] The figure of 75 % was chosen for two reasons:

a. In relative terms, it is used here as a general target figure, representing a substantially large equity majority.

b. In absolute terms, under the Indian Company (Amendment) Act of 1960,[18] certain rights of shareholders, changes in administration, and liquidation of a company can be altered or arranged only with the agreement of the holders of 75 % of the issued voting shares.

While the distribution of responses did not suggest a significant trend in variation by size of the foreign parent company, it did appear to confound two prior expectations related to risk-avoidance schedules. The first expectation is that equity holding might be kept to a minimum above a level which would give the foreign firm a majority, as one way of minimizing the exposure of assets to a risky environment. This concern for exposed assets was part of a foreign investment strategy

[17] Attitudes were measured on a five-level scale. The relationship between the two variables was significant (at the 0.004 level) but was unevenly distributed. In no case was such a holding felt to be necessary (level 1), or unnecessary (level 4). Two small and one very large firm said that 75 % would be unacceptable to them (level 5). In 20 cases, of which 10 were medium-sized firms, 75 % would have been acceptable (level 3). For all of the remaining 47 cases, a 75 % holding would have been desirable (level 2).

[18] Company (Amendment) Act of 1960. See also Indian Companies Act, 1956, as amended, Schedule 1, Table A.

suggested by a Vice President of Merck & Co., Inc. during a seminar in 1965, in connection with operations in Brazil.[19] Second, one might expect that the importance attributed to such a method of reducing the risk in foreign investment would tend to vary inversely with the size of the foreign parent company.

There were several reasonable explanations for the rejection of the first of these predictions. Parent companies probably felt that the larger their share in the equity of a joint venture, the less the risk to their own participation through contrary action by partners. Perhaps coupled with this was the argument that while such risk was due to environmental effects, as well as to internal business variability, it was best reduced by restricting the total amount of voting equity issued, and increasing gearing through local loan capital. In other words, this means investing overseas in the "American style,"[20] rather than limiting the foreign as a proportion of total equity.

The explanation may even be much more straightforward. British firms, for historical reasons, did not seem to consider India or Pakistan to be particularly risky environments. If this were the case, these investors may simply have wished to increase their share in the return by increasing their share in the investment. This situation may be changing. Over a quarter of these British senior executives mentioned strong doubts about the future desirability of India as a locus for investment. Typical was the comment of a director of a large chemical company: "Our main reassurance for the future in India is in the fact that our experience with this joint venture has been reasonably good. We would certainly hesitate to invest in any other projects at the moment, because of the difficulty in forecasting India's political and economic development." In essence, these executives were worried about an increase in the element of uncertainty rather than in risk, to use Aharoni's distinction.[21] India's future performance and political stability were felt to be becoming less predictable.[22]

[19] Discussed by Mr. Leo Fernandez, Vice President, Western Hemisphere Operations, Merck, Sharp and Dohme, International, Division of Merck and Co. Inc., at a seminar at the Massachusetts Institute of Technology, December 15, 1964.

[20] As an example of this particular phenomenon in India, the practice of two U.S. rubber companies before 1955 was interesting. According to a Government of India report, in 1955, Firestone showed an annual turnover of Rs. 70 million on a total paid-up capital of Rs. 20,000. In the same year Goodyear had a turnover of Rs. 40 million on a paid-up capital of Rs. 15,000. (Government of India, Tariff Commission, *Report on the Fair Prices of Rubber Tyres and Tubes,* 1955.) However, both firms have since increased their local capitalization and reduced the ratios above.

[21] Yair Aharoni, *The Foreign Investment Decision Process,* Division of Research, Graduate School of Business Administration, Harvard University, Boston, 1966, pp. 35–39 and 274–282.

[22] Doubts of this kind about India's future are nothing new. See Selig S. Harrison, *India: The Most Dangerous Decades,* Princeton University Press, Princeton, 1960, pp. 54–62.

A possible reason for the apparent lack of difference in attitudes, between large and small firms, to a large majority holding in the equity of an overseas joint venture, may have been the homogeneity of the sample along the size dimension. The category "small" may perhaps only have been valid in the context of this sample. Only one British parent company had assets and sales of less than $10 million. Three others had assets of less than $20 million, but their sales were considerably greater.

The two small firms which would have found an equity holding of 75% or more unacceptable were the two smallest. At the same time, the one very large company which made this response did so in reference to a joint venture in which its participation was in the form of a long-term contract (involving set-up supervision, training, and supply of components), with a large, public sector operation. In this case, the question of foreign equity control was quite obviously irrelevant. If this case were removed, the remainder of the responses could very broadly be interpreted as showing some slight support for the argument that the size of the equity share in a joint venture desired by a British parent firm varied directly with the size of the firm.

Parent Size and Selection of Associates

Carrying further some of the arguments discussed, one would expect that if large firms were inclined to "go it alone" in their overseas invest-

Table 4.3
Foreign Parent Size in Assets and Reasons for Selecting a Specific Associate

Reasons for Selecting an Associate	Foreign Parent Size in Assets								
	Number of Cases and Cell % Based on Column Sum*								
	Small		Medium		Large		V. Large		Total
	No.	%	No.	%	No.	%	No.	%	No.
Forced choice	—	—	—	—	3	13	9	36	12
Convenience of facilities/ resources	4	36	4	36	10	42	6	24	24
Favorable past association	7	64	4	36	5	21	4	16	20
Status/identity, etc.	—	—	3	28	6	25	6	24	15
Total and (% based on row sum)	11	(16)	11	(16)	24	(34)	25	(35)	71

* Percentages do not all add up to 100 because of rounding. Relationship between variables significant at the 0.016 level.

ments, felt that they were forced into joint ventures against their wishes, and looked for control, they would also feel limited in their choice of partners. On the other hand, smaller firms, being more relaxed in attitudes toward control or choice and looking for positive benefits from a joint operation, should choose their associates because of the latter's resources or potential attributes, rather than because they felt they were forced into such a choice. These arguments were supported by the relationship between parent size and reasons for selecting specific joint venture associates as shown in Table 4.3.

The only firms forced into their choice of partners, 17% of the sample, were larger companies, three quarters of them very large. To some extent, this was due to the matching constraint. The choice of potentially compatible partners for such foreign investors was likely to be more limited. At the extreme, their only choice was the one significant local interest in the field or, alternatively, the host government. "Project size sufficient to deter a firm from investing . . . other than on terms unacceptable overseas, may also make it probable that an overseas government is the only likely local partner."[23]

This last point is particularly valid so far as the oil companies are concerned. Whatever their own inclinations may have been, all the U.K. firms in this group had the decision preempted by the local government in several ventures. This was the case, for example, in Titas Gas Transmission Company Ltd., a mixed venture involving Shell in East Pakistan. It was also the case for Burmah Oil in several mixed ventures, including: the two Sui gas projects, Sui Gas Transmission Company Ltd.,[24] and Sui Northern Gas Pipelines Ltd. (in West Pakistan); Eastern Refinery Ltd. (in the eastern wing of the same country); and Oil India Ltd. in India.

There may also be an element of forced choice for the larger British companies in the fact that they chose their partners in 25% of the cases primarily because of the status of the latter. Status was considered in terms of both financial standing and influence, especially influence with local authorities. This relationship could be expected, on the grounds that these firms would need to find comparable and compatible partners under the suggested matching constraint. It might also be expected, however, that status of a local partner would be an important reason for selection by smaller U.K. companies, largely as a feature of

---

[23] Cf. Fforde, *An International Trade in Managerial Skills,* p. 88.
[24] The origins of this joint venture were reported in detail in Wolfgang G. Friedmann and George Kalmanoff, *Joint International Business Ventures,* Columbia University Press, New York, 1961, pp. 456–466. It was also reported in the *Burmah Group Magazine,* No. 5, Spring, 1966, pp. 10–18.

their anticipated risk-avoidance schedules. Actually, in only 20% of the cases in which status is a ruling consideration, is the British parent in the medium-size category. In no cases did a small company cite status as its primary selection criterion.

This result is probably due to a fact noted earlier, that most smaller British firms go into joint ventures in the first place because they need local facilities or resources. On the other hand, the figures in Table 4.3 show that, when it comes to the selection of a specific partner, only about 36% of these smaller firms indicated that this choice was specifically determined by the potential contribution of such facilities or resources by a local interest. This appears to contradict the assumption just made. However, another section of the results in the same table may conceal the explanation.

A total of 64% of the small firms and 36% of the medium-size firms stated that favorable past association was their main reason for choosing a particular partner. For such companies, satisfactory past experiences may well have provided the most acceptable method of defining a partner's status, or for reducing the possible area of risk in associating with local interests. This consideration was especially relevant when, because of the matching size constraint, potential local partners were themselves smaller firms, firms which were not usually as reliably documented and reported as were the giants. This feature was further compounded in its effect in that a higher proportion of these smaller local interests were likely to be private firms (i.e. close corporations)[25] free from the restraining influence of publicly audited financial results.

In a similar manner, the high proportion of answers from smaller U.K. parents citing favorable past association as the prime selection criterion in a specific case may have concealed another feature. The associate chosen for meritorious past conduct may well have been contributing the facilities or resources which had motivated the decision to go into a joint venture. There was an element of the chicken-or-egg riddle in this relationship. Although it might have entered into a joint venture in order to obtain lacking facilities or resources, would the smaller British company have gone into such a project at all, without the security engendered by a favorable past association?

For 36% of these firms, the answer was presumably "yes." For the others, it seemed unlikely that past association, no matter how favorable, would have been enough to motivate a foreign firm to go into a joint venture with a partner which had nothing more tangible to offer than such association. This seemed even less likely when the joint operation

[25] See Indian Companies Act, 1956, as amended, Sec. 4 (7), for a description of the private companies in India.

would still have been short of certain facilities or resources which the foreign parent could not itself provide. Nor is there any evidence in this study to suggest such a case. When past association was the prime reason, it led to a choice between a number of possible partners endowed with the necessary attributes, or of one which had already proved the extent of its endowment.

Parent Size and Profitability of Joint Ventures

Because of some of the advantages generally supposed to accrue to size—more particularly, internal economies of scale and external ability to exert monopolistic pressures on prices and upon potential competition—it could be expected that returns on investments in joint ventures would tend to vary directly with size. Local conditions would be likely, if anything, to enhance this effect. Firms which were relatively large in the United Kingdom would presumably have even greater competitive advantages in the limited development of the Indian and Pakistani economies (especially when these advantages were amplified by tariff or import quota protection).

If these assumptions are valid, one might expect a direct and positive correlation between parent size and such ratios as the return before U.K. taxes on long-term investment by British firms in associated joint ventures. Rates of return for this group of investments[26] in India and Pakistan were classified into three categories as in Table 4.4.

Such assumptions do not appear to be entirely valid, however. There is a significant relationship[27] between size of foreign parent and return

Table 4.4
Classification of Joint Ventures by Rate of Return before U.K. Taxes
on British Parent Companies' Long-Term Investment

% Return on Long-Term Investment in a Joint Venture	Category	Number of Joint Ventures in Subsample	Weighted Group Average Return
10% or less	Low	12	6.5%
11% to 20%	Medium	17	14.5%
Over 20%	High	10	27.0%
Overall Subsample Total and Average		39	15.3%

[26] This return included fees, royalties, profits, and interest earned. The investment covered the British share in equity, reserves and surplus, plus medium- and long-term loans to the joint venture. These data were available only for a subsample of 39 joint ventures.
[27] At the 0.009 level for size in assets and the 0.018 level for size in sales.

on investment in a joint venture. As Figure 4.3 shows, this relationship appears to contradict, quite clearly, the general assumptions that this return would vary directly with the size of the British parent company.

More detailed analysis of individual cases added some further evidence. For example, out of sixteen smaller firms, only two show returns in the low category while five small and four medium-sized parent companies had investments earning over 20%. On the other hand, only one out of fifteen large firms, and no very large ones, are in the high returns category, while eight large and two very large firms are in the lowest group.

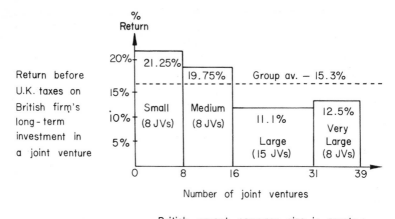

Figure 4.3
Return on Investment in Joint Ventures, According to Size
of British Parent Company

Some possible explanations for this reversal from expectations follow two lines. First, interest charges in these two countries were limited by the effect of host government tax policies. At the same time, the larger British firms were those most capable of providing loans to joint ventures—and, in fact, were the companies which did so. Thus their overall returns, as constituted here, incorporate for some companies the results of an effective limit of around $6\frac{1}{2}\%$ on interest payments.[28]

[28] Interest rates on loan funds are higher than this in India and Pakistan. See J. D. Nyhart and Edmond F. Janssens, *A Global Directory of Development Finance Institutions in Developing Countries,* The Development Center of the Organization for Economic Co-operation and Development, Paris, 1967, pp. 143–169 and 287–293. This is, however, the rate at which high levels of taxation on returns commenced.

Second, the effects of the operations of larger parent firms and larger joint ventures are more "visible" locally in terms of their significance to the host economy. Smaller firms may not, therefore, suffer quite such strict surveillance over prices and high rates of return as larger companies. The latter are likely to have their results subjected to much closer official scrutiny and regulation, because of what is felt to be the national interest.[29] There appeared, however, to be a stage at which the international leverage of the very large firms is such that these companies can themselves prevent the host government from completely limiting their advantages. Some evidence for the existence of such a stage comes from the fact that 75% of the ventures involving very large British parents show returns in the 11%–20% class (even though none appeared able to achieve a higher rate of return).

Parent Size and Methods of Evaluating Joint Ventures

How do companies assess the performance of international and overseas operations? Is this a relatively scientific or objective evaluation anchored closely to predetermined criteria, or is it a much more pragmatic type of activity, showing a close relationship to what the market will bear or offer? One might suspect that in many cases evaluation of the success, or otherwise, of overseas investments—joint ventures in particular—would not be as pure an operation in practice as in theory. More specifically this would imply that

a. Clearly specified minimum acceptable rates of return would probably not have been determined by many foreign investors.
b. Even when such "benchmarks" were established, they would tend to be treated pragmatically in the light of circumstances rather than used as a strict control over investment.

The problems and issues involved are many. Apart from the difficulty in determining what constituted a reasonable or optimum rate of return on these investments for any given case, such figures would tend to be merely a formal, even an arbitrary, financial guide. Variation in such figures would probably be less significant than levels of achievement in relation to certain more general objectives, objectives which were of underlying importance when the original decision was made to invest in a given project or market.

Among the British companies involved in this study, return on investment was cited as a primary basis for evaluation in only thirty-one of their investments in this group of joint ventures. In thirteen more, this

---

[29] This argument was supported in discussion by the comments of executives from both large and smaller British firms.

particular measure of return was recognized as one component in an evaluation matrix. For twenty-five joint ventures, no fixed levels of return were used as guides. Even among the firms which did set a minimum acceptable figure, this was treated with considerable tolerance, as typified by this comment from the managing director of an electrical company: "We feel that, once committed, it is probably too late to worry about firm performance standards, as we can't very well get out, except by incurring considerable 'write-off' losses. This would need a terrible and sustained performance."

More important to most of these foreign parent companies in evaluating joint venture performance was achievement of the more general objectives. For convenience, these are grouped into four categories:

a. Long-term development of the local market,
b. Actual performance against budgeted output and/or cost standards,
c. Contribution to integration of the international operations of the foreign parent company.
d. Achievement of returns other than dividends (i.e., fees, royalties, transfer pricing margins).

If these categories of scheduled objectives are used as a basis for comparison, the size of the British parent company turns out to be significantly related to the nature of the primary overall objectives used

Table 4.5
Foreign Parent Size in Sales and Evaluation of Joint Ventures through Performance against Scheduled Objectives

Scheduled Objectives	Foreign Parent Size in Sales									
	Number of Cases and Cell % Based on Column Sum*									
	Small		Medium		Large		Very Large		Total	
	No.	%	No.	%	No.	%	No.	%	No.	%
Long-term market development	—	—	13	77	6	43	7	25	26	42
Output or cost performance	2	67	2	12	1	7	7	25	12	19
International integration	—	—	1	6	3	21	12	43	16	26
Other returns	1	33	1	6	4	29	2	7	8	13
Total and (% based on row sum)	3	(5)	17	(27)	14	(23)	28	(45)	62	(100)

* Percentages do not all add up to 100 because of rounding.

in evaluating the success of a joint venture.[30] This relationship is shown in Table 4.5.

A concern for international integration was considered likely to and did increase with the size of the parent company. Larger firms are more capable of having, and more likely to have, a wider range of international operations. This being so, they are more likely to be concerned with the integration of this type of operation.

It was also expected that larger firms would be more likely to have longer time horizons and to seek long-term market development. This is only partly supported by the evidence. For example, 43 % of the large firms cited this as their primary objective. Only 25 % of the very large firms made this their prime criterion. However, it is worth noting that from the point of view of these companies, there is probably a certain element of continuity between this objective and that of international integration. To some extent, the latter actually involves the long-term development of a complex of markets.

A noticeable feature of this set of responses is the concern of medium-sized companies for long-term market development. In the medium category 50 % of the firms citing this objective, and 77 % of the medium-sized firms gave such development as their primary criterion for evaluation. No small companies gave this reason. This particular finding may constitute further evidence of continuity in objectives as a possible underlying explanation.

At the same time, however, the medium-sized firms were those which stated most frequently that they had gone into a joint venture in India or Pakistan primarily in order to develop a new market. Larger companies were usually defending an existing market, reacting to a tariff, or else matching competitive needs.[31] These results suggest that the hypothesis relating larger size to longer time horizons is incomplete, at best, in terms of its relevance to these companies. On the other hand, neither age of joint ventures nor type of business were significantly associated with overall evaluation criteria used by foreign parents. A better explanation than those put forward is therefore not available.

Achievement of other returns was mentioned as a primary consideration in only 13 % of these cases. This response accounted for 29 % of the answers given by foreign parents in the large class, but was not important for the others. It had been expected that this method of evaluation would be more important for smaller foreign firms or would be associated with smaller foreign shares in joint venture equity. The

[30] At the 0.003 level.
[31] These results appear to agree with those reported in Kidron, *Foreign Investment in India,* pp. 253–255.

latter relationship was not significant. The former was valid for a single case, which appeared to be slender evidence upon which to base conclusions.[32] Most of these companies were more concerned with the return to corporate objectives of a corporate package of skills, technology, and investment rather than with possible returns to individual components of such a package. This concern appeared to be as much a characteristic of the smaller as of larger foreign parent firms.

Profitability of the Foreign Parent Companies

After looking at the effects of parent company size upon various characteristics of joint ventures, one must consider another dimension of variation. Size is to some extent a measure of efficiency. A better measure for many purposes is profitability. In the context of overseas joint ventures, what sort of operation is associated with profitable foreign investor companies? In particular, how do performance and criteria for evaluating performance vary with the profitability of the foreign parent?

There are as many ways of distinguishing between firms by their profitability as by their size. Again, as argued earlier, discussion of the analytical merits of various financial ratios would be of limited direct relevance here. Briefly, therefore, three main measures were used to examine some of the effects of variations in the profitability of British parent companies. These were net profits of the company as a proportion of shareholders' capital (net return on investment, or NRI), capital employed (NPCE), or total sales (NP Sales).[33]

The distribution of the joint ventures in the sample according to these measures is shown in Table 4.6.

Profitability of British firms appears to be closely related to that of associated joint ventures in India and Pakistan. Both of the measures of parent company return on capital, NRI and NPCE, are highly correlated with similar ratios for the joint ventures in which these firms were specifically involved.[34]

---

[32] A similar reservation applied to the fact that 67 % of the small British parent companies mentioned performance against standards as a basis for evaluation, since this only involved two cases. This objective was important in 25 % of the joint ventures associated with very large foreign parents, but was not considered to be significant for the others.
[33] Profits, capital, and sales figures in these measures were all those of the British parent groups' consolidated totals.
[34] For Parent NRI and JV NRI, $r = .841$.
   For Parent NPCE and JV NRI, $r = .849$.
   For Parent NRI and JV NPCE, $r = .846$.
   For Parent NPCE and JV NPCE, $r = .853$.
   All four of these correlations were significant at the 1 % level, after allowing for N, or subsample size.

Table 4.6
Classification of Joint Ventures by Three Measures of
Profitability of the British Parent Company

Percentage Range in Profitability	Number of Cases and Cell % Based on Column Sum*					
	Net Return on Investment (NRI)		Net Profit on Capital Employed (NPCE)		Net Profit on Group Sales (NP Sales)	
	No.	%	No.	%	No.	%
5% or less	6	9	31	48	32	49
6% to 10%	39	60	22	34	28	43
11% to 15%	18	27	11	17	1	2
Over 15%	2	3	1	2	4	6
Totals	65		65		65	

* Data available for only 65 cases, from parent company reports and Exchange Telegraph Daily Statistics Service. Percentages do not all add up to 100 because of rounding.

On the whole, this relationship is what might have been expected. The fact that profitability of joint ventures varies directly with that of the U.K. parent may be a result of the latter's effectiveness, or it may reflect the nature of the two businesses. In most cases, the nature of business of the joint venture and its British parent is much the same. Each may possess some inherent competitive advantages, tending to make them comparably profitable in the U.K. and the host country. Unfortunately, however, it is not possible to distinguish between these two effects, the effect of parent company efficiency and of the nature of the business, over the cases in this sample, so their relative primacy remains un-determined.

Whatever the primary reason for the correlation between the profita-bility of British companies and that of their overseas joint ventures, there is some indication that the British companies expected this relationship to be continued. For the cases in which a specific figure was actually given by a U.K. parent as the minimum acceptable level of return on the investment associated with a joint venture, this figure varies directly with variations in the British firm's NRI.[35] The relation-ship between the two variables is outlined in Figure 4.4.

Parent companies with a higher NRI for their own activities tend to expect a higher rate of return from a joint venture. All of the cases for which a lower return was acceptable involve U.K. firms showing a

[35] Over a subsample of 32 cases for which data were available the relationship was significant at the 0.024 level.

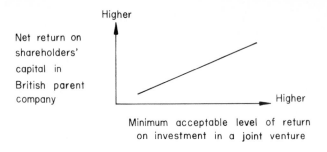

Figure 4.4
Relationship between British Parent Company's Return on Investment
and Minimum Acceptable Rate of Return on Investment
in a Joint Venture

lower level of profitability themselves. Origin of causation in this
feature is not clear. Does it reflect generally higher standards set by
more efficient parent firms? Is it the result of considered analysis of the
potential opportunity peculiar to a given joint venture? Or is it simply
that such expectations were calibrated to a continuation of the *status
quo*, in which case the relationship was "trivial"? Trivial, but possibly
an interesting indication of the way in which standards for evaluation
are set up in one area of corporate policy determination. One suspects
that a genuine answer is itself indeterminate.

More efficient firms may have set higher standards, but they do not
appear to have set them in the form of return on investment figures. In
none of the cases in which British parents are in the higher groups by
NPCE, do they evaluate joint venture performance primarily through
this criterion.[36] In 25% of these higher NPCE parents, it was cited as
part of the overall check on performance, but no more. As suggested
previously, these firms were looking at a wider matrix of returns.

For 50% of the group in which foreign parents themselves had a
higher NPCE, contribution to the international integration of their own
operations was the primary basis for evaluating a joint venture.[37] Most
of these cases involved oil companies. This finding again leads back to
the possibility that nature of business may be a more important determinant of policy of profitability than are variations in the effectiveness
of foreign parents, unless, of course, oil companies are more effective
than others, a possibility which can not be disproved from this evidence.

[36] Relationship significant at the 0.017 level.
[37] Relationship significant at the 0.015 level.

So far as "considered analysis" in financial terms is concerned, this too appears to have limited application. Some of the issues were also discussed earlier. Even after the event, in 37% of these cases, the British parent company did not know whether any additional cost or loss resulted because of operating through a joint venture, rather than through a subsidiary. Nor had they attempted to discover whether this was an effect of a joint operation. Another 20% made the comment that the issue was irrelevant. It was felt by 15% that there was merely a lower return on a lower investment, while 21% said that there was no loss; in fact, their returns were probably better than they would have been in a subsidiary. Only 7% stated that they could determine some loss through joint operations, and most of these were firms in the lower group by NP sales.[38]

In general, therefore, this evidence supports the earlier argument that optimum return on investment figures are in many cases not thoroughly determined or capable of being determined. They are probably not very important in evaluating joint venture performance, certainly not to firms considering a wider complex of investments. There also appears to be some slight indication that when such figures were felt to be important, this was part of a less flexible approach to evaluation by less effective foreign parent companies.

Among the other possible effects of variations in the profitability of foreign parent companies, it would be interesting to know if more profitable foreign investors tend to look for particular characteristics in a partner, in a relationship, or in the structure of a joint operation. The results of this study indicate that it is not possible to make predictions of this nature. The profitability measures bear little or no significant relationship to the selection criteria used in choosing associates, or to the groups of variables related to the background of that choice, or to the structure of the joint ventures.

There is a slight indication that some of the more profitable foreign parents in terms of their NRI are also more likely to be those which felt that they were forced into a joint venture.[39] It could be argued that, being more successful themselves, such companies felt more capable of operating without local assistance. On the other hand, there is also an apparently conflicting tendency for firms seeking local facilities or resources as the prime reason for going into a joint venture to be the more profitable ones.

This duality is probably explained by the existence of two different groups among the more profitable companies, as these were defined in

[38] Relationship marginally significant at the 0.057 level.
[39] Relationship marginally significant at the 0.066 level.

the relationship between parent company NRI and parent size in assets.[40] The first group consists of very large firms, powerful enough to limit officially induced erosion of their own profitability, a category which also tended to have been forced into joint ventures. The second is made up of less "visible" small firms which tended to seek complementary local facilities or resources. They therefore sought to go into joint ventures by preference.

Some Conclusions

The size and gearing of this group of joint ventures are positively correlated with size of the British parent companies, possibly because larger projects are likely to involve larger foreign and local partners. Greater ability to attract loan capital is, to some extent, a reflection of all three of these size dimensions, but primacy probably rests with the size of the foreign parent.

Few of these British companies, large or small, seem to have any inhibitions about taking a large share (75% or more) in the equity of a joint venture in India or Pakistan. Larger firms are more likely to feel they have been forced into a joint operation and, at the same time, the most likely to seek control. This may well be due to a weaker bargaining position on the part of smaller foreign investors. It may also be due to a more relaxed attitude toward control, since a higher proportion of these firms seek positive contributions from potential partners—for which they are presumably more prepared to forgo control over a joint venture. The choice of prospective associates is more limited for larger foreign firms, and these firms, the oil companies in particular, are more likely to be explicitly forced into a mixed venture.

Status of a local partner is only really significant for larger British companies, smaller ones usually choosing to continue a favorable past association with an existing associate. The tendency for partners to be matched in size enhances the importance of known associates for small foreign investors, since less substantial information is available concerning smaller local interests. There is also the fact that past associates were chosen originally by some smaller British firms because of their need for facilities or resources which these local associates could provide.

There is some evidence that profitability of joint ventures varies inversely with the size of the foreign parent. This relationship is partly due to the fact that a higher proportion of larger firms made loans to an associated joint venture, loans on which interest rates were limited by

---

[40] Significant at the 0.012 level.

local taxation. It may also be due to less stringent scrutiny of rates of return obtained and prices set by smaller companies, since these operations are less "visible" to local authorities.[41]

Return on investment figures seem to have limited importance to U.K. firms in evaluating the performance of joint ventures. Many could not, or did not, specify any acceptable minimum rate of return. In over a third of these cases, British parents had not considered, or could not determine, whether there was any cost or benefit to them in operating through a joint venture rather than through a branch or a subsidiary.

Even when a formal bench mark does exist, it is not as important as achievement (defined in more general terms) of the parent company's objectives in a wider context. Medium-sized firms usually went into these two countries in order to develop a new market, and their chief concern was with long-term development of this market. As firms increased in size, their objectives became more international in scope. Long-term development of a specific market became subsidiary to needs of international integration. Firms which did set specific minimum acceptable levels of return in evaluating joint venture performance were among the less profitable classes of British parent companies.

Profitability of joint ventures shows a high positive correlation with that of British parents, which expect this relationship to continue. It is not clear whether this relationship reflects higher standards set by more efficient parents, or simply anticipation that the *status quo* would be maintained. In the interests of a rational basis for decision behavior, one would like to argue for clearly defined standards as a function of efficiency and hence profitability. On the basis of the evidence in this case, such an argument is limited to unsubstantiated conjecture.

Since both size and profitability of British parent firms are significantly related to several of the other characteristics of joint ventures, they are useful as anchor variables in setting up a model of the joint venture process. As such, they form two separate submodels with their own network of interdependent relationships and linkages with other variables. The constitution of the model and its parts is described in Chapter 8.

---

[41] To some extent the variation in profitability depends upon the foreign parent's ability and inclination to take its return elsewhere. It was not possible to determine this extent.

5 THE NATURE OF THE BUSINESS

One of the most difficult aspects of international operations to compare across national or political boundaries is that of technological complexity.[1] Even in the same economic environment, attempts to establish a scale which can be used to distinguish corporations according to the complexity of their operations are beset with awkward problems. At the corporate level, typologies based upon capital intensity, standard international trade classifications, product, process, or market distinctions are not satisfactory as substitutes.

There are two chief reasons for these difficulties. First, methods of production vary, even domestically, more than theoretical simplification of the technical situation usually admits. Until the "perfectly competitive" state of a given product or progress market is achieved, manufacturing methods, while probably congruent over time toward some cost optimum, vary from firm to firm. The domestic product life cycle[2] can be looked at as a function of two major variables. On the one hand is the convergence of supply costs toward some perceived minimum achievable or acceptable level, largely due to gradual standardization of the methods of production. On the other hand is the rate of saturation, or effective saturation, of the market. It is the first of these variables which creates problems of classification. At any given time, the level of technical complexity involved in the methods used by two companies to produce and supply the same product can vary significantly.

The second reason is simpler. Most major corporations are actually involved in producing a range of products for different markets. The question then arises: By which of the many types of operation, product markets, and processes should they most representatively be classified?

At the level of international operations, the problems become even more complex. The same firm may be associated with different products

---

[1] The technical background to these difficulties is one of the main themes in Wickham Skinner, *American Industry in Developing Economies. The Management of International Manufacturing,* John Wiley & Sons, New York, 1968.
[2] For an excellent development of the arguments of the product life cycle theories, see Seev Hirsch, *Location of Industry and International Competitiveness,* Clarendon Press, Oxford, 1967, esp. pp. 16–41, in which the approach is developed from the findings in S. Kuznets, *Economic Change,* W. W. Norton, New York, 1953.

overseas, or with different production functions for making the same product,[3] as it extends the product life cycle by introducing an international dimension.[4] This is the case for many of the British parent companies of overseas joint ventures. They themselves are involved in a diversity of operations of varying levels of complexity, so that any single classification is more arbitrary than comprehensive.

So far as the joint ventures in India and Pakistan are concerned, the differences in production functions between operations in these two host countries and in Britain are too variable to control.[5] It is not possible to classify either parent firms or joint ventures in any meaningful way according to the level of technological complexity of their activities.[6] It is necessary, therefore, to establish some fairly arbitrary method of classification to provide a basis for analysis.

In all but one case, the nature of business of the joint venture in India or Pakistan is the same as at least some part of that of the British parent company. This provides a starting point. British firms are classified by their major type of business into seven categories; so are joint ventures. This arbitrary method of classification exaggerates slightly the overall difference between parents and joint ventures according to the nature of their respective operations. Thus the figures in Table 5.1 suggest a difference in roughly 10 % of all cases, whereas the true overall difference was in fact less than 2 %.

Given this basic similarity between the two variables, "parent business" and "joint venture business,"[7] it is possible to combine them and use either one as the basis for further analysis of joint venture activities and relationships.[8] The nature of the foreign parent usually

[3] See Kindleberger's argument for divergences in production functions as an explanation of the "Leontief Paradox," C. P. Kindleberger, *Foreign Trade and the National Economy,* Yale University Press, New Haven, 1962, p. 77.

[4] Raymond Vernon, "International Trade and International Investment in the Product Cycle," in *Quarterly Journal of Economics,* Vol. LXXX, May 1966, pp. 190–207; and also by the same author, *Manager in the International Economy,* Prentice–Hall, Englewood Cliffs, N.J., 1968, pp. 77–83. See also Hirsch, *Location of Industry and International Competitiveness,* pp. 25–41.

[5] At least at the level of analysis of technical variation which was possible under the conditions of the study. Successful research directed specifically toward the definition and classification of production functions and their variation internationally would provide a highly useful tool for future analysis of international operations.

[6] Similar problems were also mentioned in Michael Kidron, *Foreign Investments in India,* Oxford University Press, London, 1965, for example, p. 244, but the only technical classification used was by nature of business.

[7] These two variable names are used throughout the text as abbreviations for the nature of the parent company's business and the nature of the joint venture's business.

[8] Both parent business and joint venture business were tested against other variables in order to justify this procedure. In each case the significance of the resulting relationships is very similar for the two measures of nature of business against any particular third variable, while the direction of variation is the same.

Table 5.1
Classification of British Parent Companies and Associated
Joint Ventures According to the Nature of the Business

Nature of the Business	Category Description	Number of Cases		
		British Parent Firms	Joint Ventures Classified by Business of the Parent	JV
Oil, petrochemicals, natural gas	Oil	5	13	12
Chemicals, pharmaceuticals, plastics, fertilizers, pesticides, etc.	Chemicals	13	16	17
Heavy and light engineering, machine tools, instruments, mechanical handling equipment, etc.	Engineering	8	10	9
Electrical equipment, materials and cables	Electricals	9	15	14
Vehicles and transport equipment, components and accessories	Vehicles	5	7	9
Metals, metal products, glass, ceramics	Metals	5	5	6
Tobacco and food products, other	Tobacco, food	4	5	4
Totals		49	71	71

determines that of an associated joint venture. The former is therefore used in examining the effects upon other variables of variations in the nature of the business.

The nature of business turns out to be significantly associated with most of the other characteristics of joint ventures and therefore to be potentially a useful predictor of their manner and direction of variation. In terms of defining anchor variables for a model of the joint venture process, the extent of the relationships between nature of business and other variables clearly indicates that the former would be an excellent anchor.[9]

[9] The framework of the model and its parts based upon various anchor variables appears in Chapter 8. The relationships and linkages based upon nature of business are shown on pages 160–161.

It is unfortunate that there does not appear to be a significant relationship between nature of business and the reason for going into a joint venture.[10] Such an association would have provided stronger evidence for or against a hypothesis that the joint venture decision is governed by bilateral monopolistic advantage. More specifically, it would have indicated the extent to which conditions of bilateral monopoly are governed by the nature of the business. In line with this theory,[11] it would be presumed that industries associated with more modern and powerful technology would be more desirable to the host country and therefore in a stronger bargaining position. As a result, firms from such industries could be expected to state less frequently than others that they had been forced into joint ventures. An argument along these lines appeared to be supported by the experience of companies such as I.B.M., A.E.I., or English Electric in India.[12]

Attitudes toward Control

In general terms, the need or desirability for control by the foreign parent of a joint venture's operations varies with different types of industry and activity. This is partly a function of the complexity of the technology involved and of its strangeness to the host environment. It depends too upon the relative level of sophistication of the host environment. In turn, the attitudes of foreign parent firms toward such control are based partly upon objective criteria; they also reflect considerations, fears, and doubts which are more subjectively evaluated.

Both the needs and attitudes are interdependent. They each tend to vary according to the nature of business of the companies involved. Along the same lines, it was stated in an earlier study on behalf of the National Industrial Conference Board, "A company's preference for a minority or a majority position in a joint venture is very often dictated by the type of business. . . . The value of local partners will vary with

[10] Among the other variables which were tested but turned out not to be significantly related to nature of business, at least not within the limited size of this sample population, were
a. Past knowledge of the host country, or of the selected associate;
b. Availability of alternatives to the chosen associate;
c. The nature of the initial contact, or the original approach to set up a joint venture;
d. Location of responsibility within the British parent company for the initiation and promotion of a specific project.
[11] See Stephen Hymer, *The International Operations of National Firms, a Study of Direct Foreign Investment,* unpublished doctoral dissertation in economics, M.I.T., 1960, Chapters 1, 2.
[12] The cases of I.B.M. and English Electric were described in Matthew J. Kust, *Foreign Enterprises in India, Laws and Policies,* The University of North Carolina Press, Chapel Hill, 1964, pp. 148–149.

each type of business."[13] The comments of the executives of British corporations investing in India and Pakistan confirm this variation. Before the actual nature of the variation in attitudes toward control is examined, it is worth considering briefly some of the general assumptions which might reasonably be made concerning the desire for control in different industry or business groups.

It could reasonably be assumed that the vehicle and transport equipment industry would indicate a strong desire for control. This would be due in part to the fact that the aggressive competition in which these companies are almost universally involved does not appear likely to favor joint operations, or at least joint responsibilities. It would also be due in part to the scale of operations which is commonly a feature of this type of business. Bivens and Lovell argue that "companies in industries requiring large-scale production units ... generally desire controlling interests in joint ventures."[14]

Oil and associated interests are familiar with, and to some extent reconciled to, the vagaries of host nations. In general, however, they could be expected to seek control over the activities of a joint venture

Table 5.2
Nature of Business and Attitudes of British Parent Companies toward Effective Control over a Joint Venture

Nature of Business	Number of Cases and Cell % Based on Row Sum*									
	Effective Control Described as:								Totals	
	Necessary		Desirable		Acceptable		Unnecessary			
	No.	%	No.	%	No.	%	No.	%	No.	%
Oil	—	—	11	85	1	8	1	8	13	19
Chemicals	2	13	12	80	1	7	—	—	15	21
Engineering	2	20	—	—	4	40	4	40	10	14
Electricals	5	33	2	13	6	40	2	13	15	21
Vehicles	1	14	3	43	1	14	2	29	7	10
Metals	1	20	1	20	2	40	1	20	5	7
Tobacco, food	3	60	—	—	—	—	2	40	5	7
Totals	14	20	29	41	15	21	12	17	70	

* Percentages do not all add up to 100 because of rounding. Percentages in the final column are based on the column sum.

[13] Karen Kraus Bivens and Enid Baird Lovell, *Joint Ventures with Foreign Partners, International Survey of Business Opinion and Experience,* National Industrial Conference Board, New York, 1966, p. 13.
[14] *Ibid.,* p. 14.

wherever possible in order to facilitate optimum international integration of their operations. In the case of food and tobacco companies, the argument is slightly different. These firms are used to operating in other countries in monopolistic or, more often, oligopolistic markets. Unless their investment philosophies changed dramatically, they would probably tend to seek control largely in order that they could continue to operate in the manner to which they had become accustomed.

On the other hand, the basic diversity of the types of operations included in the classification used for the engineering, metals, and electricals groups suggests that their attitudes toward control should not show many consistent intragroup tendencies. Finally, one could argue that the chemicals group would probably be more relaxed than most in terms of their desire for formal control over a joint venture. This could be argued on the grounds of the leverage which could be exerted by such companies, through a joint venture's dependence upon their corporate process technology and continuing research and development results.

In fact, attitudes toward control do vary significantly according to the nature of business of the foreign parent company.[15] The ways in which the results vary are not, however, entirely as might have been expected. The actual variation is shown in Table 5.2.

Executives from the vehicles group clearly found an important distinction between the two concepts of joint venture control. Responses from this group were very different in the two measures of attitudes toward control. The opinion expressed for all cases in this group was that majority control of equity would be necessary, or desirable.[16] This evidence is in agreement with the arguments given. However, as the figures in Table 5.2 indicate, effective control is a less important consideration in 43 % of this particular subgroup of joint ventures. These foreign investors appear to consider that equity control gave them a final sanction which was consistent with their investment policies. Since, however, they were all satisfied with the effectiveness of their associates, they were prepared to leave effective control of operations to them.

Most members of the food and tobacco group considered that control was necessary, however defined. One of the two cases in this group in which control was described as unnecessary actually involves

[15] The two measures of attitudes toward control are explained in Chapter 7. The desire for majority (equity) control is probably self-explanatory. In the desire for effective control, the definition of "effective" was deliberately left to respondents. Both were significantly related to nature of business at the 0.000 level.
[16] Statement based on the cross-tabulation of nature of business and attitudes toward majority control. Results are not shown in the tables in the text because of duplication.

the one British parent which is neither a food nor a tobacco company, but is included under the heading "other." Responses from the metals and electricals group are as varied as the earlier arguments suggested.[17] On the whole, therefore, the attitudes of these three groups of foreign parent companies agree quite closely with the forecasts.

In overall terms, however, the attitudes toward control of companies in the engineering group tended to be rather more relaxed than predicted. None of these parent firms stated that equity control was necessary and only 20% felt they needed effective control. A probable explanation here is the proportion of smaller investments in this group. Some of these involved relatively "painless" participation by British firms, in the form of equity shares in a joint venture granted, under the original agreement, in return for licenses or know-how.[18] In others, the foreign participation was in the form of plant or machinery which had already been depreciated in Britain. Some of these British firms also earned additional returns from a joint venture investment through continuing technical assistance contracts, or through the supply of components. Among this group of companies were several which, according to statements during interviews, were not interested, and had not been interested in the past, in running a company in India or Pakistan under any circumstances. The reason usually given was lack of the necessary staff.

On the whole, the answers from oil and associated interests conformed to expectations. While neither effective control nor a majority share in joint venture equity was considered to be *necessary* for any of the joint operations in which these firms were involved, each of these methods of control was felt to be *desirable* in 85% of the cases. There is, perhaps, an element of philosophical resignation, or at least a pragmatic recognition of reality, in the attitudes of oil companies toward the issue of control. They would prefer to have control in a joint venture, but are quite prepared to operate without it if necessary.

Even in combination with other foreign interests, the oil firms actually held a majority position in only 45% of their joint ventures in this sample. Even these "foreign majority combinations" are not entirely reliable in some cases. Witness in this context the politically motivated "slippage"[19] of foreign partners' tankers during the Indo-Pakistan conflict in 1965. "In September, 1965, during the Indo-

[17] In the matching test of attitude toward a majority control, none of the executives of the firms from the metals group considered that an equity majority was necessary.
[18] Shares granted in this manner were often described, somewhat quaintly, as "free shares," both by Indian authorities and by British executives.
[19] "Slippage" was the failure to meet scheduled timing by supply tankers, especially, as here, failure to meet times laid down for arrival at refineries.

Pakistan hostilities, crude oil shipments to Karachi were dislocated [Esso and, to a lesser extent, Caltex tankers "slipped"] to the point where PRL [Pakistan Refinery Ltd., at Karachi] had to reduce crude runs somewhat for 13 days."[20]

Desire for control turned out to be much stronger than might be expected for companies in the chemicals group. In fourteen out of fifteen cases, both majority and effective control were felt to be necessary, or desirable (if they could be achieved). Yet these firms were confident of their ability to exert any necessary pressure upon a given joint venture through technical leverage, regardless of their own equity position. A respondent from the British parent of a 50–50 joint venture in the chemicals group actually commented along these lines: "This operation could probably now stand on its own feet without either our local partner or ourselves. It would certainly be unable to develop further, however, without our products, patents and know-how."

The implication seems to be that confidence or complacency about their own situation could be interpreted as satisfaction with the existence of a required state of affairs—namely, effective control— rather than as impartiality toward the issue of control in general, as had been originally expected and as was suggested previously. Why, then, the concern over equity majority positions by the firms in the chemicals group? Less than 30% actually had a majority position in any joint venture, and yet they appear to feel that they had effective control in most cases.

One reason may have been the strong association, by most of the British executives in the sample, of effective control with majority control—in principle, if not necessarily in effect. Thus, the chemicals companies, even though they realized the extent of their own effective control over the operations of a joint venture, appear to feel this would be enhanced by its formal recognition in the form of a majority holding of equity. A director of one large chemicals company explained, "If we control financially, it is easier to provide technical interchange with a joint venture, since we have control over the eventual use of the technology. This applies especially to corporate know-how, which tends to be best transmitted through free interchange. Sharing technical responsibilities tends to bring difficulties."

There were realistic deviations from this concern. One of the more impressive performers in the chemicals group originally received permission from the host government to hold 50% plus one share in the equity of a joint venture which it set up with a major Indian company.

[20] Shell International Petroleum Company Ltd., "Aide Memoire on Pakistan," 17th November, 1966.

At the time, the issue had not been equity control in the joint venture but rather the possibility of consolidating the latter's financial results with those of the British parent for U.K. tax purposes. At the time of the interview, this same British firm was considering disposing of two shares in the Indian joint venture in question. This maneuver would have changed the status of the joint venture, under the U.K. tax system, to that of an associated company, and the two sets of accounts would henceforth not be consolidated.

The whole operation was being carried out in order to improve the debt: equity ratio of the British company. In general, Indian companies were permitted a higher gearing ratio than was common in the United Kingdom,[21] and this particular joint venture took full advantage of this opportunity. By reducing the proportion of debt in its own overall capital structure, the British firm was hoping to become a more attractive proposition for additional financing in Britain. The question of control over the joint venture was not considered to be significant in terms of relative equity holdings between partners.

This particular British firm was obviously satisfied with its Indian partner and the local joint operations. In fact, this satisfaction was tangibly expressed in a deliberate policy of offering this local partner a 50% share in all its other Indian operations. Most of these other interests had arisen from the acquisition in Europe of other foreign parents of Indian subsidiaries, in particular of a large British-controlled operation in India, bought from the original owner in the United Kingdom.

A more explicit reason for this apparent contradiction in the attitudes toward control held by companies in the chemicals group may be an offshoot of what could be called the "50–50 phenomenon." One third of the chemicals cases are 50–50 joint ventures. In more than half of this group, the British share is in the 49% to 51% range and said to be legally and firmly restricted by the host government. This is a higher

---

[21] The debt:equity ratio officially approved by the Indian Capital Issues Controller was theoretically limited to 2:1. (Capital Issues Control Act, 1947, Sec. 12; and also Capital Issues [Application for Consent] Rules, 1954.) However, purely short-term loans were not apparently counted in the computation of the debt side, since they were allowed as working capital. The result was a high proportion of overdraft and other short-term financing. The effective limit thought to be realistic by respondents in this sample was about 3:1 (although the U.S. rubber companies' figures described earlier suggest that this estimate might have been a bit low). Over the subsample in this study of cases, in which financial data are sensitive enough to permit the necessary calculations (43 cases), gearing of the joint ventures averages about 2.4:1. This compares with an average of approximately 1.6:1 for the total sample of British parent companies, according to figures from their consolidated group accounts.

proportion than in any of the other groups as defined by nature of business.

In several of these cases involving equal shares in equity between partners, the joint venture apparently came up against the problem of increasing investment to permit growth at a rate which the British partner felt was justified by market demand and potential. When the local associates were Tata interests, or firms with a similar access to financial liquidity, matching investment increases were no problem. In fact, they appeared to be sought equally by the local partner. In some of the other cases (at various stages, most of the 49 % to 51 % group), the local associates' inability or unwillingness[22] to match an increase in British investment created difficulties. These were reinforced by host government insistence upon the maintenance of relative shares in equity.

As a result of these problems, the growth of these joint ventures was, at certain times, stultified. These experiences appear to conflict with those described by Friedmann and Kalmanoff, who state: "There is considerable evidence that serious conflicts have *not* arisen, and that joint ventures have followed a liberal policy of reinvestment for growth."[23] The present study indicates there appears to be evidence on both sides of this particular argument.

Even though problems of the kind described arose, they apparently led the foreign[24] partners in such cases to consider that control would be desirable in order to avoid their repetition. This led, in some cases, to strategies designed to obtain host government permission to increase investment as needed by a joint venture to a level, or in a manner, which would cause the foreign share in equity to exceed 50 %.

In this context, another strategic advantage of an equity majority in a joint venture was put forward in discussion by one executive from a chemical company. In essence this revolves around the added leverage which it might be possible, given a foreign equity majority, to exert upon a host government in order to permit increased unilateral foreign investment. The main theme of this particular argument is that, if foreign majority control were to be a fait accompli, then an increase in

[22] Unwillingness, due partly to what Hirschman called "the milking so often practiced by local capitalists" (Aibert O. Hirschman, *The Strategy of Economic Development*, Yale University Press, New Haven, 1958, p. 39), in which profits from a reliable source, such as a sound local industrial enterprise, were applied to high-risk, but also high-return, local alternatives.

[23] Wolfgang G. Friedmann and George Kalmanoff, *Joint International Business Ventures*, Columbia University Press, New York, 1961, p. 172, italics supplied.

[24] The reminder is offered that "foreign" means foreign to the host country. While the strategies discussed in this section were based on British firms' experiences, they are perhaps capable of extrapolation to the general "foreign" case.

the foreign share in equity would not appear to be so significant or "damaging" to the host country's interests.

The whole question of the relationship between willingness to increase commitment in an investment and the desire for a majority equity position raises another issue. This was the added argument in favor of perceived financial control through an equity majority in order to justify to parent company shareholders (and home office senior executives) the investment of any needed additional funds in the form of nonvoting equity or long-term loans to an overseas joint venture. (Presuming, of course, that the strategies suggested did not work, or that the foreign parent decided that loans were a more suitable form of investment within the constraints of its own investment decision matrix).

Although difficulties of the type just discussed are not peculiar to investments in chemicals, they appear to have arisen most frequently in the joint ventures associated with British chemicals companies. They are major contributing factors to the unanticipated desire of these firms for majority holdings in equity in addition to effective control. These arguments appear broadly to be consistent with the comments of a large U.S. chemical company, as quoted by Robinson, "We feel that it is best to have either a minority interest, or a controlling interest." The author continued, "The firm had a number of fifty-fifty interests abroad, and in some instances problems had arisen in reaching decisions."[25]

Responsibility for Decision

The location of responsibility within a British parent firm for initiating and promoting a specific project does not appear to vary significantly according to the nature of business. There is, however, some indication of the characteristics of the decision process in the relationship between nature of business and the final responsibility for the decision to go into a proposed joint venture,[26] as shown in Figure 5.1.

A theory of general interest in connection with the foreign investment decision process suggests that overseas investments are likely to be motivated primarily by influential individuals or groups. Thus, for example, it has been stated that "Even in giant firms, the most important decisions are effectively taken by very small groups."[27] More

[25] Richard D. Robinson, *International Business Policy,* Holt, Rinehart and Winston, New York, 1964, p. 161.
[26] Significant at the 0.001 level.
[27] Tibor Barna, *Investment and Growth Policies in British Industrial Firms,* National Institute of Economic and Social Research, Occasional Papers, 20, Cambridge University Press, London, 1962, p. 32.

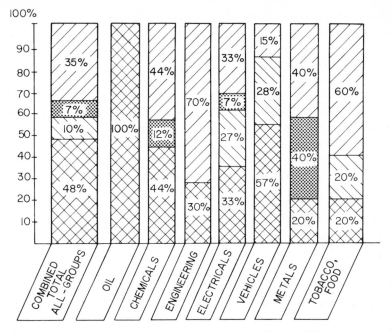

Percentage of cases in each business group when final decision was made by:

A familiar individual (i.e., an individual familiar with local conditions in the host country)

An individual

A special group

Through normal channels *

Figure 5.1
Nature of Business and Location of Responsibility for Decision to Go into a Specific Joint Venture

* For example, "normal channels" were described in two cases as follows:
a. Project proposal to International Division Coordinator/to Executive Board of Product Division/to Board of British Holding Company/to Main Board (Oil company). The statement was made that, once a project team or promotor had put forward a proposal to the coordinator, it was no longer an individual responsibility.
b. Project proposal to Chief Executive of local subsidiary in the host country/to International Group (or division)/to Executive Board of Product Division/to Executive Management Committee (or Board)/to Main Board (Vehicle accessories company).

specifically, it seems that such people would also be those who have either considerable experience in the country concerned,[28] a special interest in promoting overseas investments,[29] or both.

The history of investment decisions made by the sample of British firms in connection with their joint ventures in India and Pakistan appears to support such a hypothesis. So does the explicit statement by an executive director of a chemicals company: "Support for any such policy of international development of operations usually comes from those who are familiar with it. These decisions are usually pushed through by one or a few individuals." In 30 out of 71 cases, the decision to go into a particular joint venture investment was said to have been made by an individual. In 25 cases, the decision maker was also familiar with the host country in question, and in many, with the chosen associate. In a further 7 cases, the decision was said to be the responsibility of a specially defined group other than the main board of the company.

Who exactly were these influential individuals, and how far down the hierarchy were such decisions effectively determined? For the British parent companies of these joint ventures, the actual breakdown of the individual decision makers and their levels of responsibility is as follows:

1. Chief executive of British parent company (as distinct from main board) 37.5%
2. Executive director of British parent company 20.0%
3. Chief executive of international or overseas division 17.5%
4. Chief executive of local branch or subsidiary in host country 25.0%

Decision making in oil companies is an exception, however. In view of their overall international orientation, it was perhaps natural that all the decisions involving oil and associated interests should be made "through normal channels" rather than by individuals. If these 13 cases were removed from the sample, the decision was said to have been made by an individual in 52% of the remaining joint ventures, while in a further 12%, it was ascribed to a group other than the board. Only in 36% of the "oil-less" sample was the decision said to have been made through normal channels.

Another exception to the wider pattern of individual responsibility for the joint venture decision occurs in the vehicles group. Among these

[28] Raghbir S. Basi, *Determinants of United States Private Direct Investments in Foreign Countries,* Bureau of Economic and Business Research, Printed Series No. 3, Kent State University, Kent, Ohio, 1963.
[29] Yair Aharoni, *The Foreign Investment Decision Process,* Division of Research, Graduate School of Business Administration, Harvard University, Boston, 1966, pp. 56–61, 197.

firms, an individual was responsible for the decision in only 1 case, while 4 out of 7 joint ventures were reported as being decided upon through normal channels. There is a good explanation for this exception in one of the features of the foreign investment decision process of these companies. Several major component and accessories producers for the motor industry are included in this group. These turned out to have an interesting problem in connection with the decision to invest abroad.

For these firms, the decision to set up local operations in a new country or market is quite clearly determined exogenously. Because of their close interdependence with the car and truck manufacturers, these suppliers have to be prepared to provide their own products wherever, and whenever, their customers require them in any specific market. A director of one of these firms explained: "We have no hard or fast rules on overseas investment, because of the ancillary nature of our operations to the motor industry. We have to be where the motor industry is. The motor industry was developing in India. As part of the motor industry in the United Kingdom, we had to be in India with them." The ultimate sanction described by these respondents in discussion was the potential loss of major customers in other markets, especially the large markets in the developed nations, if they failed to support them in countries like India.

Thus the component and accessories manufacturers are caught in a squeeze between two monopsonists. On the one hand are their customers, who demand universal service. In theory, this could be provided through exports to each market area where it is required. On the other hand, the presence of a vehicle manufacturer immediately presents the host government with an indirect monopsonistic advantage over that firm's suppliers. The government can then raise tariffs or impose import quotas in order to force the latter either to manufacture locally, or else lose their customer in that market—and therefore, in other markets.

As a result of this squeeze, this group of companies, more than most others, make a practice of keeping in step with their customers in local investment, rather than strictly initiating new operations themselves. Such a situation tends to provide less scope for individuals to persuade, guide, or direct their companies into overseas investments which are initially stimulated by their own personal interests and their experience of a given set of conditions.

Attitudes Toward Potential Associates

One of the most interesting features of the joint venture process is the difference in foreign investors' attitudes toward potential associates and the bearing they have upon decisions and structure. These attitudes will be discussed again, especially in connection with the selection of associates and the way in which attitudes appear to change with experience—in most cases becoming more favorable. In order to provide a basis for such discussion, however, it is necessary to structure the variation in attitudes according to the nature of business of the British firms in this sample.

To begin with, possible types of associates are divided into five categories:
1. Fellow nationals: Other interests from the same country as the foreign parent company (in this case, Britain).
2. Other foreigners: Interests from other developed nations.
3. Local private: Local private business interests from the host country, excluding investment consortia.
4. Host government: Agencies of the host government.
5. Local public or investors: Investment consortia, or the general public in the host country.

The first four categories are clearly defined business or politico-economic concentrations. In theory, they would take a participatory interest in any joint venture. In the fifth category are included investing interests which are essentially nonparticipating associates.

Attitudes toward possible associates are considered from two aspects. The first defines attitudes as explicitly stated. The second provides an additional check, in which the relative favorability of attitudes is represented by the order in which the various types of potential associates were ranked by respondents with respect to their preferability to the British parent companies for their joint ventures in India and Pakistan.

Nature of business and attitudes toward the different types of potential associates are significantly related, and a series of weighted attitude scores has been calculated. (The relationships and calculations are shown in Appendix C.1.). The results are summarized in Tables 5.3 and 5.4. In general, the lower the score in these tables, the more favorable is the attitude toward that type of associate and the higher is the associate's ranking in preferability.

If attitudes toward associates tend to vary with the nature of business of the foreign investor, what underlying patterns of variation are likely to arise? Before the results based upon the actual responses from the group of British executives are considered, it is worth outlining some of the preconceived basic patterns which could reasonably be expected and some of the possible explanations for these preconceptions. One can then see how closely the actual patterns conform to expectations, both overall and by nature of business.

Table 5.3
Attitudes of British Respondents toward Potential Associates
According to Nature of Business of U.K. Parent

Nature of Business of U.K. Parent	Attitudes Toward Potential JV Associates				
	Fellow National	Other Foreign	Local Private	Host Government	Local Public/ Investors
	Weighted Average Score and (Rank) for Each Group				
Oil	2.08 (1)	2.32 (2)	2.92 (5)	2.54 (3)	2.69 (4)
Chemicals	3.07 (3)	3.33 (4)	2.27 (1)	4.07 (5)	2.47 (2)
Engineering	2.00 (2)	3.10 (3)	2.00 (1)	4.00 (5)	3.40 (4)
Electricals	2.20 (1)	2.33 (2)	2.53 (4)	3.87 (5)	2.47 (3)
Vehicles	2.71 (3)	3.14 (4)	2.00 (1)	3.71 (5)	2.57 (2)
Metals	3.20 (4)	3.00 (2)	2.20 (1)	3.80 (5)	3.00 (2)
Tobacco, food, other	2.00 (2)	2.00 (2)	2.20 (4)	3.60 (5)	1.60 (1)
All-industry score	177 (2)	194 (4)	166 (1)	255 (5)	184 (3)

Table 5.4
Ranking of Potential Associates by British Companies According
to Nature of Business of U.K. Parent

Nature of Business of U.K. Parent	Rank Ordering of Potential JV Associates				
	Fellow National	Other Foreign	Local Private	Host Government	Local Public/ Investors
	Weighted Average Score and (Rank) for Each Group				
Oil	1.85 (1)	2.85 (2)	3.38 (3)	3.38 (3)	3.54 (5)
Chemicals	2.60 (3)	3.67 (4)	1.87 (1)	4.67 (5)	2.20 (2)
Engineering	2.90 (2)	3.30 (3)	1.90 (1)	3.80 (5)	3.40 (4)
Electricals	2.13 (1)	3.00 (4)	2.60 (2)	4.33 (5)	2.93 (3)
Vehicles	2.57 (2)	3.57 (4)	1.29 (1)	5.00 (5)	2.57 (2)
Metals	2.60 (2)	3.20 (4)	2.00 (1)	4.60 (5)	2.60 (2)
Tobacco, food, other	2.80 (2)	3.40 (4)	2.20 (2)	4.60 (5)	1.80 (1)
All-industry score	169 (2)	228 (4)	161 (1)	298 (5)	197 (3)

Because of the possible uncertainty and risk involved in operating in a different environment, there might well appear to be some preference for a fellow national associate, or at least for one from a comparable background. The advantages of associates from a background comparable to one's own were specifically remarked upon by several respondents in a 1966 study for the N.I.C.B.[30] The basis for this particular preference

[30] Bivens and Lovell, *Joint Ventures with Foreign Partners*, pp. 34–35.

was roughly that, through such a choice, the area of uncertainty in the environment and the operation was perceived to be reduced, while the risk would be shared by a partner of similar capability and standing.

No matter how preferable fellow national associates might appear, however, this option is academic for investments in many less-developed nations. Even though Burmah-Shell has been a major force in India for fifty years, a repetition of such a relationship would now appear to be virtually impossible for any long-term investment in that country. If there is the assumption that participation with local capital is virtually a necessity, then a second strategic pattern of preference might be thought to depend upon a desire to maximize control over actual operations. Such a strategy would presumably lead these British firms to seek local investors, or the public, as potential "sleeping partners." The N.I.C.B. study quotes the comment of a British managing director in support of this particular argument, "Stockholders in the mass are essentially inarticulate, and, provided dividends are forthcoming on a regular basis, it follows that interference with parent company policy will be minimal."[31]

Least of all would foreign investors be expected to favor partnership with host government interests. This argument is based upon the perceived capability of such interests for interference with the policies and operations of a joint enterprise. Coupled with this potential threat is the fear of conflicting goals and standards for evaluation in an association between private business interests and a government agency. This fear appears to have been part of the outlook of many companies from "free enterprise economies."[32]

How do the actual patterns of attitudes compare with the general forecasts? The order of preference indicated by the attitudes of the British firms in the electricals group shows agreement with the general pattern forecast. This is the only exception, however, and is not even supported by the actual ranking of possible associates by this same group, let alone by the all-industry order, as shown in the tables. In general, the forecast certainly appears to be correct at the bottom end of the scale. Host government partners are felt to be least desirable by almost all groups in terms of both the attitude and the ranking test.

Only the oil companies fail to place host government associates last. This is partly due to the scale of investment required in their operations, which made public issues, or local private interests, appear to be less feasible alternatives—at least in the less-developed nations. It is also

---

[31] *Ibid.,* p. 34.
[32] For a comparable finding in the U.S. case, see Robinson, *International Business Policy,* p. 164.

due in part to a philosophy of recognizing realities, stated quite explicitly by a respondent from one company:

Since Partition, our policy has been that our interests in India and Pakistan can only continue to exist if the host government is given some share or interest in oil operations. We are therefore quite prepared to teach the government the oil business, and to trust them, partly in an effort to get them to trust us in turn. In general, oil companies now have to be in partnership with local governments if they wish to operate locally. We have decided, therefore, to accept this position, and to try firmly to like it.

Since its own operations were exploiting (in the nonpejorative sense) the natural resources of the host country, or were alternatively importing a crucial raw material, this firm argued that it was reasonable to expect that the host government should wish to be closely involved. This attitude was coupled with a history of what were said, by the company concerned, to be fairly satisfactory joint venture relationships with host government interests. The fact that mixed ventures of this type are by no means always unsatisfactory to foreign private investors has also been described for the case of U.S. companies by Robinson.[33]

Local public and investing interests are third in the actual results as well as in the original forecast. However, the order above and below this type of associate in the ranking lists changed between prediction and findings because of transposition of local private and other developed-nation interests. This latter feature is perhaps the most striking deviation from the forecast. Only host government partners appear to be less desirable than partners from another developed nation. Although this type of associate is fourth on both the attitude and the ranking measure, the latter is probably a better indication of the true facts of the matter.

No executives expressed a strongly negative attitude toward other foreign interests. Time and again, the responses given were along the lines, "no point, no advantage, nothing to offer as a partner in a local joint venture that could not be better supplied by ourselves, or by local interests." In particular, another foreigner could not offer local know-how, contacts, or identity to a joint venture, and so was ranked behind local interests. At the same time, other foreigners were not felt to offer any noticeable technical or financial advantage to most British firms that the latter could not get more easily from fellow British companies. Thus, in overall terms, this type of associate is simply considered to be fourth in rank, or level of preferability, rather than undesirable per se.

[33] *Ibid.,* pp. 165–170.

Both in their attitudes and specific ranking, the U.K. companies in this sample indicated a preference for local private interests as the best potential choice of partner for a joint venture in a less-developed country. No respondents gave a strongly negative answer, and only 14 % appeared to be at all negative in their attitudes to this type of partner. Half of these negative responses were from oil companies. Typical of the comments from this last group is the following: "Private sector interests in these countries (less-developed) are rarely of sufficient standing, or have adequate resources, to be of much use to oil companies. If they have the right ideas, they may be useful political adjuncts, but little more."

On the other hand, 72 % of the attitude responses concerning local private interests were positive or strongly positive. In 43 % of all cases in the sample, this type of associate is also ranked as the first choice of potential partner for a joint venture. Only in connection with two joint ventures which involved oil companies, are associates of this type ranked in fifth position.

Two subgroups are discernible among these favorable responses. In the first, companies forced into joint ventures chose local private partners as the best alternative, subject to the constraint that they had to take in some kind of local associate. In the second subgroup are those British firms which sought local facilities or resources in a joint venture. These naturally tended to favor local companies which possessed such attributes. For both these subgroups, however, the positive contributions which local partners could offer were seen to be much the same. The preference of these British parent firms is clearly indicated in terms of three attributes[34] offered by a good local company.

First is local influence and standing, especially the ability to lobby effectively on behalf of the joint venture's interests, and, less directly, in the general interests of the foreign parent company. An ability described by Kidron as the "paramount ... importance of Indian partners in the role of ... coping with officialdom."[35] This was considered to be an important contribution in the general case, even by British firms which firmly felt they could themselves conduct negotiations with the authorities as effectively as could their local associates (at least in the special case of India or Pakistan); firms, furthermore, which maintained permanent representatives in New Delhi for just this reason.

Second is the corporate asset of good local managerial personnel, especially significant to smaller British companies, but in recent years a

---

[34] These attributes exclude fixed assets, especially sites, which were certainly important in many cases.
[35] Kidron, *Foreign Investments in India,* p. 263.

consideration which became important even for the giants. This is essentially a reflection of wide, internationally encountered pressures for "localization" of personnel exerted upon foreign enterprises in the underdeveloped nations. This phenomenon is strongly represented by the Indian case. Over three quarters of the respondents mentioned in discussion the difficulties of employing expatriate staff in India. In the general foreign case, these difficulties could arise directly in the form of restrictions on the renewal of visas, or the unavailability of new entry visas, for individuals who were not nationals of British Commonwealth nations. For most of the employees of firms in this sample, pressure had been exerted indirectly, through prohibitive rates of personal taxation.

Theoretically, the Indian system of personal taxation was selective and biased toward the employment of necessary foreign technically qualified staff.[36] In practice, it appeared to work somewhat haphazardly and, at times, irrationally. A manager of one British parent company was granted a tax waiver for a tour of duty with an associated joint venture in a role which was essentially administrative in nature. The waiver was granted on the grounds that, in a previous job with another employer, the man in question had obtained considerable experience in crop-spraying (and was therefore obviously a technician). Yet a year later, the same British parent company sent to the same joint venture a technical manager with an honors degree qualification who failed to obtain a waiver from personal income tax as a technician.[37]

A third attribute of local partners among those mentioned most frequently is the possession of a sound domestic marketing network. Some joint ventures had grown out of associations with previous local distributors, a sequence of events which has been widely described as a common strategy for "dynamic development" or "evolution of overseas investment"[38] in the literature of the field. (Unfortunately, the evidence usually cited does not provide any firm basis for comparison

[36] Following the amendments in the Finance Act of 1966, foreign technicians are allowed exemption from income tax for three years (as before 1966), plus a further period of five years in which, if government approval is obtained for their continuing employment, they are not liable for taxation on the personal tax paid on their behalf by their employers. (Indian Income Tax Act, 1961 [as amended by the Finance Act of 1966], Sec. 10 [6] [vii].)

[37] For a full discussion of Indian taxation and appropriate source material, see Kust, *Foreign Enterprise in India, Laws and Policies,* pp. 342–418; and also Matthew J. Kust, *Supplement to Foreign Enterprise in India, Laws and Policies,* The University of North Carolina Press, Chapel Hill, 1966, pp. 73–81.

[38] See, for example, W. B. Reddaway, *Effects of U.K. Direct Investment Overseas, An Interim Report,* University of Cambridge, Department of Applied Economics, Occasional Papers, 12, Cambridge University Press, London, 1967; also Howe Martyn, *International Business, Principles and Problems,* The Free Press of Glencoe, New York, 1964, pp. 133–134.

in quantitative, or even qualitative, terms). For the companies in the present sample, this case appears to have occurred less frequently than might have been expected. It seems to lead to the hypothesis that this particular strategic sequence has been less important to British than to U.S. companies, certainly for investment in India or Pakistan. (One should add, however, that this is a hypothesis which needs to be tested more specifically in future research).

The argument upon which such a hypothesis is based would attribute any difference in strategy to the longer experience of British investors and managers of the local marketing channels in India and Pakistan. Coupled with this would possibly be a greater informal awareness of the power points in such channels. If these arguments are valid, British companies would have felt the need for local associates in these countries who could provide marketing facilities rather less than did U.S. firms.[39]

Whatever the validity of such an argument for past operations, this particular attribute of a local associate appears to be increasing in importance in India and Pakistan, largely because of host government discrimination; that is, discrimination along the lines that trade should be a suitable activity for local, rather than foreign, interests and that marketing constitutes trade. "The marketing of oil products is treated as trade, not industry, by the Pakistan Government, whose declared policy is to let Pakistanis handle all trade and to eliminate foreign interests."[40] More generally, the Government of Pakistan, in its statement of industrial policy with respect to foreign direct investment, distinguishes between industry and trade or banking, where Pakistani interests are expected to have control, both in equity and in practical terms.[41]

All three of the attributes described are positive contributions to local operations. None of them were felt to be available from a local public shareholding. Only rarely, and in part, are they likely to be provided by a local investor. In general, most of the British firms in the sample, with the exception of the tobacco and food group, stated explicitly that they looked for such positive contributions, rather than just for local capital. Hence a local private partner was ranked as more

[39] Thus, in the case of several joint ventures in the electricals, chemicals, and oil groups, not only did the British partner take responsibility for marketing the products of the joint venture, but it also handled those of its Indian or Pakistani partner, usually through its own local branch or subsidiary operation. This appears to be evidence of the often under-emphasized pragmatism of these governments, when an apparent exception to the general rule is encouraged because of technical realities. These were goods which required sophisticated, technically complicated methods of distribution that were not available locally, except from the foreign partner.

[40] *The Financial Times,* 10th November, 1965.

[41] Government of Pakistan, *Industrial Policy Statement,* 1958.

desirable, in most cases, than a public shareholding or an associate which was purely an investor. Only when a local shareholding was felt to be essentially a token gesture toward pressures for local participation was this order reversed. This reversal was, for example, the argument given in relation to most of the cases in the food and tobacco group.

In several responses, there is an indication that fellow-national interests aroused stronger antipathy among British executives than did other foreigners. In this respect, the intraindustry antagonism among British ceramic producers appears to be comparable to that between some of the U.S. rubber companies.[42] One British executive director in this group stated flatly, "Under no circumstances would we ever go into a joint venture with one of our British competitors," a statement supported by stronger comment in discussion. In view of the fact that geographical concentration of the industry is a feature in both cases (Akron, Ohio, for the U.S. rubber companies; Stoke-on-Trent and the Potteries, for the British ceramics producers), there appears to be some argument for further research into this phenomenon—an argument for a study of the possible correlation between frictional effects of competitive asperity and intraindustry juxtaposition.

Selection of Associates

Upon moving from attitudes to the actual selection process carried out by firms from different industries, we find a significant relationship between nature of business and the main reason given for selecting a specific associate for a particular joint venture.[43] The relationship is shown in Table 5.5. In this selection process one would again expect that certain patterns should emerge.

For example, oil companies are more likely than other firms, in general, to consider that they were forced into their choice of associate. The basis for such an argument is along the lines that host government ambitions would require local participation in an industry as strategically significant as oil; the scale of investment involved in a typical oil company operation would severely limit the range of feasible local partners available; the matching limitation, combined again with host government aspirations, might even mean that association was virtually preempted by a government agency. In any case, the choice would appear to be forced upon the oil company.

[42] The comments upon the attitudes of the U.S. rubber companies were based upon interviews with some of these companies carried out in Akron, in 1965, by the author of the present study.
[43] Significant at the 0.019 level.

Table 5.5
Nature of Business and Reasons for Selecting Specific Associates

	Reason for Selecting an Associate								
	Forced Choice		Convenience of Facilities/ Resources		Favorable Past Asso- ciation		Status/ Identity		Totals	
Nature of Business	Number of Cases and Cell % Based on Row Sum*									
	No.	%	No.	%	No.	%	No.	%	No.	%
Oil	6	46	2	15	4	31	1	8	13	18
Chemicals	3	19	7	44	5	31	1	6	16	23
Engineering	—	—	4	40	5	50	1	10	10	14
Electricals	3	20	4	27	4	27	4	27	15	21
Vehicles	—	—	2	29	—	—	5	71	7	10
Metals	—	—	3	60	—	—	2	40	5	7
Tobacco, food	—	—	2	40	2	40	1	20	5	7
Totals	12	17	24	34	20	28	15	21	71	100

* Percentages in the final column are based on the column sum. Percentages do not all add up to 100 because of rounding. Classification of reasons for selecting associates is discussed in Chapter 7.

The results shown in Table 5.5 clearly support the prediction of a difference in pressures upon the oil companies. Although this group of companies were said to have made a forced choice in less than half (46%) of the joint ventures in which they were involved, these cases represented 50% of the forced-choice category, taken over all industries. The chemicals and the electricals groups are the only others reporting cases in which the choice of partners was thrust upon them. For these two groups, the forced-choice cases involve 19% and 20%, respectively, of the joint ventures in which they participated, proportions which are very much smaller than in the oil company joint ventures.

Facilities or resources offered by a prospective associate appear to have been most important to the chemicals and the metals groups. This reason was also cited by many British engineering firms (i.e., in 40% of the cases in which they were involved). These included some companies which had been looking for a local "going-concern" that could use British technology and operate effectively with a minimum of direct contribution and close supervision by the U.K. parent. As one executive stated, "We prefer to develop overseas manufacturing out of licensing agreements, with a minimum necessary commitment ourselves. We therefore also prefer a local associate with staff and facilities, as well as contacts and political know-how."

For the chemicals companies, two features are said to have been most important. One is the need for a suitable site, with adequate water, power, and effluent disposal facilities. Adequate sites were described as having been very limited in number and usually under the control of local companies already in the field. The cost of making a contribution to the development of an infrastructure sufficient to support a new site for chemical operations was felt to be prohibitive, except where a large proportion of such costs would be borne by the State Government.[44]

The second important feature for chemicals companies is the need to find local personnel of a suitable level of education for employment as chemical plant operatives. This is in addition to the need for competent managerial and technical staffs, a cause for concern also cited among firms in the metals group. The problem was solved neatly by one of the companies in the chemicals group in a joint venture not included among the present sample.

In this case, a small Indian chemical engineering firm had a highly competent staff and had proved itself in adapting foreign patents and technology into forms suitable for domestic production capabilities. The British firm in question had set up what was, in effect, a consultancy joint venture with the Indian company. The main reason for establishing this particular joint operation had been to obtain the services of the local interest as a consultant organization to help in developing and starting up new projects in India. The British partner had even employed the Indian firm as consultants in the United Kingdom (although this appeared to have been something in the nature of a *quid pro quo* arrangement, enabling the local personnel to obtain a source and overseas depository for foreign exchange).

Confidence arising out of a favorable past association is the criterion most often chosen by British firms in the engineering group. It also

---

[44] Acquisition of the land was apparently not a problem, although long-term rights of foreign enterprises in India were not clear in this respect. Article 19 (1) (f) of the Indian Constitution includes the basic freedom to acquire, hold, and dispose of property, but these rights are clearly limited to Indian citizens. The Supreme Court ruled in 1963 and 1964 that companies were not entitled to the rights guaranteed to citizens, *even through all the shareholders were Indian citizens.* (*State Trading Corporation of India Ltd.* v. *The Commercial Tax Officer et al.* [Decision, July 26, 1963]; *The Automobile Products of India Ltd.* v. *Sales Tax Officer, Bombay* [Decision, February 25, 1964].) Companies were however, persons, according to Section 3 (42) of the General Clauses Act and, therefore, under Article 31 of the Constitution, could only be deprived of property—once acquired —upon payment of due compensation. Justice Bose of the Supreme Court has suggested that "in the absence of such a law (to the contrary), non-citizens can also acquire property in India. If they do, they cannot be deprived of it any more than citizens, save by authority of law." (Justice Bose of the Supreme Court, in *Dwarkadas* v. *Sholapur*, A.I.R. [1954] S.C. 119, 137–38.) Expropriation under due authority of law would involve adequate compensation, and India's compensation record has been excellent.

accounts for a significant proportion (roughly 30 % of the joint ventures in each group) of the decisions made by British companies in chemicals, electricals, tobacco and food, and even for oil and associated interests.

This reason was not mentioned at all in connection with joint ventures of the vehicles and metals groups. Most of the firms in these latter two groups had the opportunity to choose a past licensee, distributor, or major customer. In roughly 50 % of these cases in which past associates were available, they were selected. Other considerations were said, however, to be more important than past association per se.

Status and standing of a local associate appear to be most significant to the vehicles group. This is also an important consideration for British firms in the metals group; it is second only to the search for local personnel and resources. These are the only two groups in which this reason for selecting an associate was a major consideration. Together, they account for nearly 50 % of the times when it was cited.

It is difficult to see just why this criterion should be relatively so much more important for the vehicle group companies, except possibly through a process of eliminating their possible alternative reasons. In most cases, the local partner was actually described in discussion as a very competent and effective business interest with excellent managerial personnel. Yet the partners were said to be chosen in most cases either for their political influence or for their general financial standing.

There is no immediate explanation of why these two reasons should necessarily be of peculiar significance for this type of British company. On the other hand, the choice was not said to be forced, nor, apparently, was it based upon favorable past association. In the majority of this subgroup of joint ventures, a new operation was set up and managed, at least in the early stages, by the British partner. Thus it seems reasonable to assume that previously existing facilities and resources were of limited importance to the British parent. This assumption leads to a rather unsatisfactory interpretation for these companies. Since three out of the four suggested alternative reasons for choosing partners did not appear to be relevant for these cases, there is perhaps a higher residual probability that the selection would be said to have resulted primarily from the status and standing of the potential local associate.

Summary

It appears to be rare for the nature of business of a joint venture to differ from that of its foreign parent. However, the variation in technology between British, Indian, and Pakistani operations, even under the auspices of the same parent company, means that no overall measure of technological complexity is appropriate within the limitations of the data in the study. It is, though, possible to set up somewhat arbitrary and broad-scale groupings of operations by nature of business.

Attitudes toward control over joint venture operations vary according to the nature of business. There is a strong association by British executives of effective control with a majority share in equity. Even firms having considerable technical leverage in controlling a joint venture, such as in the oil and chemicals industries, tend to seek a majority position as an additional safeguard. Oil companies, however, appear to become resigned to local restrictions on their control over local operations.

Among these groups, the most relaxed in their attitudes toward control appear to be companies in the engineering, electricals, vehicles, and metals categories. These are also the most variable in terms of the intragroup differences in concern over control.

On the whole, 50-50 joint ventures are felt to be frustrating, especially by firms in the chemicals group, the group most frequently involved in this type of arrangement. There is some evidence that the nearer the relative equity shares approach equality, the greater is the frustration, especially over issues concerned with reinvestment and increasing investment.

Individuals were responsible for the decision to go into a joint venture in nearly half the cases in this sample. These people were usually familiar with conditions in the host country. The chief exception to this practice occurred in the oil and vehicles groups. Oil companies are concerned primarily with international integration of their operations, leaving less scope for individual decision making. Vehicle accessories manufacturers virtually have the decision to invest made for them by a combination of monopsonistic pressures from their major customers and from host governments.

Except for the oil companies, all British parent companies rank host government associates the least desirable alternative for joint venture partners. The oil companies have little alternative and are, to some extent, resigned to association with such interests. For most groups, local private interests are described as the best type of partner, usually because they can offer some tangible contribution to a joint venture. Other foreign companies are considered preferable only to host government partners, largely because there is felt to be little point in associating with such companies rather than with fellow nationals or with local interests.

The oil companies are the only group in which a large proportion of associates were forced upon the British parent company. An associate's provision of local facilities or resources is important to all except the oil group. This contribution is felt to be particularly valuable by companies in the chemicals, metals, and engineering groups.

Favorable past association is the most frequently mentioned reason for choosing partners in the engineering joint ventures. The status of an associate is apparently of major interest only to companies in the vehicles and, to a lesser extent, the metals group.

6 NATURE OF BUSINESS—STRUCTURE AND EVALUATION OF JOINT VENTURES

The way in which joint ventures are set up seems to produce certain patterns. Some of these have already been examined. There are also noticeable patterns in the resultant structure of the joint relationships, in the assessment of associates, and in the comments of parent company executives upon the success of the operations. These patterns vary according to the nature of the business. In addition to direct comments, it is interesting to look at an indirect form of comment which may be a better reflection of genuine attitudes toward this type of investment. This depends upon the stated readiness of investors to participate in other joint ventures whether in developed or in less-developed environments. The readiness of British firms to invest in other joint ventures also varies with the nature of the business.

Structural Characteristics of Joint Ventures

The structure of joint ventures, as of any corporate form, can be laid out in a number of ways. The format used, however, should depend for greatest effectiveness upon the analytical use to which it will be put. In joint ventures, certainly from the aspect of the foreign partner, the most significant structural feature is probably the level of interdependence with the parents. This means, really, the degree of dependence of the joint venture upon its parents. The degree of dependence, or effective independence, of joint ventures can be described and measured. Three particular methods come immediately to mind, each of which represents a different aspect of possible dependence of joint ventures upon their foreign parent companies.

First, independence in financial terms is partly a function of the partners' relative shares in equity. Thus, from the aspect of dependence upon the foreign partner, in this study the measure is represented by the percentage of the voting equity in a joint venture held by the British parent.[1] Second, the degree of independence from the foreign partner is likely to be closely related to the level of dependence upon the local partner. In operational terms, this measure involves determining the

---

[1] This measure is called "parent share in joint venture equity" in the text.

extent to which a local partner is responsible for certain functional areas of joint venture operations. British executives were therefore asked specifically to define the local associates' responsibility in nine functional areas:[2]

1. Marketing and distribution,
2. Purchasing and procurement,
3. Engineering and technical matters,
4. Production,
5. Administration and control,
6. Finance (including obtaining capital),
7. Recruitment and personnel,
8. Relations with the host government and with local authorities,
9. Public relations.

Finally, independence can be expressed as freedom from control by the foreign parent in policy matters—in this case, a measure represented by the level of control expressly stated to be exercised over the joint ventures by their British parents in eleven areas of policy determination:[3]

1. Capital expenditure,
2. Pricing,
3. Dividend policy,
4. Organization,
5. Product selection, design, and planning,
6. Production planning and control,
7. Quality control,
8. Marketing and sales,
9. Purchasing,
10. Wage and labor policy,
11. Selection, promotion, and compensation of executives.

If these three measures are used as the basis for describing joint venture structure in respect to its dependence upon a foreign parent firm, how does such dependence vary according to the nature of business? The calculations of dependence scores along each of the measures for British joint ventures in India and Pakistan are explained in Appendix C.2. Results of these calculations are laid out in Table 6.1. In the table, the lower the score, the lower the level of dependence of that subgroup of joint ventures upon the foreign parent, in terms of the criteria of the measure concerned.

The figures in Table 6.1 indicate that, on all three methods of scoring for dependence, the joint ventures in the engineering group were the

[2] This measure is referred to as "associate's responsibility for joint venture's operations."
[3] This measure is "joint venture's independence in policy areas."

Table 6.1
Structural Dependence Scores of Joint Ventures According
to Nature of Business

Nature of Business	Number of JVs	Equity Share of U.K. Parent	Associate's Responsibility for Operations	Joint Venture's Independence in Policy Areas
		Weighted Average Group Score and (Group Order Rank)		
Oil	13	2.31 (3)	3.23 (6)	2.54 (3)
Chemicals	15	2.93 (6)	2.73 (5)	2.57 (4)
Engineering	10	1.90 (1)	1.90 (1)	2.10 (1)
Electricals	15	2.20 (2)	2.33 (3)	2.27 (2)
Vehicles	7	2.57 (4)	2.00 (2)	2.71 (5)
Metals	5	2.60 (5)	2.40 (4)	3.00 (6)
Tobacco, food	5	3.60 (7)	3.40 (7)	3.60 (7)
All-industry average score		2.50	2.57	2.55

least dependent. At the other extreme, food and tobacco joint ventures, at least in India and Pakistan, were more dependent than any other groups upon their foreign parents. Before the implications of the scores are discussed in more detail, it is worth clearing up the question of inter-dependence between the three measures themselves. Statistically they are not significantly related,[4] but the share in equity probably helps to explain the results in the other two measures for the extreme cases.

Thus, for example, British parent firms held a majority of the equity in four out of five tobacco and food group joint ventures. In the fifth, the British partner held a minority share with a management contract which gave them effective control over the operations of the joint venture. At the other extreme, a British parent held a minority in nine of the engineering joint ventures (in three of them, the holding was less than 25 %). The tenth joint venture in this group involved a foreign equity majority and also a management contract granted to the *local* partner.

The thesis that the foreign parent's share in joint venture equity is the major determinant of the level of dependence could also apply to joint ventures in the electricals group. The argument in this case would again be that the lower level of dependence is due to the higher proportion of

[4] A separate pair of tests indicated that the British share in joint venture equity was not significantly related, in statistical terms, for the limited size of the sample, with either the level of responsibility assumed by associates or the joint venture's independence in areas of policy.

minority and small British shares in the equity of joint ventures in this category (i.e., 11 minority holdings out of 15 cases, of which 4 were less than 25%).

Such an explanation does not appear to be entirely satisfactory, however, for joint ventures associated with British companies in the oil, chemicals, vehicles, and metals groups. It is especially unsatisfactory in helping to predict

a. The level of the contributions which were attributed to associates by British firms in the oil and, to a lesser extent, in the vehicles groups.

b. The dependence of joint ventures in the chemicals and the metals groups.

For each of these pairs, the two groups concerned deviate from the level which would be predicted from foreign parent shares in equity. At the same time, the deviation is in opposite directions so that there appears to be no consistent explanatory trend.

The variance of the joint ventures in the oil group is probably due to the fact that seven of them were mixed ventures that had certain peculiar characteristics. In particular, it turned out that whatever the relative shares in equity of the partners, the actual operations were almost entirely run by the British parent company. Whether carried out with the help of a formal management contract or not, the net results are much the same. The host government partner merely assumed a watching brief. It took an interest in policy matters and watched over the actual operations of a joint venture to make sure they did not conflict with what was considered to be the national interest. It made little contribution, however, in the sense of assuming direct responsibility for such operations.

The experience of these British corporations with their host government partners was consistent with the comment made in an earlier study of joint ventures by Friedmann and Kalmanoff: "Generally, government agencies are content to leave management to the experienced foreign partner, at times through formal management contract arrangements."[5] As a result dependence of these joint ventures in terms of the responsibilities undertaken by associates was not as low as would have been predicted by the relatively low score of the British share in equity. An important implication of this relationship for the general case is, therefore, that some of the alleged fears of foreign investors concerning potential interference in joint venture operations by host government associates are not justified.

[5] Wolfgang G. Friedmann and George Kalmanoff, *Joint International Business Ventures,* Columbia University Press, New York, 1961, pp. 175.

According to the dependence scores among the vehicles group, the contribution from associates is greater than might have been expected if one looks at their scores on the other measures. A probable explanation lies in the high level of competence attributed to their local associates by practically all the British companies in this group. A fairly typical comment was the following by an executive of one of these firms: "Our local partners are pretty good and run the operation well. They are keen, and achieved profitability after two-and-a-half years. They are generally 'on the ball', and have sent over some excellent people to the U.K. for training." Given such competence and given this satisfaction with their associates, it is reasonable to expect that local partners in this group would be granted a greater opportunity to make an effective contribution—and that they would in turn be able to take advantage of it.

All of the highly commended local partners in the vehicles group were from the South of India, where these joint ventures were themselves located. It was remarkable how much warmer were the attitudes expressed toward South India, especially Madras, (and toward partners from that area) than toward the rest of the country. Most of these associates were Chettys, or Chettiars, one of the major Indian business communities, most important and influential in Madras and South India.[6] In this area, the work force was alleged to be as effective as anywhere else in the country but was not prey to the disruptions caused elsewhere. (In the Bombay area such disruption was said to be caused by militant labor organizers; in Calcutta, by politically motivated agitation.)

As a topic of wide importance in connection with investment in India, it would be interesting to examine relative wage rates, living standards, employment levels, and work force satisfaction in the three areas. The objective would be to determine whether comments such as those made by the group of British executives described a genuine state of affairs, or whether they were open to a less charitable interpretation. In particular, did they represent managerial satisfaction over a relatively quiet life in the South?—a quiet life made possible by a local labor force possibly less sophisticated in its awareness of the benefits available through collective bargaining.

[6] For discussion of the business communities in India, see L. A. Joshi, *The Control of Industry in India, A Study in Aspects of Combination and Concentration,* Vora, Bombay, 1965; R. K. Hazari, *The Structure of the Corporate Private Sector, A Study of Concentration, Ownership and Control,* Asia Publishing House, New York, 1966; Gokhale Institute of Politics and Economics, *Notes on The Rise of The Business Communities in India,* Institute of Pacific Relations, International Secretariat, New York, 1951.

In all fairness to the British executives and firms in the sample, there was no hint of such sentiments in their actual comments. They accepted the high labor costs around Bombay as a fact of life. They became worried over the increasing antagonism toward foreign interests in the Calcutta area. They were simply pleased at being able to get on with doing business in Madras.

The dependence of joint ventures associated with British companies in the metals group is partly due to the technological complexity of continuous and integrated processing operations. This contributed to a need for foreign control in some of the local operations. This interpretation is especially plausible in view of the fact that the one case in which a joint venture in this group was classed as highly independent involved one of two batch-type and less-integrated production systems. (The second of these also involved a British majority share in equity, together with a local partner whose main contribution was in marketing and, to a lesser extent, administration.) However, because of the small subsample size and the indeterminate nature of the assessment of technological complexity, this explanation should be offered only as conjecture.

As far as the chemicals group is concerned, the relatively lower dependence of these joint ventures in policy areas, despite the fact that foreign shares in equity are higher than in most other groups is probably due to three features. In the first place, these ventures include a majority of the 50–50 ones, which receive a relatively high value under the weighting system used. This has the effect of allocating a higher apparent level of significance to the foreign share in equity than is perhaps justified.

Second, in over half of the cases in this group, a British firm joined an established local business in what previously was the latter's own private operation—an operation which had probably been free from "internal" interference in policy matters and therefore free to be run in any manner which the local owners might desire, subject only to official "externally derived" restraints. In this type of situation, there is likely to be a certain amount of difficulty for the foreign partner in altering the existing *status quo.*

In the third place, the 50–50 form of joint ventures generally appeared to create problems for foreign partners in their efforts to determine or influence policy. The fact that partners were formally equal in authority, as shown by their relative shares in equity, had the latent effect that equality was jealously guarded by local associates, even to the point at which determination of policy was hindered. This evidence again indicates an important implication for the general joint venture process.

The implication of this type of situation is that it would quite possibly be easier to influence policy in a joint venture with a minority equity holding than from a position of "unstable equilibrium" (in a 50–50 joint venture) in which local partners might become nervous about possible dangers of erosion of their equal rights. Possible existence of such a phenomenon has been reported for the general case in earlier studies.[7] It was also cited specifically in connection with the experiences of U.S. firms.[8]

There appears, therefore, to be a clear difference, according to the nature of business, in the structure of joint ventures as represented by these three measures. Independence from the U.K. parent and the level of contribution by associates could be partially explained, for the extreme cases, by the foreign share in joint venture equity. When this explanation is not satisfactory, the nature of the associate sheds some further light, as does the nature of the process and the techniques involved. Even the locus of operations and the nature of the labor force appear to be influential.

What was more difficult to forecast or interpret, however, was the effect upon the foreign parent share in joint venture equity if the nature of business varied. This share was the result of an amalgam of circumstances. At one level of analysis it depended upon what the foreign parent company wanted or would accept, what the local associates wanted, and what the host government would permit. At another level these, in turn, depended upon the nature of the business and the point in time at which the original negotiations took place. These begin to approach an interpretation in terms of the effects of bilateral monopolistic advantage. Unfortunately, an analysis in these terms is, itself, limited in its capacity for definitive interpretation by the lack of an adequate scaling method for classifying technological complexity.

The evidence indicates, however, that the comparative advantage of firms in achieving a desired share in the equity of a joint venture varies according to the nature of the business. Firms that are best able to obtain and most likely to maintain a larger share in equity are those in the following groups:
1. Tobacco and food,
2. Chemicals, including plastics, pharmaceuticals, pesticides, and fertilizers,

[7] Karen Kraus Bivens and Enid Baird Lovell, *Joint Ventures with Foreign Partners, International Survey of Business Opinion and Experience,* National Industrial Conference Board, New York, 1966, pp. 20–22.
[8] Richard D. Robinson, *International Business Policy,* Holt, Rinehart and Winston, New York, 1964, p. 161.

3. Metals, including glass and ceramics,
4. Vehicles, including accessories and components.

It turned out that, with the exception of the first, these were the technologies which India and Pakistan appeared to need most. The tobacco industry was probably a special case as it was an exporter and an earner of both revenue and foreign exchange. Its companies had, in some cases, been established locally for over 40 years, and the pattern of their operations was relatively difficult to disturb. As for the food industry joint ventures in this group, they qualified as badly needed technology, and the foreign parent shares in equity were correspondingly high.

Oil technology and products are also quite obviously highly desirable, but they appear to constitute another special case. The nature of the oil companies' status, together with suspicion of their international oligopoly and transfer pricing practices, tends to stimulate some of the strongest countervailing thrusts by host governments. The Greek-meets-Greek situation of bilateral monopoly is best shown in the encounters of the oil companies.[9]

The less-complicated and more widely diffused technologies of the engineering and electricals groups are those in which India and Pakistan are themselves more competent. Even in 1960, *The Economist* commented upon the improving productivity in a number of engineering works and stated: "Indian railway carriages now cost less than the ex-works cost in Switzerland. Hindustan Machine Tools can now produce and sell in India, at a profit, for about £2,000, a 1,000 mm. lathe of a type that costs £3,000 to import from Europe."[10]

It seems that potential foreign investors were both capable of seeing for themselves, and were encouraged to see, that opportunities for participation in these two industries were more limited than in others. This was, to some extent, the case in Pakistan; it was certainly said to be true in India. "In these industries, we need only the very latest results of R and D, plus certain advanced management techniques. India has by now developed a very solid competence and a wide base, especially in engineering."[11]

Evaluation of Associates and Joint Ventures

If a joint venture is successful, the relationship between the partners is usually a success. Conversely, a successful relationship is likely to

---

[9] There is an excellent discussion of the vicissitudes of the oil companies in India in Michael Kidron, *Foreign Investments in India,* Oxford University Press, London, 1965, pp. 166–175.

[10] "Advance in India," *The Economist*, March 25, 1960, p. 1227.

[11] Comment in discussion at M.I.T. in 1968, by the Director of the Indian Institute of Management at Calcutta.

lead to a successful joint operation, although this statement cannot be made quite so strongly. In either case, the level of satisfaction of a foreign partner with the local associate is a reflection of the success of the joint venture. Thus, the extent to which foreign parent executives assess their associates as effective or important to a joint venture provides a direct measure of the quality of the relationship between partners and indirectly reflects the success of a joint venture.[12]

In a further dimension, it is reasonable to assume that such assessments are quite likely (though not necessarily certain) to vary with the nature of business. In particular, there should be some correspondence with the level of an associate's functional responsibility for a joint venture's operations and this varies with the nature of business. British executives were therefore asked whether their companies' associates were considered to be effective in relation to a specific joint venture (and outside India or Pakistan, for other joint ventures in general).

First to be dealt with, the comments on effectiveness were classified and assigned a value—plus one for a positive, zero for a neutral, minus one for a negative response. An average score was calculated over the values for each group by nature of business, and these scores are charted in Figure 6.1. Other tests, using measures of actual returns achieved and comparisons between subsidiary and joint venture types of operation, did not appear to be successful, at least not over the available sample data.

If, as suggested before, these assessments corresponded to the level of responsibility attributed to a particular group of associates, they should therefore vary inversely with the scores shown in Table 6.1 for each group by nature of business. However, one should build in a deliberate "hedge." If the associate was considered effective in practically all cases, one alternative interpretation of this overall finding could quite reasonably be considered trivial. More precisely, if all firms were satisfied with their associates, this might represent a universally successful selection process, or simply *post hoc* rationalization to support the actual choice which had been made. This would have been a "trivial" interpretation, consistent with theories concerning the "freezing" of values through the decision process,[13] or efforts to reduce cognitive dissonance following commitment.[14]

---

[12] The actual definition of "effective" was not specified, since an overall impression was all that was sought in this particular response. A later question was designed to determine the manner in which importance of an associate was decided. The relationship between nature of business and the stated effectiveness of associates was marginally significant at the 0.073 level.

[13] Kurt Lewin, "Group Decision and Social Change," in Theodore M. Newcomb and Eugene L. Hartley (eds.), *Readings in Social Psychology*, Holt, Rinehart and Winston, New York, 1947.

[14] Leon Festinger, *A Theory of Cognitive Dissonance*, Stanford University Press, Stanford, 1957.

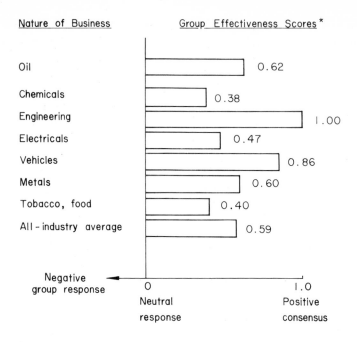

Figure 6.1
Relationship between the Stated Effectiveness of Associates
and Nature of Business

* In the diagram, a score of 1.0, as in the case of the engineering group, represents a 100%
favorable response covering all the associates in that group. A score of zero would
indicate either a generally neutral assessment of a group of associates or else a bimodal
distribution of an equal number of positive and negative responses. The theoretical
minimum of minus one would require a negative consensus of opinion concerning their
associates by all the British executives in a given group.

Actually, 68% of these cases were described as having effective
associates. Only in six of the whole sample of joint ventures was the
answer a flat "no." Four of these were related to companies in the
chemicals group, and the other two involved joint ventures in electricals.
This negative response corresponded to the earlier measure of associates' responsibility for chemicals, but not for the electricals group. For
the latter, these two were cases in which an ineffective (strictly, when
unbusinesslike practices had been proved) local partner had had to be
replaced.

Only in the tobacco and food group were more neutral than positive
answers given, and these can be explained by the fact that local asso-

ciates in these joint ventures were primarily investors. In view of the marginal significance of the relationship and the preponderance of positive answers by all other groups, the hypothesis of triviality cannot be disproved. It simply appears that most British companies were quite satisfied with the effectiveness of their associates.

Importance Attributed to Associates

Another major issue of this section concerns the importance to a joint venture, attributed by British companies to their associates. These comments were simplified into four categories:

a. Very important, in some specified manner,
b. Useful,
c. Necessary, with a negative connotation,
d. Useless.

Table 6.2
Nature of Business and Importance Attributed to Associates
in Specific Joint Ventures in India and Pakistan

Nature of Business	Importance Attributed to Associates									
	Very Important		Useful		Necessary /Negative		Useless		Totals	
	Number of Cases and Cell % Based on Column Sum*									
	No.	%	No.	%	No.	%	No.	%	No.	%
Oil	3	7	4	33	4	40	2	33	13	18
Chemicals	8	19	4	33	4	40	—	—	16	23
Engineering	9	21	1	8	—	—	—	—	10	14
Electricals	10	23	1	8	—	—	4	67	15	21
Vehicles	6	14	1	8	—	—	—	—	7	10
Metals	4	9	1	8	—	—	—	—	5	7
Tobacco, food	3	7	—	—	2	20	—	—	5	7
Totals and cell % based on row sum	43	61	12	17	10	14	6	9	71	100

* Percentages do not all add up to 100 because of rounding. Nature of business and importance attributed to associates in India or Pakistan were significantly associated at the 0.024 level.

The results are shown in Table 6.2. Again, British executives stated that their firms' associates were very important in 61 % of the joint ventures and were useful in another 17%. Only six were felt to be useless, two of which were in the oil and four in the electricals groups. This response was not unexpected for the oil and associated companies because of the nature and scale of their operations and the conformity with the earlier measure of associates' responsibility. Two of the electricals cases were those described earlier as involving specifically ineffective partners. In one of the others, the associates were primarily investors and distributors. In the last, the British parent firm had been invited by the host government to take up a large majority holding in a local company which was on the verge of bankruptcy.

Of the ten answers in the necessary/negative category, four each were from companies in the oil and the chemicals group, for which the limitations of the associates have already been discussed. Two were from firms in the tobacco and food group. All of these appear to correspond satisfactorily with the ordering, according to the level of responsibilities assumed by associates. Apart from the oil group, and

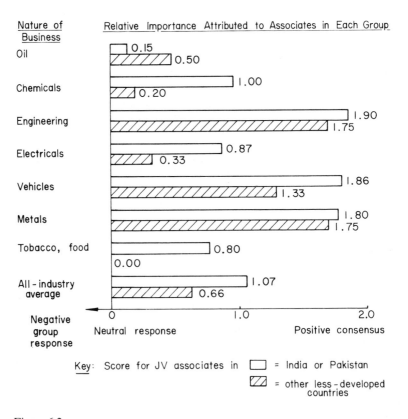

Figure 6.2
Nature of Business and Importance Attributed to Associates
in Less-Developed Countries

allowing for a marginal 50 % in chemicals, associates were described as being important in some specified manner for a clear majority of the cases in all groups.

The question also arose of associates in other less-developed nations and how they compared with those in India or Pakistan. Figure 6.2 provides a basis for such a comparison.[15]

Figure 6.2 indicates the reduction in the overall importance ascribed to associates, as compared with what may have been the special case of India and Pakistan. In six cases, the British respondents actually stated that they were unable to judge the importance of associates in other countries. Only in 31 % of all cases were such other associates described as being very important, while in another 31 % they were said to be useful.

For 30 % of these cases, associates in the less-developed nations in general were classified as either necessary, in a negative sense, or useless. This reduction in attributed importance is most marked in the chemicals group. Although many of these chemicals companies actually operated through joint ventures in other less-developed nations, they were said to be much more selective than most of the other firms. According to these respondents, this was because of the nature of their business and the difficulty in finding local partners of adequate caliber in countries other than India or Pakistan.

As usual, the oil companies appear to differ from the others. Associates were considered by respondents from this group to companies to be slightly more important in other countries than they were in India or Pakistan. The chief reason given was that the oil companies had run major operations in India for over half a century. Their ranks were studded with O.B.E.s and C.B.E.s,[16] earned by a lifetime of service there. Since they considered that they themselves knew as much about these two host countries as any local associate, the latter could really offer only political expediency—not that the oil companies were particularly impressed with what local partners had to offer in any underdeveloped nation. It was merely that they were prepared to concede that such associates did provide some marginal benefits in countries other than India or Pakistan. More specifically, these were

[15] Comments were again assigned a value, this time: very important = 2, useful = 1, necessary = −1, useless = −2, "can't judge" comments were deleted. An average score was calculated over the values for each group by nature of business. The maximum possible score would therefore have been 2.0. Nature of business and importance attributed to associates in other less-developed countries were only marginally significantly associated at the 0.063 level.

[16] Order of the British Empire and Commander of the British Empire, honors awarded for service to the British Commonwealth.

benefits such as local knowledge or personnel in locations where the oil companies were not themselves so well endowed as in these two host nations.

Readiness to Invest in Other Joint Ventures

While on the subject of indirect evaluation indices, it is worth considering briefly one other measure of the success of the joint venture process. If a given joint venture is successful, the foreign partners concerned are more likely to be ready to invest in further operations of this type than if their prior experience was unfortunate. Thus the level of readiness of such investors to participate in other joint ventures provides an indirect measure of their satisfaction with existing joint operations and an insight into their evaluation of the latter.

British executives' comments upon the readiness of their corporations to participate in further joint ventures, whether in developed or in less-developed countries, also helped to clarify another matter. This was the underlying question, of whether India or Pakistan, because of historical relationships, appear to constitute a special case for British firms in terms of their readiness to invest abroad in joint ventures. These comments are summarized, for both types of host country, in Table 6.3.[17]

The main dissenting groups with respect to investment in other under-developed nations were

a. The "selective" chemicals companies, for the reasons already discussed.

Table 6.3
Readiness of British Firms to Participate in Joint Ventures
in Countries Other than India or Pakistan

	Suggested Location of Joint Ventures			
Answer Given	Other Less-Developed Countries	Other Less-Developed Countries, Less Oil	Developed Countries	Developed Countries, Less Oil
Yes we would and we do	45%	35%	51%	39%
Yes we would	13%	15%	15%	19%
Summarized as "it depends"	27%	31%	14%	17%
No	15%	19%	20%	25%

[17] Nature of business was significantly related to answers for the less-developed case at the 0.025 level and for the developed case at the 0.009 level. For Table 6.3, variation by nature of business was not shown, in order to provide as concise a summary as possible of both sets of answers.

b. A subgroup of engineering firms, which considered their operations to be unsuitable for less-developed countries, largely because of a lack of complementary activities and resources.

c. The majority of the companies in the vehicles group, some of them for the same reason as in *b*, others for the reason discussed in connection with the structure of joint ventures. These were the firms which judged a country according to whether or not their motor industry customers were already established or preparing to invest in it. Since the motor industry's operations in less-developed countries tended to be limited, so also was the interest of their suppliers.

So far as investment in the developed countries is concerned, the chemicals group had no objections. Here the other dissenting opinions for the case of investment in less-developed countries were joined by 40% of the responses from the electricals group. The latter preferred outright acquisition as the most suitable method of operating in developed nations and their markets.

On the whole, although British firms were reasonably cautious about committing themselves to general, rather than specific and definable, joint venture opportunities in less-developed countries, only one in seven (one in five if oil cases were excluded) would not have considered them. This can be taken as reflecting a fairly high level of satisfaction over their past experience with joint operations. The satisfaction in turn implies that the joint ventures were successful on an overall basis. There is really no evidence here that India or Pakistan constituted a special case in the sense that these firms were clearly and strongly not prepared to invest elsewhere.

Summary

The structure of joint ventures, in terms of dependence upon a foreign partner, varies considerably according to the nature of business. For groups in which there is a marked predominance of foreign majority or minority equity holdings, these holdings appear to offer a reasonable explanation for the level of dependence of joint ventures.

Many of the cases in the oil group are mixed ventures which depend upon the technical and managerial skill of the British partner. In spite of the fact that a formal equity majority was held in most of these mixed ventures by a host of government agency, the latter did not assume responsibility for operations but merely concentrated upon supervising policy.

In the vehicles group, local associates were said to be highly competent and undertook considerable responsibility for operations, even though these joint ventures were subject to foreign control in policy areas more than were most others. Over a small subsample, it is possible to conjecture that dependence in metals group joint ventures varies with the complexity of the process.

Many of the chemicals cases were 50–50 joint ventures which tended to be relatively independent, with respect to policy determination, of influence by the foreign parent. This was partly a result of a stalemate between partners, and is further evidence of the existence of problems in this area, a frequent feature of joint ventures involving formal equality of associates.

Approximately two thirds of the British companies in the sample stated they were satisfied with the effectiveness and importance of their associates. A few doubts were expressed in relation to associates in the oil and chemicals groups. This is consistent with the earlier evidence that associates tend to assume rather less responsibility in these two than in other groups. Opinions concerning associates were generally neutral for cases in which the latter were primarily investors.

As a whole this group of foreign investors considers that the importance of associates in other underdeveloped nations is less than in joint ventures in India and Pakistan. An exception to this general assessment arises in connection with joint ventures in the oil group. The oil companies were even more familiar with Indian conditions than were the other British firms. As a result, local associates were, for them, merely a political necessity.

Over one third of these British companies were involved in joint ventures in other countries, both developed and underdeveloped. Excluding oil companies, less than one in five would not consider joint ventures in other less-developed countries, while one in four made the same reservation for developed countries. For the less-developed case, the objections were usually one of the following:

a. Unsuitability of the business for such countries,

b. Lack of local partners of suitable caliber,

c. Absence of particularly significant customers.

In the developed case, *a* and *b* were not important. Reason *c* was joined by the preference of some firms for outright acquisition, rather than for setting up joint ventures in such markets.

The strong preferences expressed by some respondents, notably from firms in the vehicles group, for associates and the labor force in South India suggest that this subject would be worth studying further in order to determine whether the alleged regional differences are, in fact, significant for foreign investors.

7 ATTITUDES TOWARD CONTROL

Ownership and control strategies provide fascinating topics for analysis and theoretical discussion. As such, they have been relatively well explored in the literature on international business, foreign investment policy, and comparative management.[1] It is not proposed to recapitulate all of these arguments here but rather to look at some of the relationships between attitudes toward control by British companies and certain aspects of their associated joint ventures in India and Pakistan.

Although basing their opinion on a small sample, Friedmann and Kalmanoff comment, "In the United Kingdom and Germany, virtually all the firms interviewed prefer arrangements in which they have majority control."[2] This was not quite true for all the respondents in this study, but it certainly applied to the majority. In any case, a majority share in equity[3] is not the only form of control open to foreign investors. For some corporations other methods of control are equally desirable, even preferable.

If one wishes to examine attitudes toward control, one needs more than just opinions regarding majority control. For the joint ventures in

---

[1] For example, there are excellent discussions of the significance of control:

a. In very general terms by Wolfgang G. Friedmann and George Kalmanoff, *Joint International Business Ventures*, Columbia University Press, New York, 1961, pp. 151–186.

b. In considerable detail with respect to U.S. companies by Richard D. Robinson, *International Business Policy*, Holt, Rinehart and Winston, New York, 1964, pp. 146–170, and in rather less detail by Jack H. Behrman, "Foreign Associates and Their Financing," in Raymond F. Mikesell (ed.), *U.S. Private Government Investment Abroad*, University of Oregon Books, Eugene, Oregon, 1962.

c. In a legally structured context for the Indian case by Matthew J. Kust, *Foreign Enterprise in India*, The University of North Carolina Press, Chapel Hill, 1964, pp. 141–184.

d. In conprehensive detail for the general case of investment in India by Michael Kidron, *Foreign Investments in India*, Oxford University Press, London, 1965, pp. 274–296.

e. In theoretical terms as part of a generalized theoretical framework by Richard N. Farmer and Barry M. Richman, *Comparative Management and Economic Progress*, Irwin, Homewood, Ill., 1965.

[2] Friedmann and Kalmanoff, *Joint International Business Ventures,* p. 107.

[3] The term equity refers to the voting shares of the company, the total voting stock.

135

India and Pakistan, two measures are used to classify such attitudes. These are the levels of desirability described by British executives with respect to control in terms of
1. A majority share in the equity of a joint venture.
2. Effective control over the operations of a joint venture.

The actual definition of what constitutes "effective" control was deliberately left to the interpretation of individual executives. In organization theory, control involves successful acts of influence, i.e., the controller's influence being strong enough to ensure completion of the desired cycle of behavior. The power to control "refers to potential acts rather than to transactions actually occurring."[4] Power itself is described by Weber as the probability that one actor within a relationship will be in a position to carry out his own will, despite resistance. What is really sought here, therefore, is an assessment of the extent to which foreign parent companies consider they should be able to exert such power and control. Detailed definition of the actual areas and the direction in which these are to operate are not of prime concern, depending upon each firm's own peculiar requirements. In simpler terms, effective control is the ability of foreign parent companies to do what they feel they want to do, when they want to do it.

Many of these foreign investors actually found it difficult to distinguish control along these two dimensions. For many of them, effective control was virtually synonymous with a majority equity holding. This was in spite of the fact that most companies were well aware of the leverage they could exert upon a joint venture through their own technological advantage, through special conditions written into agreements, and, in many cases, through their control over the supply of vital materials and components. Kust has suggested that a reaction of this type is largely due to the convenience of control through a majority holding, or what he describes as an "effective majority."[5] The attitudes of British investors with respect to their joint ventures in these two countries certainly support such a theory.

There appears to be little formal recognition by most of these British companies of any potential countervailing power of resistance by local associates against equity control, either directly or via host government intervention. This seems to contradict the argument: "One could anticipate that in fact control could be assured only so long as the policies of the firm coincided with the interests of the host government and of local associates. If conflict arose, control could be lost with or

---

[4] Daniel Katz and Robert L. Kahn, *The Social Psychology of Organizations,* John Wiley & Sons, New York, 1966, p. 220.
[5] Kust, *Foreign Enterprise in India,* p. 147.

without ownership, contractual relationships, or (foreign) management."[6] This threat has been specifically described as relevant for investment in India, "A large Indian house is usually able, if it wishes, to persuade the licensing authorities of the virtues of economic nationalism."[7] This lack of recognition is one reason for the association of effective control with majority control. The reason for such an attitude is not entirely clear. At times it appears to be a product of a realistic appraisal of the actual situation in India and Pakistan. At others it seems to be due to little more than blissful ignorance.

In general, the effects of host government action were felt to be limited to their nuisance value (especially in the areas of high taxation levels, pressures for "localization" of personnel, and a certain amount of disruption of supply and price levels), if a foreign partner had financial control. (This assumes that such a majority position could actually be achieved.) However, the view was not universally held. One oil company respondent commented, "The host government is probably the best local choice (of partner), we must get on well with them as they have eventual authority in any case."

Ranking of Associates

Attitudes of foreign investors toward various types of associates are colored by their attitudes toward control over a joint venture. This is basically due to their expectations concerning the degree of congruence or conflict between different kinds of associates and their own aspirations toward control. In other words, they are concerned over the extent to which a given partner will be likely or able to interfere with the foreign firm's ability to control. This concern is reflected in the relationship between attitudes toward control and ranking of associates, in which certain patterns can be expected to emerge.

If effective control is felt necessary or desirable, then the firm concerned could be expected to prefer the nonparticipating class of investors or public. This would be argued on the grounds that "Effective control by a foreign collaborator without majority ownership is . . . not difficult to obtain today [1964]. . . . A 40% equity participation, where the Indian collaborator has 30% and the balance is distributed widely, gives the foreign collaborator effective control."[8] This distribution is favored by the Indian Government according to Kust. (The Indian Chairman and Managing Director of a large joint venture in the metals

[6] Robinson, *International Business Policy*, p. 148.
[7] Kidron, *Foreign Investments in India*, p. 278.
[8] Kust, *Foreign Enterprise in India*, p. 147.

group also added to this, however, the proviso, "New Delhi usually prefers the Indian collaborator to be a strong local company and an effective partner.")

From the point of view of a foreign company concerned over control, a reasonable second choice would seem to be a local private interest. This is so because many of the local interests are limited in their own scope of activities to certain functional areas, outside of which they would be unlikely to interfere. Also, because of the relative size and strength of the foreign vis-à-vis the local partner, the former could reasonably expect to be able to dominate the latter by *force majeure* if necessary, rather more easily than dominating another company from a developed country or an agency of the host government. Least probable for a foreign corporation of this type would be the choice of a partner from the host government.

There appears to be no strong reason why companies to whom control is relatively unimportant should show a marked preference for any particular type of associate, at least not on the basis of the issue of control alone. On the other hand, companies might well rank host government interests lowest in preferability. Even for foreign companies which are relaxed in their attitudes toward control, association with the local government would be a special situation and perhaps would be felt to carry such attitudes too far. Behind these predictions is the general assumption mentioned earlier : Foreign companies, on the

Table 7.1
Ranking of Various Types of Potential Associates According to British Company's Attitude toward Effective Control of a JV

Stated Level of Necessity for Effective Control	Rank Ordering of Potential JV Associates*				
	Fellow National	Other Foreign	Local Private	Host Government	Local Public/ Investors
	Weighted Average Score and (Overall Rank) for Groups				
Necessary	2.21 (1)	3.21 (4)	2.71 (3)	4.47 (5)	2.28 (2)
Desirable	2.17 (1)	3.14 (4)	2.41 (2)	4.24 (5)	3.03 (3)
Acceptable	2.13 (1)	3.13 (3)	2.12 (1)	4.47 (5)	3.13 (3)
Unnecessary	3.43 (3)	3.75 (5)	1.65 (1)	3.65 (4)	2.50 (2)
All-group score	167 (2)	228 (4)	160 (1)	298 (5)	197 (3)

* Relationships between attitudes toward effective control and ranking of the five types of associates were significant at the 0.007, 0.091, 0.038, 0.091, 0.005 levels respectively.

whole, expect the host government to be most likely to interfere in the operation of joint ventures, largely because of potentially conflicting basic goals, philosophies, or even ideologies. An assumption based upon extrapolation from the "doctrinaire, free enterprise approach" alleged to be found in U.S. firms and typified for the general case by one respondent in an earlier major study is "Mixed companies almost always lead to conflict and the influx of political pressure in the business operation."[9]

How do such generalized assumptions agree with the attitudes expressed by this group of British executives, with respect to control over their joint ventures in India and Pakistan? One way of providing an overall basis for such a comparison is to calculate a score based upon the ranks allocated to each type of associate according to a British parent firm's attitudes toward effective control over joint venture operations. For this group of corporations, a series of scores[10] are shown in Table 7.1, where the lower the score, the more preferable the associate.

The results shown in Table 7.1 do not appear to verify all of the assumptions mentioned. Host government partners are certainly the least attractive alternatives for companies to whom control is important. At the same time, however, they are also least attractive overall. Firms which consider control to be unnecessary seem to find a poor choice among interests from developed nations, the host governments, or fellow nationals. They show a clear preference for local private interests, with the investor category a poor second.

There is an indirect linkage[11] in the evidence which probably explains this clear preference for local private partners. Most of the British firms which considered control to be unnecessary are the smaller ones. These are also the firms which tended to look for facilities and resources from a local associate. Hence the order shown in this table—the smaller firms are most likely to choose a local private interest. In fact, 75% of these companies ranked such a partner their first choice.

A major deviation from the forecasts appears in the preference shown by the control-conscious companies for fellow national associates. This is especially true for companies classing control desirable. In actual fact, for the group with the strongest predilection for control, the

---

[9] Quoted in Robinson, *International Business Policy*, p. 164.
[10] Scores and overall ranking between associate types were calculated in the same manner as in the comparisons by the nature of parent business in Chapter 5. A first-place ranking received a score of 1 and a fifth-place, a score of 5.
[11] A more direct explanation in the relationship between attitudes toward control and reasons for selecting specific associates is not strictly available as these variables are not significantly related.

preference for fellow nationals seems to be only marginally greater than for the predicted investor category. However, fellow nationals were clearly preferred to the second predicted class of local private investors, whether or not control was considered necessary or desirable.

This preference for fellow nationals in cases where there was a strong desire for control can probably be explained by a better definition of what was really felt to be involved in control. The general predictions discussed are, in effect, based upon an implicit assumption that concern would be related simply to control over the operations of a joint venture. The attitudes of these U.K. firms also incorporated an element of concern regarding control over the uncertainty induced by the environment in which the joint ventures operated. If this were so, then preference for fellow national associates would be a feature of a reasonable strategy through which to improve this control by reducing the area of uncertainty in a partner/environmental matrix. This would be consistent with the primacy of reducing uncertainty in the foreign investment decision process suggested by Aharoni.[12]

Within the group stating that control is desirable are most of the joint ventures involving oil companies. Given the choice, these firms also indicated a strong preference for fellow national partners. This explains the apparently stronger preference of this group for fellow nationals over other types of associates as compared with firms considering control to be necessary. In a similar manner, this group also includes a large subgroup of chemicals joint ventures. British parent companies of these joint ventures also show a preference for local private partners offering facilities and resources. Their responses weight the group score in favor of this type of associate. Hence the group stating that control is desirable also prefers local private participating partners to investors, an ordering contrary to the forecast.

Structural Characteristics of Joint Ventures

If a foreign parent company were greatly concerned over the issue of control of joint operations in which they might be involved, it would be reasonable to expect that this would be reflected in the structure of a joint venture. In terms of the structural measures used in this study, this concern could be reflected in several ways. In particular it should result in a higher level of dependence of joint ventures upon the British parent company.

[12] Yair Aharoni, *The Foreign Investment Process,* Division of Research, Graduate School of Business Administration, Harvard University, Boston, 1966, p. 37.

As a general rule, the fact that effective control was equated with a majority share in equity naturally suggests that companies requiring effective control are likely to seek a majority position in any joint venture in which they are involved. To some extent, the actual equity position achieved would reflect the share sought. Differences between levels of aspirations and achievements are, of course, likely to show the effects of intervening variables, in particular, the effects upon relative bargaining power of such features as the nature of business, size of the foreign company, and significance of the project to the economic and social development of the host country. In general, however, companies which actively seek control would be more likely to achieve it than those to whom the issue was of less concern. An extreme example was quoted in an earlier study, "We just kept on insisting upon 100% ownership for fourteen months until we got it."[13]

Admittedly, the situation was not as simple as the above remark by an executive of English Electric suggests. On the whole, however, the evidence of this present study indicates that the attitudes of U.K. companies toward both effective and majority control were significantly related to the actual equity share in joint ventures which they were able to obtain.[14] This relationship is shown in the third column of Table 7.2, which provides an overall basis for comparison of the effects of attitudes toward control upon structure in terms of dependence scores along each of the three main structural variables.

Independence of joint ventures with regard to their own authority in policy areas is also likely to be affected by the attitudes toward control of the British parent companies. The greater the parent's concern for control over this type of investment, the less would be the level of independence expected in an associated joint venture. The last column in Table 7.2 shows there is some indication that such an assumption is valid.[15]

Another way in which the predilection for control on the part of the foreign parent company could be expected to affect the structure of a joint venture would be in the level of the contribution made by associates. Determination of cause and effect cannot be said to be complete,

[13] Quoted in Kust, *Foreign Enterprise in India*, p. 148.
[14] Significant at the 0.001 and 0.011 levels respectively. Cases in which the British parent actually held a majority position were involved in 75% of cases when majority control was said to be necessary and in 72% of those in which effective control was necessary. At the other end of the scale, companies holding a minority position in joint ventures accounted for 85% of those who felt that effective control was unnecessary and 88% of those who considered that majority control was no more than acceptable.
[15] Of the firms which considered majority control necessary, 75% actually controlled their joint ventures. For 50%, the control in areas of policy was close.

Table 7.2
Structural Dependence Scores of Joint Ventures According to
Foreign Partners' Desire for Effective Control

Stated Level of Necessity for Effective Control	Number of JVs	Equity Share of Foreign Parent	Associate's Responsibility	JV's Independence in Policy Areas
		Weighted Average Score and (Group Order Rank)*		
Necessary	14	3.43 (4)	2.89 (4)	2.86 (4)
Desirable	28	2.46 (3)	2.86 (3)	2.36 (1)
Acceptable	15	1.93 (1)	2.13 (1)	2.60 (3)
Unnecessary	12	2.08 (2)	2.16 (2)	2.57 (2)
All-group average score		2.48	2.60	2.55

* Significance levels were 0.001, 0.050, and 0.063 respectively. Scores and overall ranks were calculated in the same manner as in the comparisons by nature of parent business in Chapter 6. Dependence was ranked for each structural variable according to the strength of the British parent company's stated need for effective control. Table 7.2 presents the results of these calculations—the higher the score, the greater the dependence of the joint venture upon its British parent.

however, merely because an association exists between these two variables. For example, a powerful or highly competent local associate may well make a considerable contribution to the effectiveness of a joint venture in spite of a foreign partner's desire for control. Alternatively, the latter may rest secure in the knowledge that it has the potential to exert control if it so wishes, while leaving much of the responsibility for the actual operations of a joint venture to a local partner. With these reservations, a strong desire for control would tend to imply a similar desire to obtain maximum benefit from the ability to supervise operations. If this were so, it would appear in a tendency for the local partners to assume less responsibility, mainly because they would be afforded less opportunity to participate effectively by a control-conscious foreign parent company.

On the whole, the findings in this study support such an argument. Relationships between the level of associates' responsibility and attitudes toward majority and effective control were significant[16] and are shown in the fourth column of Table 7.2. Associates were said to have made little or no contribution in over 70% of joint ventures involving U.K. companies which considered majority or effective control neces-

[16] Significant at the 0.001 and 0.050 levels, respectively.

sary. On the other hand, they assumed considerable responsibility when the British parent's attitude toward control was more relaxed.[17]

These results do not appear to be consistent with Kidron's statement, "In practice, whatever the arrangements for allocating functions between the Indian and foreign partners, whatever the distribution of capital between them . . . , almost invariably, it appears, works management remains in non-Indian hands."[18] It is not entirely clear from this statement just what definition of "works management" was used. In view of an earlier comment on the importance of quality control, in the paragraph from which this excerpt was quoted, "works management" appears to be essentially management of production and quality control. The measure of associates responsibility in the present study covers a much broader scope. Production and the technical or engineering functions, which between them also covered quality control, were only two out of the eleven functional areas included in this measure. Even for these two areas, however, the figures do not appear to agree with those of the earlier study. The breakdown of the raw data of this study is shown in Table 7.3.

Table 7.3
Associates' Responsibility for Production, Technical, and
Engineering Functions in Joint Ventures

| Functional Area | Level of Associate's Responsibility | | | | | | Total Cases |
| | Full | | Joint | | None | | |
	Cases	%	Cases	%	Cases	%	
Production	23	(33)	14	(20)	33	(47)	70
Technical and engineering	3	(4)	21	(30)	46	(66)	70

The term "non-Indian hands" is also misleading, although one suspects that this is rather a case of splitting hairs in criticizing an author working on a broad canvas. The figures shown understate the number of occasions when these two functions were actually in Indian hands, but hands which were in the employ of the foreign partner, and therefore classified here in the "none" category (in that ultimate responsibility lay with the British partner).

[17] When effective control was unnecessary, 75% of cases; 73% when it was merely acceptable. Alternatively, 83% of cases when majority control was acceptable.
[18] Kidron, *Foreign Investments in India*, p. 279.

To recapitulate briefly, the underlying hypothesis is that the level of concern over control on the part of foreign parent companies is directly related to the level of dependence of joint ventures in which they are involved. Such concern would lead to greater dependence, except when other factors interfere with this tendency. Actual relationships between attitudes toward control of British companies and the structural characteristics of joint ventures did not disprove this hypothesis.

The direction of cause cannot strictly be proved. In theory, a strong desire for control could conceivably reflect a wish to perpetuate the *status quo*, in which dependence may have arisen for some other reason than a foreign partner's desire for control. Alternatively, a combination of a desire for control and other factors could have led to dependence, but the other factors, especially those affecting relative bargaining power, could have been the major determinants.

The first of these two alternatives is probably unlikely. It would imply that control may not have been sought deliberately. The question of control over investment was too basic an issue in over 60 % of the cases discussed for it to be other than a specific objective. The second alternative is probably true but is not sufficient to refute the hypothesis. Even though bargaining power may have made control possible, it did not necessarily explain why control was actually assumed, at least not beyond the stage when control could be relaxed without jeopardizing the effectiveness of a joint venture. There was no suggestion by any of the British companies citing control as necessary that, if control was achieved, it might be relaxed in the future—except under duress.

The only suggestion of this nature came from firms which were more relaxed over the issue of control, typified by the following statement of a parent company director in the vehicles group who actually set up two operations in India:

Our policy over control is fairly flexible. In less-developed countries, it depends upon our partners. Control is useful in early days, in order that the new operation can be put into shape as soon as possible. In the long run it is better for the country if local interests have control over local operations. This reduces the impact of the conflict of interests which is always there between local partners, the host country, the foreign investor and, to some extent, the latter's parent government.

Look again at the figures in Table 7.2. The analysis can be simplified and summarized by grouping the four categories of attitudes toward effective control into two sections. The "necessary" and "desirable" responses constitute the group of companies which considered that control was important. "Acceptable" and "unnecessary" responses indicate a lower level of concern. With one exception, there is a clear difference between these two sections. Dependence was consistently greater where control was important and less where the attitude toward control appeared to be more relaxed.

The exception arises in the low level of dependence in policy areas for joint ventures associated with companies citing control as desirable. It is explained by the presence in this group of responses on behalf of oil interests. In 85% of the responses from such interests it was suggested that control was desirable, but, at the same time, just over half of the joint ventures in this sample involved host government partners. These partners took considerable interest in policy issues, even though their contribution was not significant in other respects. Hence the dependence of these mixed ventures upon the foreign partner was lower than the latter would prefer along this dimension.

The general conclusion which arises from this evidence is that British companies appeared to have the ability to achieve control in joint ventures when the issue was felt to be important. This ability is represented in Figure 7.1. These companies were usually able to obtain or maintain an equity majority position when it was considered necessary, in spite of host government policies to the contrary. Such a conclusion has some interesting implications in the context of the bilateral monopoly thesis.

One must accept the possibility that some companies may have failed to invest in these host countries because they were unable to obtain a majority share in a joint operation, or because they were unable to invest in a 100%-owned subsidiary.[19] With this reservation, even though two of this subgroup of companies were small and one was medium-sized, the apparent ability to achieve control when necessary to a firm's own interests seemed to be evidence against the thesis of bilateral monopoly. More specifically, it was inconsistent with the argument that the joint venture decision was governed primarily by relative bargaining power in terms of technological and economic desirability to the host nation.[20]

Profitability of Joint Ventures

Underlying most of the arguments put forward for control of operations by a foreign partner is the implication that this will result in a

[19] The study was not organized to provide details of such firms.
[20] The argument is discussed in Stephen Hymer, *The International Operations of National Firms, A Study of Direct Foreign Investment,* Unpublished Doctoral Dissertation in Economics, M.I.T., 1960.

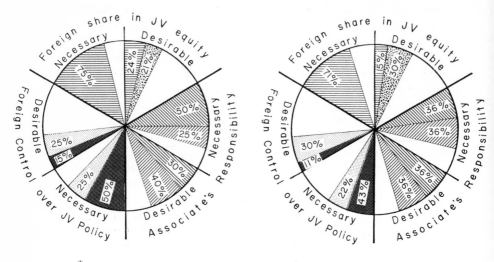

KEY *

 Majority share in equity held by British parent.

 No responsibility on part of local associate.

 Close U.K. control over JV policies.

 50-50 share in equity.

 Little responsibility by local associate.

 Considerable U.K. control over JV policies.

Figure 7.1
Aspirations and Achievements of British Parent Companies Concerning Control
(as indicated by structural dependence of JVs)

* Figures are percentages of total cases in each aspiration group, i.e., in 75 % of cases when
majority control was felt to be necessary, foreign majority in JV equity was achieved.

better performance of a joint venture. Performance of a given operation
is most commonly measured and described in terms of its profitability.
In general, therefore, the same argument implies that a greater level of
foreign control should lead to greater profitability. If this is true, then
British companies which are concerned over control (these are the firms
which are more likely to achieve control) should be associated with

higher rates of return on the long-term U.K. investment in a specific joint venture in India or Pakistan.[21]

Actually, the evidence indicates that higher levels of return were obtained from joint venture investments by U.K. firms with a more relaxed attitude toward control. Over 70% of the cases in which the British parent considered majority control to be no more than acceptable were in the high return class. The remainder were in the medium class. Those in which the British parent stated that control was acceptable made up 50% of the joint ventures earning a high return. Of the cases in which the foreign parent considered that majority control was necessary or desirable, 30% were in the low and 50% in the medium return classes. The association between these two variables is outlined in Figure 7.2.

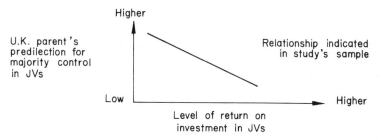

Figure 7.2
Relationship between Foreign Parent's Predilection for Control and Return on Joint Venture Investment

This relationship appears to rebut some of the arguments generally put forward for control over this type of investment. In particular it casts some doubt upon the theory that control is necessary in order to improve the operational effectiveness of a joint venture, from which would be expected to come a better rate of return. However, while this rebuttal is valid to some extent, it is also probable that other considerations have a significant bearing upon the relationship. In particular, the nature of business and the overall objectives of the foreign parent company[22] are likely to have been major determinants of the level of return on a specific investment.

---

[21] This simple measure of the percentage rate of return, net of host country taxation, was described in Chapter 4. Details were available only for 38 joint ventures, but the relationship with attitudes toward control was significant at the 0.009 level. Levels of return were grouped into three categories: low = 10% and under, medium = 11% to 20%, high = over 20%.

[22] Especially location of the cost/profit center at which a corporation with internationally integrated operations found it most rewarding to take or record its returns.

The data are not sensitive enough to indicate the magnitude of the effects of these other variables. In actual fact, the only other relevant evidence in this study appears to support the argument against control. Analysis of some of the effects and relationships associated with varying size of parent companies indicates that smaller foreign companies appear to obtain the highest returns on investment in joint ventures in India and Pakistan. These companies were also more relaxed in their attitudes toward control.

Importance of Associates

If a foreign investor is worried about control—a worry possibly expressed in terms of fears for profitability of a joint venture if control is not obtained or is lost—he is also implying that local associates are unlikely to be effective or important from the foreign partner's point of view. Thus U.K. firms concerned over control should tend to have a lower opinion of their associates. At the same time, this opinion is indirectly a publicly expressed evaluation of their own competence in choosing associates. A poor opinion may be said to reflect a poor level of competence, and respondents may therefore try not to recognize or publicize such an opinion.

This reservation is valid for the comments of British executives upon the effectiveness of the participation of their joint venture associates. Sensitivity of analysis is limited by the high proportion of cases (68%) in which associates were said to be effective. In spite of this effect, there is some association between concern over control and a poor opinion of partners.[23] Over 80% of joint ventures in which associates were said to be ineffective, and a similar proportion of neutral responses, involved U.K. parent firms whose executives stated that effective control was necessary or desirable. On the other hand, only one negative and three neutral responses were given out of twenty-seven cases in which British firms stated that control was unnecessary or merely acceptable. The pattern of this relationship suggests a kinked curve along the lines indicated in Figure 7.3.

A kink in the curve is probably explained by the high proportion of chemical companies in the group stating that control is desirable. Chemical companies also tended to look for local partners which would be effective participants in a joint venture. If they were successful in this search, they were also likely to state that their associates were effective.

The reservation concerning possible cognitive dissonance reduction also seems to suggest the possibility of some "noise" in the high pro-

---

[23] Marginally significant at the 0.087 level.

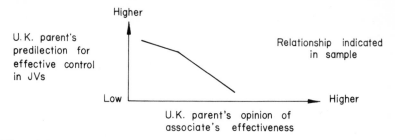

Figure 7.3
Relationship between Foreign Parent's Predilection for Effective Control
and Effectiveness of Associates

portion (60%) of executives stating that associates are important in
some specified and tangible manner. Again, however, in spite of this
possible distortion, the responses clearly indicated that U.K. firms
which found control important tended to find their partners less so.[24]
Again, the importance of associates in chemicals joint ventures caused
a kink in the overall trend of the relationship. The actual cross-
tabulation of responses, grouped by U.K. parent firms' attitudes
toward effective control, appears in Table 7.4.

Table 7.4
British Parent Companies' Attitudes toward Effective Control and their
Comments on Associates' Importance to the JVs

Stated Level of Necessity for Effective Control	Importance of Associates to this JV*				Row Total
	Important (Specified)	Useful	Necessary (Negative)	Useless	
Necessary	6	2	3	3	14
Desirable	13	8	7	1	29
Acceptable	13	—	—	2	15
Unnecessary	10	2	—	—	12
Column total	42	12	10	6	70

* Figures represent actual numbers of cases in each category.

To emphasize the extremes of the trends, the four central rows and
columns of Table 7.4 can be looked at as four quadrants centered on the
middle of the table. This reveals the fact that 88% of the negative
opinions concerning associates are in the northeast quadrant and

[24] The "importance of partners" variable was significantly related to both attitudes
toward majority and attitudes toward effective control at the 0.037 and 0.015 levels, respectively.

therefore associated with parent companies stating that effective control is necessary or desirable. At the same time, 93% of the responses by British companies which consider that control is unnecessary or merely acceptable are in the southwest quadrant, associated with positive opinions concerning partners. Actually, 85% of these responses are in the far west of this quadrant, indicating that partners are important in some specified manner to the joint venture.

The northwest quadrant explains the kink mentioned previously which compares with that in Figure 7.3 (with the curve back-to-front). It includes twelve joint ventures of British companies in the chemicals and associated interests group, seven involving oil and three involving vehicles group companies, all of which stated that control was desirable. It also includes five joint ventures associated with companies in the electricals group considering that effective control is necessary. The only two cases in the southeast quadrant are those in which ineffective partners had to be replaced.

To move on to the general case, a relaxed attitude toward control also tended to be related to a higher stated importance of associates for joint ventures in less-developed countries in general. Again, there was a kinked trend in the relationship.[25] The curve ran from a strong desire for control, coupled with a low opinion of associates' importance at one extreme, to a relaxed desire for control and a high assessment of associates at the other. As might be expected from previous comments on the relationships between other variables and the nature of business, there was also a reduction in the importance ascribed to associates in other host countries. Table 7.5 shows these responses classified by the felt or stated need for effective control.

Table 7.5
British Parent Companies' Attitudes toward Effective Control and their Comments on the Importance of Associates to JVs in Less-Developed Countries

Stated Level of Necessity for Effective Control	Importance of Associates to JVs in LDCs in General*					
	Important (Specified)	Useful	Necessary (Negative)	Useless	Can't Judge	Row Total
Necessary	1	3	8	1	1	14
Desirable	6	10	10	1	2	29
Acceptable	8	5	—	—	2	15
Unnecessary	7	4	1	—	—	12
Column total	22	22	19	2	5	70

* Figures represent the actual number of cases in each category.

[25] Significant at the 0.024 level for effective and the 0.004 level for majority control.

In this case, too, the table could be divided into four quadrants, (this time ignoring the last two columns, since the "can't judge" responses do not add to the interpretation). The overall reduction in importance of associates is then shown by the shift toward the center or central intersection of responses in the two western quadrants, when Table 7.5 is compared with Table 7.4.

Readiness to Invest in Other Joint Ventures

How much do a foreign investor's attitudes toward control affect its readiness to participate in joint ventures? The firms in the present study were already involved in such operations. How did the attitudes affect their interest in further joint ventures? As these attitudes are partly a function of risk aversion schedules and the latter are in turn a function of environmental uncertainty, one would expect that readiness to invest would vary with different countries in which joint ventures might be located. Firms concerned over control would tend to look for a familiar, established environment and would prefer joint ventures in developed countries—or India and Pakistan, where uncertainty was reduced by experience.

Readiness to invest in other joint ventures should be a direct reflection of a British parent company's general policies on investment. Indirectly, it would likely be affected by the experiences of these firms with the particular joint ventures under study, especially those British companies not already involved in other similar operations in the three investment locations specified. This last point would also be relevant with respect to attitudes toward possible further investment in India or Pakistan.

Responses were organized into two categories, according to the attitudes toward control described by U.K. executives as representative of their own firms. "Necessary" and "desirable" were reclassified as "concerned"; "acceptable" and "unnecessary" as "relaxed." The results appear in Table 7.6.

Certain figures stand out in Table 7.6. A high proportion of "concerned" companies were already involved in other joint ventures in all three groups of host countries. This proportion increases but only slightly when the investment location is in a developed country. With firms *not* involved in other joint ventures in the area in question, there is a marked tendency on the part of "concerned" companies to prefer developed countries. Most of these firms not so involved would not even consider joint ventures in less-developed countries, or other joint ventures in India or Pakistan. Two thirds of them, however, would consider such operations in developed countries.

Table 7.6
Relationships between Attitudes toward Control and Readiness of
British Firms to Invest in Other JVs*

Locus of Investment	Attitudes toward Effective Control of U.K. Partner	Response Categories Indicating Level of Readiness**				
		Yes, We Would And We Do Cases (%)	Yes, We Would Cases (%)	It Depends Cases (%)	No Cases (%)	Row Total Cases
Host country (India/ Pakistan)	Concerned	22 (51)	1 (2)	9 (21)	11 (26)	43
	Relaxed	10 (37)	5 (19)	9 (33)	3 (11)	27
	Column total	32	6	18	14	70
Other less- developed countries	Concerned	26 (61)	1 (2)	6 (16)	10 (23)	43
	Relaxed	5 (19)	8 (30)	13 (48)	1 (4)	27
	Column total	31	9	19	11	70
Developed countries	Concerned	28 (65)	5 (12)	5 (12)	5 (12)	43
	Relaxed	7 (26)	6 (22)	5 (19)	9 (33)	27
	Column total	35	11	10	14	70

* Attitudes toward effective control were significantly related to the readiness of
British firms to invest in other joint ventures at the following levels: in India or
Pakistan—0.000; in other less-developed countries—0.000; in developed nations
—0.003.
** Cell percentages are based upon row sums. Percentages do not add up to
100 because of rounding.

This distinction suggests that developed countries were felt to be
safer milieux for investment by companies concerned over control. Such
an argument would be consistent with that mentioned earlier, namely,
that the control over which these firms were concerned was, at least in
part, control over the investment environment. To the extent that this
environment was similar to that of a foreign investor's parent country, it
was probably felt to be either easier to control or less threatening to
foreign control. An international survey of business opinion and
experience published in 1966 adds support to this argument for the
general case:

The very significant differences in customs and language, management ability,
and long-range business and investment objectives are cited as primary reasons
for requiring a majority position in a joint venture in an under-developed area ...
[but] ... In the countries ruled by political and economic instability, [even] a
majority position does not seem very advantageous .... The privilege of free

enterprise, which is an essential condition of a majority participation, is unsafe under these circumstances.[26]

With regard to the readiness of firms in this sample to invest in further joint ventures in less-developed countries, including India and Pakistan, a higher proportion of "relaxed" British companies were prepared to carry out such investment, while a higher percentage of "concerned" companies were not. The figures in Table 7.6 suggest that this situation was reversed to some extent for the case of developed countries, where 33% of "relaxed" companies were not prepared to consider a joint venture. This phenomenon is due to a reversal in the policies of these companies rather than a dislike of investment in developed nations. The reversal is accounted for by the group of electricals companies which preferred outright acquisition as their investment strategy in such countries.

Summary

The concern of British parent firms for control over some of their joint ventures in India and Pakistan involved the felt need to reduce the area of uncertainty in overseas operations as well as the desire to dictate the course taken by a joint investment. As a result, fellow national partners tended to be favored as potential associates by companies concerned over control. Where control was felt to be less important, local private partners were preferred because of the likelihood of their positive contribution to a joint venture within the political, economic, and social desirability constraints of host countries.

It appears that, in general, firms feeling strongly about control are usually capable of achieving it, even though the desire for control is probably only one of the factors likely to contribute to such achievement. Whether or not they actually hold a majority share in the equity, such companies appear to permit their associates to undertake less responsibility for the operations of a joint venture. They also maintain a closer supervision in areas of policy, allowing joint ventures limited independence in these areas. An exception occurs in the case of mixed ventures (most of which were associated with oil interests), in which host governments tend to exert their countervailing power in policy areas. The dependence upon foreign partners appears to be less, in terms of both the level of responsibility undertaken by associates and

---

[26] Karen Kraus Bivens and Enid Baird Lovell, *Joint Ventures With Foreign Partners, International Survey of Business Opinion and Experience,* National Industrial Conference Board, New York, 1966, p. 8.

the joint venture's autonomy in policy areas, when foreign companies are more relaxed in their attitudes toward control.

There is some evidence in this study that the profitability of joint ventures was inversely related to the level of concern over control of the foreign partner. This suggests that one of the most important justifications often given for seeking foreign control may not be valid.

Most of the British companies interviewed gave a favorable assessment of the importance and effectiveness of their associates. Within this general euphoria, however, there was a tendency for the level of favorability to be inversely related to the strength of a British parent company's desire for control. There is clearly a danger that such assessments were the second part of self-fulfilling prophecies, or were the result of corporate attempts to reduce cognitive dissonance. With this reservation, however, the evidence suggests that there may be a linked progression along the following lines:

From relaxed attitudes toward control on the part of foreign partners,

To greater assumption of responsibility by local associates,

To more effective contribution by local associates,

To a greater return upon investment in a joint venture,

To a more favorable assessment of local associates by foreign partners, and finally

To a greater readiness by such foreign partners to invest in further joint ventures in less-developed countries.

8 FRAMEWORK OF A MODEL OF THE JOINT VENTURE PROCESS

This study is concerned mainly with the detailed examination of a series of relationships involved in the joint venture process—an analysis of the interactions between groups of variables representing decisions and structural characteristics. The emphasis has been upon limited relationships among certain dimensions rather than upon the overall pattern involved in setting up and operating joint ventures. Behind this detailed analysis is the gradual delineation of a group of components which can form the framework of a model.

In establishing such a model, it would be reasonable to expect that one could predict and describe certain series of motivations, decisions, and relationships associated with a joint venture. This should be true even with limited information concerning parts of the model. Initially it would probably be necessary to make the limiting condition that the constraints affecting the situation should be similar to those under which the model was set up.

At the same time, certain of the implications would be open to direct extrapolation and interpretation for the general case. Even if the validity of further generalization were limited by what might appear to be special features of a particular set of constraints, the limiting conditions could be relaxed later. This would involve the extension of a study such as the present one, or its repetition with different parent and host countries.

To recapitulate briefly, because of the range of potential variability in the subjects and their environments, the research strategy attempts to concentrate initially upon validating the basis of a model for a clearly defined subset of the total population of joint ventures. In line with this strategy, the initial environment was limited to a two-country group, India and Pakistan, while foreign parent corporations were limited to those of one nationality, British.

There are many possible alternative forms in which the framework and the appropriate analysis could be organized in order to set up this type of model. For example, an attractive possibility would be to hang the structure of the model on three fairly obvious "pegs," namely, the three major decisions involved in setting up a joint venture:

1. The decision to invest.
2. The decision to use the joint venture form.
3. The decision to select a specific associate.

Without dismissing this as a possible long-term solution to defining a comprehensive model, there are certain considerations of sample size and relative scope of different parts of the analysis which make the approach less attractive in the present context. Such a format has not been adopted for two main reasons. First, the foreign investment decision covers a wider domain than that of joint ventures and therefore constitutes a major area of study in its own right. On the basis of the evidence of the present study, it is quite clear that unless this decision is itself analyzed in depth, there will be little apparent variation in the motivation suggested by respondents. At the level of analysis of business objectives, most investments are likely to be made because of market considerations, particularly developing a new market or protecting an existing one. The position of this decision in a model would be that of a constant rather than variable dimension.

As a second reason, certain other variables offer a simpler basis for classifying dimensions useful in a model. Particularly relevant in this respect are the groups of variables which can be used to classify characteristics of the foreign investors, the local associates, and the joint ventures themselves. Among these are the size, nature of business, and performance, or profitability of all three of these interests. In addition, the question of control is always likely to be a basic issue and a determinant, in any joint operation, of the resultant relationships.

Thus, rather than the three decisions, the initial format of the analysis designed to identify a model of the joint venture process used eight sets of variables. Two of these were actually modifications of the decisions already described. The analysis and model start from the premise that a decision to invest in a particular country or market has been made, at least in principle. These variables are not all equally useful. Some are significantly related to other critical variables and provide the basis for a framework. Others have little validity as predictors of variation and have not been examined further.[1] The framework has finally been defined in terms of the following eight groups of variables:

1. Size, and to a lesser extent profitability, of the foreign parent firm.
2. The nature of the business involved—in general, much the same for both joint venture and foreign parent, and therefore defined in terms of the latter's business.

[1] Some of the characteristics of foreign parent companies and of joint ventures show high positive correlation or highly significant association by chi-square and have therefore been combined.

3. Attitudes toward control on the part of the foreign parent company.
4. A diversified group of variables which appear to have an immediate bearing upon the two decision processes:
   a. Attitudes toward and ranking of different types of potential associates;
   b. Location of responsibility within the foreign parent for initiation and promotion of a joint venture project and for the actual decisions involved;
   c. Availability of alternative associates and the extent to which chosen associates were known prior to their selection.
5. The decision to go into a joint venture (i.e., the reasons given for using the joint venture form).
6. The reasons for which specific associates were selected.
7. Broad-scale structural characteristics of joint ventures, expressed chiefly in terms of their dependence upon parent companies.
8. A group of measures used by parent companies, or set up as part of the analysis, in order to evaluate different features of performance and of relationships between partners in the joint venture. These include:
   a. Methods of evaluation said to be used by parent companies;
   b. The importance and effectiveness attributed to associates;
   c. Readiness of the foreign parent firms to participate in further joint operations;
   d. Measures of return on investment (over a subsample for which data are available).

The size of the sample limits the power of the model.[2] As a result, most of the statistically valid analysis of the relationships structured in the model has been limited to two-dimensional form. What remains is to present a brief overall view of the framework and the series of linkages involved. This is done largely in diagrammatic form.

One of the difficulties in establishing complete patterns or nuclei to form parts of a model lies in the gaps that exist in the sets of relationships based upon some of the anchor variables. These gaps may be either a genuine, permanent feature of these relationships or merely a function of the limited sample size. For the purpose of establishing some approximation to an overall set of relationships for decision criteria within each part of the model, it is necessary to find a way around this problem.

[2] It was not possible to obtain statistically significant results for multiple relationships between variables representing different parameters of the model. In terms of chi-square, for example, the ratio of occurrences to the potential number of cells in anything more than a two-way cross-tabulation would have been too small to be useful.

The general assumption has therefore been made that for cases in which there does not appear to be a direct association between measures, a weaker, second-level linkage can be obtained for prediction purposes by working through indirect relationships.[3] A similar argument can also be applied in order to define lower-level linkages. For example, there does not appear to be a significant direct relationship over the responses in the sample between nature of business and

a. Size of the foreign parent corporation,
b. Availability of associates, or
c. The methods used by parent corporations in evaluating joint venture performance.

Examining each of these in turn, however,

a. Parent profitability is significantly related to both parent size and nature of business.[4] It can therefore provide a second-level linkage between the other two variables.
b. A second-level linkage exists between nature of business and availability of associates in the significant relationships between these two variables and the reasons for selecting specific associates.
c. The nature of interactions between nature of business and methods of evaluating joint ventures can be predicted through a third-level linkage. This involves working through the following relationships: nature of business, profitability of foreign parent, size of foreign parent, methods of evaluating performance.

A model described in this manner, involving a complex series of interdependent relationships, is like a complicated rooting system. For diagrammatic purposes, it soon grows out of control. The horticultural remedy would probably be to divide up parts of the plant and pot them separately in order to control the growth. A similar strategy is adopted here for convenience in laying out the model. The diagrams (Figures 8.1–8.6) describe a group of models which are in fact related components of a conceptual whole. Each model, or submodel, incorporates a set of relationships or linkages built around one of the "anchor" variables described earlier as bases for the structural grouping of variables.

---

[3] The true nature of any gaps could be confirmed in further studies incorporating a larger range of sample data.

[4] "Parent business" is significantly related to "net return on investment" of parent corporations at the 0.004 level. The latter variable is in turn related to "parent size in assets" at the 0.012 level. In order to avoid possible misunderstanding, it is perhaps worth stressing that these variables are not correlated in a relationship which is necessarily linear. The chi-square tests merely indicate that certain parts of one distribution of characteristics are significantly related to certain parts of another distribution.

In terms of its predictive capabilities, the most useful anchor is the nature of the business. Within the overall structural groupings it is significantly related to one or more of the variables in each of the other main groups of the framework. The pattern of established associations and linkages between variables based upon nature of business appears to constitute the best approximation of the decision processes and relationships involved in joint venture operations. This pattern is laid out in Figure 8.1, while some of the more important linkages in this particular model, together with appropriate chapter references for convenience in application, are listed in Table 8.1.

Although nature of business provides the most comprehensive and powerful set of relationships, the overall accuracy of prediction is likely to be improved by using some of the other sets based on other anchors which are laid out in Figures 8.2 through 8.6. In each case the approach is the same. It is possible to work back from any variable in a set to the anchor and then out again through a lower-level linkage to any other variable, either within the set or within the overall model. In Figure 8.1, for example, one can work through any linkage, say "attitudes toward potential associates" along the spoke to the hub, "nature of business," and then out again along any other spoke, say to "attitudes toward control." Such variables as the "ability to achieve control" (Figure 8.3) can be linked up. Along with each diagram is a table providing references in the relevant chapter of the text to detailed descriptions and figures for the relationships between variables.

The size of the sample limits the validity of probabilities assigned on the basis of some of the research findings. If this reservation is kept in mind, however, the model appears to be operational. With the aid of the actual figures shown in the tables presented earlier, probabilities can be assigned to the likelihood of various outcomes in the form of predicted relationships. Such probabilities can be modified further on a more subjective basis, using the comments made in the descriptive parts of the text. They are also amenable to refinement through Bayesian analysis.[5]

To carry the horticultural analogy further, such a combination of elemental and subjectively determined probabilities provides the basis for analysis of various possible outcomes by use of the decision tree approach.[6] It should be possible not only to predict the varying likeli-

[5] See for example, Robert O. Schlaifer, *Probability and Statistics for Business Decisions,* McGraw-Hill, New York, 1959.

[6] For a simple account of this technique, see John F. Magee, "Decision Trees for Decision Making," *Harvard Business Review,* July–August, 1964, pp. 126–138; also, by the same author, "How to Use Decision Trees in Capital Investment," *Harvard Business Review,* September–October, 1964, pp. 79–96.

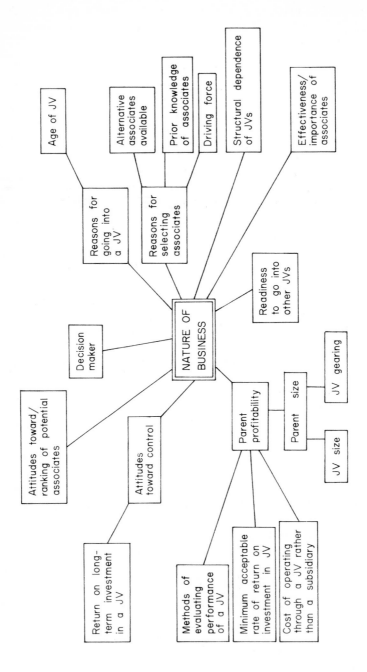

Figure 8.1
Model of Relationships and Linkages Based upon Nature of Business

Table 8.1
Linkages Associated with Nature of Business

First-Level Linkages (Related Variables)	Tests Used To Define	Level of Measurement	Chapter Reference	Data Presented	Major Second-Level Linkages
Parent profitability	χ^2	Nominal	4		Parent size; various measures used for evaluating joint ventures
Attitudes toward control	χ^2	Nominal	5	Table 5.2	Return on long-term investment in a joint venture
Attitudes toward and ranking of associates				Tables 5.3 & 5.4	
Decision maker	χ^2	Ordinal	5		
Reasons for going into joint venture	χ^2	Nominal	5	Figure 5.1	
Reasons for selecting associates	χ^2	Nominal	2	Table 2.4	Age of joint venture
	χ^2	Nominal	5	Table 5.5	Prior knowledge of associates; driving force; alternative associates available
Structural dependence of joint ventures	χ^2	Ordinal	6	Table 6.1	
Associates effective	χ^2	Ordinal	6	Figure 6.1	
Associates important: In India or Pakistan	χ^2	Ordinal	6	Table 6.2	
In LDCs in general	χ^2	Ordinal	6	Figure 6.2	
Parent readiness to participate in other joint ventures	χ^2	Ordinal	6	Table 6.3	

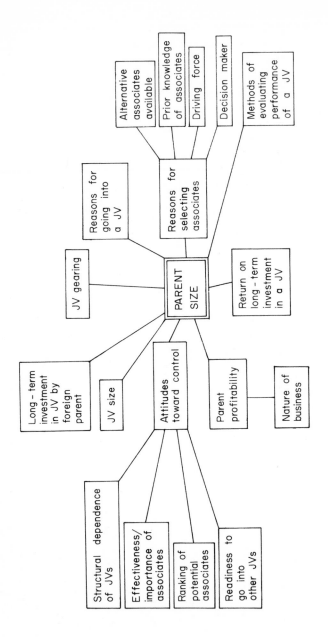

Figure 8.2
Model of Relationships and Linkages Based upon Size of Foreign Parent Firm

Table 8.2
Linkages Associated with Parent Size

First-Level Linkages (Related Variables)	Tests Used To Define	Level of Measurement	Chapter Reference	Data Presented	Major Second-Level Linkages
Joint venture size	Correlated	Ratio	4		
Long-term investment in joint venture by foreign parent	Correlated	Ratio	4		
Joint venture gearing	Correlated	Ratio	4	Figure 4.1	
Attitudes toward control	χ^2	Ordinal	4	Figure 4.2	Ranking of associates; structural dependence; associates effective; associates important; parent readiness to invest in other JVs
Reasons for going into joint venture	χ^2	Nominal	4	Table 4.2	
Reasons for selecting associates	χ^2	Nominal	4	Table 4.3	Prior knowledge of associates; driving force; decision maker; alternative associates available
Return on long-term investment in JV	χ^2	Nominal	4	Figure 4.3	
Methods of evaluating JV performance	χ^2	Nominal	4	Table 4.5	
Parent profitability	χ^2	Interval	4		Nature of business

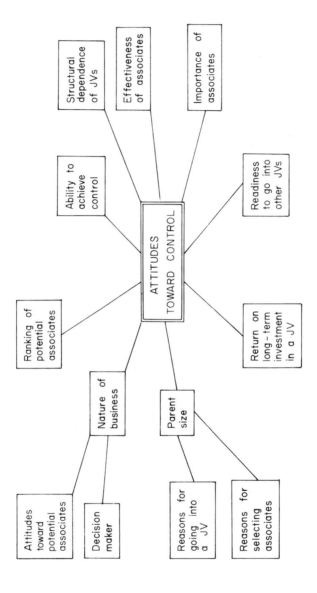

Figure 8.3
Model of Relationships and Linkages Based upon Attitudes toward Control

Table 8.3
Linkages Associated with Attitudes toward Control

First-Level Linkages (Related Variables)	Tests Used To Define	Level of Measurement	Chapter Reference	Data Presented	Major Second-Level Linkages
Parent size	χ^2	Ordinal	4	Figure 4.2	Reasons for going into joint venture; reasons for selecting associates
Nature of business	χ^2	Nominal	5	Table 5.2	Attitudes toward potential associates; decision maker
Ranking of associates	χ^2	Ordinal	7	Table 7.1	
Structural dependence of joint ventures	χ^2	Ordinal	7	Table 7.2	
Ability to achieve control	χ^2	Nominal	7	Figure 7.1	
Return on long-term investment in JV	χ^2	Ordinal	7	Figure 7.2	
Associates effective	χ^2	Ordinal	7	Figure 7.3	
Associates important:					
In India or Pakistan	χ^2	Ordinal	7	Table 7.4	
In LDCs in general	χ^2	Ordinal	7	Table 7.5	
Parent readiness to participate in other joint ventures in:					
India or Pakistan	χ^2	Ordinal	7	Table 7.6	
Other LDCs	χ^2	Ordinal	7	Table 7.6	
Developed countries	χ^2	Ordinal	7	Table 7.6	

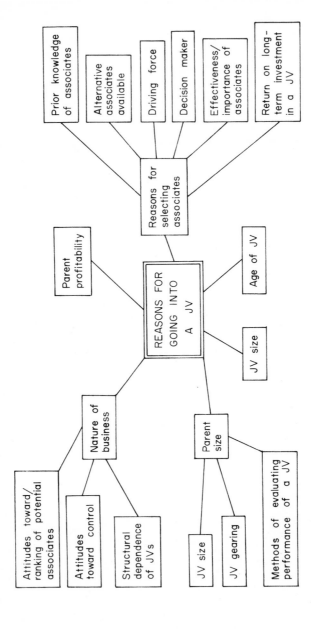

Figure 8.4
Model of Relationships and Linkages Based upon Reasons for Going into a Joint Venture

Table 8.4
Linkages Associated with Reasons for Going into a Joint Venture

First-Level Linkages (Related Variables)	Tests Used To Define	Level of Measurement	Chapter Reference	Data Presented	Major Second-Level Linkages
Parent size	χ^2	Nominal	4	Table 4.2	Methods of evaluating JV performance; joint venture gearing; JV size
Parent profitability	χ^2	Nominal	4		
Nature of business	χ^2	Nominal	2	Table 2.5	Attitudes toward control; attitudes toward and ranking of associates; structural dependence of joint ventures
Age of joint venture	χ^2	Ordinal	2	Figure 2.1	
Size of joint venture	χ^2	Nominal	2	Table 2.3	
Reasons for selecting associates	χ^2	Nominal	2	Table 2.4	Prior knowledge of associates; driving force; decision maker; alternative associates available; associates effective; associates important; return on long-term investment in joint venture

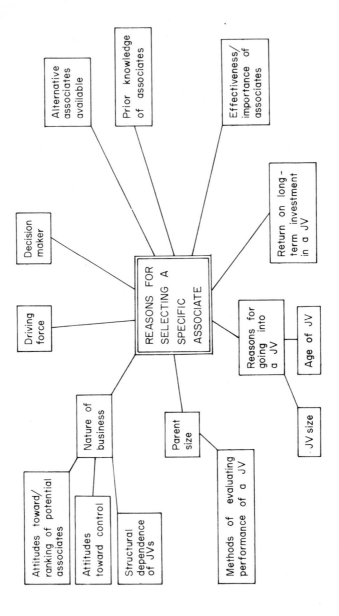

Figure 8.5
Model of Relationships and Linkages Based upon Reasons for Selecting a Specific Associate

Table 8.5
Linkages Associated with Reasons for Selecting a Specific Associate

First-Level Linkages (Related Variables)	Tests Used To Define	Level of Measurement	Chapter Reference	Data Presented	Major Second-Level Linkages
Parent size	χ^2	Nominal	4	Table 4.3	Methods of evaluating JV performance
Nature of business	χ^2	Nominal	5	Table 5.5	Attitudes toward control; attitude and ranking of associates; structural dependence of joint ventures
Reasons for going into joint venture	χ^2	Nominal	2	Table 2.5	Age of joint venture; size of joint venture
Prior knowledge of associates	χ^2	Ordinal	3	Table 3.4	
Alternative associates available	χ^2	Ordinal	3	Table 3.5	
Driving force	χ^2	Nominal	3	Figure 3.1	
Decision maker	χ^2	Nominal	3	Figure 3.1	
Associates effective	χ^2	Ordinal	3	Figure 3.2	
Associates important in India or Pakistan	χ^2	Ordinal	3	Table 3.6	
Return on long-term investment in JV	χ^2	Ordinal	3	Figure 3.3	

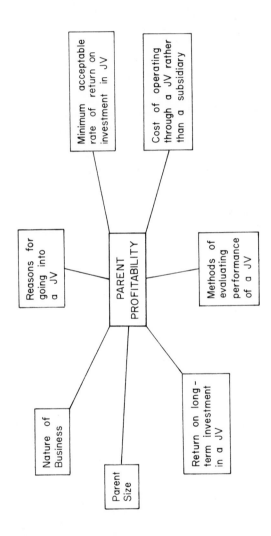

Figure 8.6
Model of Relationships Based upon Profitability of Foreign Parent Firm

Table 8.6
Linkages Associated with Profitability of Foreign Parent Company

First-Level Linkages (Related Variables)	Tests Used To Define	Level of Measurement	Chapter Reference	Data Presented	Major Second-Level Linkages
Return on long-term investment in a joint venture	Correlated	Ratio	4		
Parent size	χ^2	Ordinal	4		
Nature of business	χ^2	Nominal	4		
Reasons for going into joint venture	χ^2	Nominal	4		
Methods of evaluating JV performance	χ^2	Nominal	4		
Minimum acceptable rate of return on investment in JV	χ^2	Ordinal	4	Figure 4.4	
Cost of operating through JV, rather than subsidiary/branch	χ^2	Nominal	4		

hood of a set of relationships but also to provide a basis for decision making incorporating cost and return data. If expected values could be assigned to a series of possible outcomes in a given situation, then the effects of these outcomes could be summarized in "rolled back" estimates of

a. The likelihood that a project will succeed, and

b. Costs and benefits accruing to various levels of success, or lack of it.

A strategy of appropriately cautious behavior in the face of uncertainty and limited knowledge suggests an ending with a recognition of some of the major weaknesses in such a model as it stands. Warnings have been emphasized right along. Most of the weaknesses arise from the limitations in sample size, and from the range of variability. The power of the model is restricted, by lack of a larger number of observations, to working through a series of significant two-way relationships rather than through overall composite relationships that are multidimensionally significant. The environment within which the sample of joint ventures operated is limited, as is the range of definition of foreign parent corporations. The findings may, in some respects, be atypical since the relationship of the particular firms in this specific environment are special in nature.

One must also recognize that there are "lies, damned lies, and statistics." There is always the danger of assigning too much importance to relationships that appear to be statistically sound or significant within a given context. Alter the context, and what happens to the validity (especially when the sample size is small and the conclusions are wide)? However, statistical inference is one way of defining the rules of a game, a particular method of analysis, a theoretically sound approach to establishing a basis for making decisions, or for wider interpretation. By accepting the general constraints and advantages laid down by such rules, this study endeavors to abide by them. All of the reservations and limitations associated with the present model can probably be overcome by the incorporation of further evidence of findings from research carried out along the same lines on additional host countries and foreign parent corporations.

9 CONCLUSIONS AND IMPLICATIONS

The results of the study as a whole are reviewed briefly here from three aspects. First, what are the possible implications for investors and managers in the findings? Second, what are the implications that apply only to joint ventures in India or Pakistan? Third, what are the conclusions to be drawn from the results of the research, conclusions of wider and more general interest than the implications for management?

A final word should be in regard to the future. As a postscript, some suggestions for further research are listed in Appendix E. These suggestions cover a number of topics encountered during the course of the study on which there is currently little or no definitive information available.

Implications for Investors and Managers

Until a similar study can be repeated in the context of different environments with foreign parent firms of other nationalities, the results of this study can be considered valid only for British joint ventures in India or Pakistan. There are, however, some grounds to compare these findings with the limited amount of information presently available on joint ventures. On the basis of these comparisons and at the risk of reducing validity, it seems reasonable to consider some of these findings relevant to the general case of joint venture investment, at least that in less-developed nations. This section deals with some of these generalized implications. The next section includes implications for management and investors that are more likely to be peculiar to India and Pakistan as the host countries.

Size of Parent and Gearing of Joint Venture Capital. In general, the larger British firms were associated with joint ventures that had a high proportion of loan funds in their capital structure. The debt:equity ratio which is officially permissible appears to be higher in less-developed countries than in the security-conscious stock markets of the developed nations. It is not really clear just how much the status of the local associate or the project itself had a bearing on the availability of loan funds. Some of the local partners in this set of joint ventures were able to obtain short-term loans and overdraft facilities for a joint venture, particularly when they were themselves associated with a large business group that included financial institutions.

The evidence suggests that long-term and foreign exchange loans have most often been associated with joint ventures in which one of the partners was a large foreign company. In some cases, as in the oil joint ventures, this association has arisen because loans have actually been made by the foreign partner to the joint operation. Even after allowing for this fact, it seems clear that funds from development finance and other financial institutions have been attracted by the project soundness believed to accrue from the presence of a prestigious foreign firm.

Size of Parent and Profitability of Joint Ventures. Data on the size of foreign parent and profitability of joint ventures are incomplete, as they cover just over half the sample. The profitability figures for these joint ventures show an inverse relationship with the size of the foreign parent. This may be due to the fact that some of the larger foreign companies have been taking their returns at different profit centers or were more concerned over the international integration of their operations than over the return in any one market.

An alternative explanation having some validity is based upon the "visibility" to the local authorities of a project and its parents. This suggests there is a less stringent scrutiny of the pricing practices and achieved levels of return of smaller operations and less obviously dominant foreign concerns. Such an explanation is reasonable even on purely practical grounds. If the host country has a limited auditing capacity, the policing of pricing policies would tend to be based upon selectivity, in the sense of concentrating first on those prices that are most significant to the national economy. This has interesting implications in terms of trading off economies of scale against theoretical diseconomies of "visibility" in determining critical project size.

Evaluating the Performance of Joint Ventures. Once past the stage of commitment of funds and resources, the actual rate of return on the joint venture type of overseas investment has limited validity for evaluating performance. The theme of this group of investors was rather that, once in, one had to accept what one could get. This was partly due to the costs and difficulties of disengagement. It was also due to pragmatic acceptance of the potential variances attributable to environmental factors and to the difficulty in making accurate detailed predictions of performance.

Such a statement in no way invalidates the importance of efforts to improve accuracy in forecasting rates of return before investment, or of efforts to reduce the area of unpredictability. The case was simply that most of the executives in the sample considered continuing control and supervision of this type of investment could be carried out more realistically in terms of overall objectives of the parent company. They also considered that devotion to specific figures of rates of return on a given project was unrealistic and merely compounded a fallacy of misplaced concreteness. In support of this argument, there is some evidence that inflexibility over this particular issue tends to be a feature of less profitable foreign parent corporations.

Attitudes toward Control and Profitability. Most of the executives in this study appear to equate a majority share in equity with effective control over a joint venture. This could be a rather short-sighted view. A foreign majority position in an operation is immediately open to accusations of foreign dominance. As a result, it becomes more "visible" to local countervailing forces. Because of the existence of such forces, it is not necessarily safer in the long run than would be a foreign minority share-holding. In the short run, these forces may also work to restrict a foreign majority's freedom of operation.

There is some indication that the profitability of these joint ventures was inversely related to the level of concern over formal control expressed by its foreign parent. Apart from the fact that effective control in this type of operation may be a feature of technical more than financial leverage on the part of foreign investors, there is also the question of the local partner's contribution. The implication of the evidence here is that a relaxed attitude toward control tends to leave a local partner more responsibility. This, in turn (and presumably under some technical guidance from the foreign parent), induces the local partner to perform more effectively. Such a combination of events also appears to be associated with greater profitability in a joint venture.

The data from the study also suggest that joint ventures are in general no less profitable than foreign branches or subsidiaries. Comparison with the figures from other studies may be suspect because of the possible incompatibility of measurements and calculations. On the basis of the results of a subsample of these cases, however, the rate of return, after host country taxes, on the foreign parent's long-term investment in a joint venture was higher than comparable figures in the Reddaway report. The latter dealt mainly with the results of overseas branches and subsidiaries.

Selecting a Specific Associate. One should add that the sequence of favorable events arising from a relaxed attitude toward control already described also depends on the positive attributes of the chosen associate. In most of these joint ventures, the foreign parents selected associates for their positive potential contributions rather than primarily because of their status or because no others were apparently available. Even when the actual choice was forced upon the foreign partner, in over a third of such cases the choice was accepted only because the associate in question had something more tangible to offer. The threat of compulsion or the attribute of local nationality was not in itself sufficient justification for selection. In terms of profitability, the best returns were in general associated with joint ventures in which partners were chosen because of the positive contributions they had to offer.

The 50–50 Joint Ventures. An attractive compromise over the issue of control appears to be to set up a 50–50 joint venture. There is some danger, however, that these may be somewhat of a snare and a delusion. In theory, the compromise is excellent, provided that the parties are experienced and industrially mature interests; provided, too, that there is a clear definition beforehand of potential problem areas in operations and prenegotiation of mutually acceptable solutions or accommodations.

In such operations there is always the danger that the partners may become preoccupied over maintaining their own equality, even at a cost to the joint venture and to their own best interests. This situation was particularly relevant with respect to the issues of reinvestment and increasing investment for desirable growth among the joint ventures of this study. The net result was a stalemate which hindered a joint venture's development.

There is some implication that this type of issue becomes less of a hindrance and problem if the foreign partner is prepared to accept a minority position. There is effectively little danger in such a solution. The foreign company's technical leverage gives them as much control as needed, plus the authority to stimulate growth and development. At the same time, local partners are more likely to be prepared to find additional funds for one of their own operations, what to them is formally a subsidiary.

Availability of Potential Associates. India and, to a lesser extent, Pakistan constitute a special case among less-developed nations because of their extensive industrial sectors. Although in per capita terms, the fact that their gross domestic product is spread over vast populations means that they rank well down in any "development league," and that they actually have a fairly large amount of industrial development in absolute terms. As a result, there is less of a shortage of potential associates in these two countries than in most which are classified as less-developed or underdeveloped.

On the other hand, the number of such associates recognized in India and Pakistan by British, as compared with U.S. investors, suggests a further generalization. In practical terms, there are likely to be more feasible, potential joint venture associates available for foreign investors in less-developed countries than is suggested in the literature, or in the "folklore" of foreign investment. Usually the existence of many of these suitable alternatives is not recognized, except by investors familiar with the particular environment.

Host Government Associates. In the business "folklore" of countries with allegedly free-enterprise economies, there is also considerable emphasis upon the undesirability of host government partners in joint ventures. The evidence in this study does not support the validity of such emphasis. British firms had certainly experienced some restrictions in mixed ventures on the pricing practices which they would themselves have preferred. They also found that the host government partner in such a venture was concerned over major issues of policy insofar as these issues affected the national interest. In these cases, however, British parent firms also found that, even when a host government held a majority position in a mixed venture, it did not interfere in the actual running of operations. The general experience seemed to be that the government partner adopted what was largely a watching "brief," leaving the foreign partner to get on with the business.

On the whole, the corporations that were actually involved in mixed ventures were more in favor of this type of operation than were less experienced firms. The implications of these findings are most relevant for investors in countries which are less-developed than India and Pakistan, in countries where a large foreign corporation may be genuinely limited in its choice of potential local associates to the host government or its agencies.

In these countries, the host government may be more than simply the only partner available for political or legal reasons; it may also have some positive attractions. In particular, it may be the only potential local associate with time horizons, conception of problems of scale, and an overall view of the market compatible with those of a foreign investor. To ignore the possibility of association with government interests on dogmatic grounds is to run the danger of passing up excellent investment opportunities for reasons which are largely subjective and which are often unjustified.

Technology and Pressures for Localization. The favorite strategy of these foreign firms in the face of pressures for localization of personnel was to select a partner endowed with sound local management. Technical knowledge necessary to a joint venture's operations was then grafted onto this management. In this way, the need for foreign technical personnel was kept to a minimum, their role being concentrated in start-up, trouble-shooting, and training activities. For some companies, this strategy provided a solution for a different problem, in that they were themselves short of technically competent staff for overseas operations in any case.

Implications Peculiar to India and Pakistan

Managing Agencies a Source of Local Personnel. One of the sources of sound local management in India was the managing agency system. British firms were well aware of the advantages in grafting special technical expertise onto the competent and experienced managerial personnel available from this type of partner. This is less true of other foreign investors. There were long-standing ties between these agencies, most of which were previously British-owned, and corporations in the United Kingdom. Such ties help to explain the greater awareness of the potential of the managing agencies on the part of British investors.

One suspects that other foreign investors may have been disturbed by the apparent strength of the local agitation against managing agencies in India. In the past, agitation does not appear to have done much to impair the effectiveness of these local interests, being met by a Hydra-like proliferation of alternative methods of operation and legal forms. They are currently under intensive fire. Managing Agency and Secretaries and Treasurers agreements have been officially outlawed since May 1969. It is not yet clear how this will affect the strategies of the Indian business communities who have used these instruments.

In the long run, mechanisms of centralized control such as the managing agencies may become obsolete as and when the cadre of competent local managers grows to proportions sufficient to replace the agencies' functionally necessary activities. This appears to be a situation of the fairly distant future, in view of the vast need for managers likely to be generated by India's projected industrial development.

Until such a millennium arrives, India will need to utilize its limited managerial resources as effectively as possible. The congruence of national and corporate interests makes it likely that the business communities will find some alternative method of centralizing control. Whatever this method, these interests offer a useful source of local management to the foreign investor. It is a source, moreover, which is oriented toward "Western" business practices.

Importance of Local Associates. Except in the oil industry, associates in India and Pakistan were said to be more important to local operations and more effective than those in less-developed nations. This was, in part, another result of the relatively higher levels of industrial development in these two countries. The oil companies' lower opinion was a result of their own vast experience of Indian conditions over more than half a century.

Effects of Regional Variation in Location. For the special case of India, there appears to be some preference among this group of executives for associates and conditions in South India, especially the Madras area. Without necessarily deprecating other associates, stronger and warmer sentiments were expressed with regard to the South. Particularly emphasized were the technical competence, cooperation, and willingness to learn of this group of local partners. In addition was their concentration upon business rather than political or social parameters affecting operations.

It was also stated that the labor force in the Madras area tended to be more cooperative and less subject to agitation induced by external sources than in other parts of the country. In this respect, the Calcutta area was said to be becoming especially difficult as a location for foreign-associated operations.

Technological Desirability of Different Industries. It was not possible to establish a sensitive overall scale of technological sophistication or desirability and therefore of leverage in bargaining with host governments. At one extreme, the negative end of any such scale, there is some relevant evidence. It was felt to be easier to get government approval for foreign participation in a project in any industry other than those classified here as engineering or electricals.

Engineering and electricals were stated to be industries in which India was best endowed, largely as the result of past development efforts. In these two industries foreign investors face the likelihood of being directed to operate with local partners. On the other hand, however, these are also industries most likely able to offer a choice of competent and compatible local partners to a prospective foreign investor.

Conclusions

Examination of the experiences of this sample of British firms, and of the ways in which a group of associated joint ventures were set up in India and Pakistan, led to the conclusion that there are three separate major decisions involved in what is here called the joint venture process. As already indicated, these are the decision to invest in a given host country, the decision to use the joint venture form, and the selection of a particular associate. Although the decisions may be run together in terms of chronological order and may be interdependent to some extent, in most of the cases in the study they were made in the order listed, each one depending upon the previous decision. As a result, the problems of examining a complex and interdependent overall decision process, whether through techniques of sequential analysis or systems analysis, can be reduced through division into separate parts.

A vast majority of investment decisions in India and Pakistan were said to be motivated primarily by market considerations, either developing a new market or protecting an existing one. The decision to use the joint venture form was made most often in order to obtain local facilities or resources which were required by the foreign parent company. In spite of the fact that host government legislation in both these nations appeared to make joint operations virtually a necessity, this compulsion was felt to be of subsidiary importance in over half of the decisions. In a quarter of the joint ventures, compulsion was not an issue at all.

As far as the selection of associates was concerned, the status of a local partner and the benefits of local identity also appear to be subsidiary considerations. This may have been the result of a special relationship between British firms and these two host countries. Many of the corporations already had a local identity and considerable local status on their own account. On the basis of somewhat limited profitability figures, such an attitude seems to be justified. Joint ventures in which partners were chosen for their past or potential contributions of facilities or resources were the most profitable. They were clearly more profitable than those in which associates were selected because of their status, or in order to provide an operation with local identity. Similarly, associates chosen on the grounds of their status were felt by British executives to be less effective and less important to a given joint venture than were those selected for more tangible considerations.

Responsibility for Promotion of a Project and Decision. The evidence in this study supports the theory that the initiation, development, and promotion of new foreign investments tend to be the responsibility of individuals or of special interest groups. In these joint ventures, it was especially individuals who were responsible, individuals who were familiar with local conditions in the proposed environment. Among cases in which an associate was chosen primarily because of a favorable past association, practically all were the result of the promptings of a "familiar" individual. It appears, therefore, that such favorability was largely the result of personal recommendation.

As a general rule, the greater the scope for judgment on subjective and apparently less rational grounds, the greater the likelihood that the decisions associated with setting up a joint venture would be the responsibility of an individual. When this scope was limited, the decisions were more likely to be made as part of a formal, objectively designed procedure.

Familiarity and Awareness of the Environment. India and Pakistan were not recognized by the executives as constituting a particularly threatening environment for foreign investment. Obviously, by the time this study took place, they had some experience in that environment and were aware of actual conditions. On the other hand, only a small proportion of the executives stated that the spreading of risk had originally been a motivation for going into a joint operation. This indicated that conditions in India or Pakistan were apparently not threatening at the time the investments were actually made.

Such confidence would be compatible with the argument that British investments in these two countries form a special case in the field of overseas joint ventures. Comparison with the comments of potential U.S. investors upon the same countries leads to a fairly obvious observation concerning the general case: familiarity with an environment tends to reduce the impression that overseas investment is risky or threatening, an impression in itself largely induced by suspicion of the unknown characteristics of a strange environment.

Uncertainty and Concern over Control. Uncertainty related to investment in India or Pakistan was indeed recognized by the executives. There was an indication that a concern for control on the part of some British firms involved the desire to reduce the area of uncertainty in overseas investment as well as the desire to have a free hand in running an operation.

The strength of such a desire to reduce uncertainty was related to and indicated in the type of potential associate preferred for a joint venture, in principle if not in practice. If control was felt to be important in a particular case, then fellow nationals of the foreign investor were favored as the most desirable possible partner. When control was not considered so essential, the tendency was to favor local private interests which could make some kind of positive contribution to a joint operation.

The Squeeze between Two Monopsonists. An interesting aspect of the foreign investment decision process appeared in the experiences of some of the manufacturers of vehicle components and accessories. These firms were caught in a double squeeze so far as their own freedom to make a decision was concerned. When their major customers set up local operations in a country, these suppliers had to be ready to provide their own products in that country or else run the danger of losing the customer in other, more lucrative markets. At the same time, a host government that was aware of this threat could take advantage of it by forcing the supplier to go into local manufacturing through imposition of tariff or quota restrictions on imported components.

As a result of these dovetailing pressures, the investment decision for these suppliers was largely exogenously determined. In the present study, this situation appeared to have been a problem only in connection with the motor industry. It appears to be relevant in the general case, however, for all industries in which there is a strong interdependence among members and ancillary firms.

Bilateral Monopoly and the Joint Venture Decision. On the basis of the comments of this group of executives, the theory of bilateral monopoly appears to have only limited validity. The theory that relative bargaining power would determine the form taken by foreign investment does not provide a complete explanation of the way in which these joint ventures were set up. In 42 % of the cases, the British parent firms recognized host government pressure to go into a joint operation. If one considers the officially stated policies of these governments, this was a lower proportion than expected. For the other 58 %, such pressure did not influence their decision to use the joint venture form, except as a subsidiary consideration. Nor did this appear to be due to peculiar advantages possessed by the foreign firms in this second group of cases.

Another deviation from the implications of the theory occurred in the relationship between host government pressures to go into a joint venture and the point in time at which the latter was established. According to the theory, these pressures should become increasingly influential over time. Actually, there was some indication that these pressures became less important over time.

The only case which appears to fit a pattern of relationships and development consistent with one determined by bilateral monopolistic advantage is that of the oil companies. These were among the most powerful of the foreign companies in the study, and also offered some of the most desirable technology. It is not clear, in terms of the theory of bilateral monopoly, why this should be true.

An alternative explanation favored here is that the size of the foreign parent company is likely to be a determinant of the arousal of countervailing powers on the part of a host government, largely through fears of economic imperialism. The larger the company, the greater would be the fear. Once such local powers were aroused, an interpretation in terms of relative advantage in bargaining provided a convenient model for explaining the ensuing relationships.

On the whole, it appears that the theory of bilateral monopoly provides a useful abstraction and rationalization of a complex process which is not itself very rational. It constitutes an abstract framework from which specific analysis and explanation can commence but which requires considerable modification before explanation can be satisfactory.

Readiness to Participate in Other Joint Ventures. Perhaps the most fitting and optimistic note on which to finish is to emphasize the following findings: only one in seven of the foreign firms in this sample were not prepared to take part in other joint ventures in underdeveloped nations; only one in five made the same objection for developed nations. Even the dissenters seemed to have sound objections on technical and specific grounds. Approximately half of the companies were already involved in other joint ventures in both types of host countries.

It appears quite possible that the joint venture form of operation will become an increasingly important bridging mechanism between the resources of international corporations and the aspirations of host countries. If so, the readiness of experienced firms such as these to participate in further joint ventures is an encouraging sign and a good advertisement to other potential overseas investors.

Appendix A.1.
Research and Analytical Methods

Interviewing the Sample

The measures that the study was intended to test covered over 350 variables, including financial indices. The basic variables were organized into a questionnaire format. This was then printed, together with a précis of the research and a description of the researcher. Although it was intended to send these forms out only to a control group, organization of the data to simplify collection and later analysis was assisted by using the same questionnaire as a vehicle and agenda or guide during the actual interviews. Whenever possible, when respondents requested an agenda prior to discussion, a copy of the form was sent in advance.

Interviews were almost all held at company head offices; their duration ranged from one to eight hours, averaging about three and a half to four hours. According to the wishes and nature of each respondent, the interviewer either used the questionnaire directly as an agenda or conducted open-ended discussions, with the executives initiating many of the topics themselves.

For example, an executive who began the interview by complaining bitterly about the plethora of questionnaires awaiting completion on his desk was obviously not approached with the form and did not realize that he was in effect completing another. In either case, the net result was much the same. When an agenda was used, the discussion was encouraged to become open-ended through various stages. When the interview took the form of an open-ended discussion, it was possible to ensure that all the variables on the questionnaire were covered.

After the interview was completed, a brief transcript was prepared, and questionnaire forms were edited. In some cases, these forms were kept by the respondents for final completion and checking, to be sent on later. For a subsample, the accuracy of recording and interpretation was checked through follow-up interviews or correspondence. As accuracy was established for these cases, it was assumed that the whole sample of recorded information was also likely to be accurate.

Originally it was intended to tape-record some of the interviews, both for convenience in recording and to substantiate the evidence used in the study. In a trial interview with an executive outside this sample, certain difficulties appeared. Because of the volume of noise included in a tape recording of a two-and-a-half-hour interview, editing of the tape proved less efficient than accurate note taking during the interview.

There was also some hesitation in responding fully to certain questions when it was known that the conversation was being recorded verbatim, even though anonymity was guaranteed. At the end of the interview, the executive concerned admitted that he felt inhibited by the tape-recorder and would prefer that his evidence should not be used. This experience might have turned out to be atypical, but as the first British executive interviewed reacted so adversely, it was decided to discontinue tape-recording.

As far as substantiating the evidence was concerned, tape-recording a subsample of interviews appeared no more effective than letting a similar subsample of respondents check the information recorded on behalf of their firms, especially when this option was offered to all the people interviewed. (None took up this option of his own volition.)

In four cases, a member of the Indian associate company or the Indian chief executives of the joint venture happened to be available at the British firm's head office during the time of the interview; in one instance, he was a member of the respondent group. In each case, a brief discussion was held with the Indian executive. These discussions turned out to be of only marginal interest for the study. The Indians had severe constraints on their time in the United Kingdom which precluded discussion in depth. Their comments tended to support those of the U.K. partner, but under the limiting circumstances such support was hardly significant.

A reverse study over the same sample of joint ventures would be useful in rounding out the examination of the decision process. Such a study would require much more than a duplication of the research time and costs. It would be desirable to carry out a parallel study of this kind in the future, but it was felt that such a dimension was outside the immediate terms of reference of the current research.

Organization and Analysis of Data and Secondary Research

In the text chapters, the measures used in the study and some of the hypotheses and results associated with them are described. These measures were arranged into 277 separate basic variables and then into 45 questions in five sections of the questionnaire. These sections covered in turn:

1. Descriptive and financial data,
2. Selection and decision criteria,

3. Organization and control,
4. Evaluation, and
5. Effects of host government policies.

Wording was phrased so that the same form could be used in later studies with parent firms of different nationalities operating in other host countries. (The complete questionnaire appears in Appendix A.2.)

The questionnaire was sent out to the control group in two parts. The first consisted of questions 1–5, 14–20, 25, 29–31, 42–44. In the covering letter firms were asked especially if they would complete this part at least. The remaining questions were separated into a second form on which firms were asked to provide additional information if this was available. Half of the control group received both parts of the form under the same covering letter, while the rest received only the main questionnaire. It was hoped that in this manner some details at least would be obtained from respondents who might find an abbreviated form rather less overwhelming than the full version. As it happened, the only companies that completed the questionnaire filled in both parts at once. Even those which promised to complete the form and later defaulted appeared initially to be quite prepared to fill in the complete list of all the questions.

After the information collected was edited, it was encoded and then transferred onto punched cards and tape for analysis. The computer program which was written to perform the analysis ran under the Data-Text System,[1] a system which was admirably suited to the requirements of this study. The actual computer analysis was carried out at the Harvard Computing Center through the courtesy of that installation.

With the exception of financial data and the units used in certain of the measures of size, most of the variables used to examine decision criteria were strictly capable of analysis only at the nominal or ordinal levels of measurement.

Correlations were calculated between measures of size, profitability, and financial structure. Analysis of variance was carried out for certain selection criteria against these measures. The major part of the statistical analysis, however, involved testing significance levels and strength of association in the contingency tables which laid out the relationships between nominal- or ordinal-level variables. Unfortunately, the

---

[1] This is a system set up by the Department of Social Relations at Harvard for use on an IBM 7090/94. Its vocabulary is modeled on FORTRAN, and it operates under the Standard FMS with regard to monitoring. The system also operates quite successfully on an IBM 360/65, under EMULATE 7090/94, using the standard IBM allocation of tapes and channels for the FMS monitoring, at the Harvard Computing Center. The system is particularly useful for the type of data analysis which is common in research on management subjects.

limited size of the sample made it pointless to examine anything more than two-way contingency tables.

This factor limits the overall statistical power of the model since the relationships described are a series of two-way linkages. Ideally, it would have been desirable to use an eight- or seven-way analysis combining different groups of measures from each of the eight sectors. This may be possible in the future with a larger sample and modified variables.

All of the contingency tables resulting from cross-tabulation of variables were greater than two-by-two, so the regular chi-square statistic was chosen as the most appropriate measure of the significance of relationships between variables. Where more than 20% of the expected cell frequencies were less than 5, the exact mean and variable technique was used.[2]

An assumption was made that independence of responses would not be significantly affected if all analysis was carried out over the full sample of 71 joint ventures, rather than over the sample of parent firms. The arguments upon which this assumption was based were

a. Different divisions or respondents from the same U.K. firm answered differently for different joint ventures.

b. The same respondent answered differently (consciously) for different joint ventures.

c. In a duplicate run of tests over the two samples, the hypothesis was tested that variation in significance would merely reflect sample size. This hypothesis was not rejected.

The changes in level of significance were approximately the same for those cases in which the measure could possibly have been parent-related as for those in which it was obviously joint venture-related. Since parent- and joint venture-related associations appear to move either way in similar proportions as the sample size was varied, generally deteriorating as expected with sample size, there is no clear evidence that all measures could not be associated over the population of joint ventures.

The strength of these relationships was assessed through calculation of Cramer's V coefficient and Pearson's contingency coefficient C, for tests based on the chi-square statistic.[3] In addition, certain other tests were used which were based upon more probabilistic approaches to examining the strength of association. Where measurement was at the nominal level, the Goodman and Kruskal lambda statistic was

[2] W. G. Cochran, "Some Methods for Strengthening Common Chi-Square Tests," *Biometrics,* December 1954, Vol. 10, No. 4, pp. 417–451.
[3] See Hubert M. Blalock, *Social Statistics,* McGraw-Hill, New York, 1960, pp. 225–230.

calculated for the symmetric and the asymmetric cases.[4] Where it was at the ordinal level, Kendall's tau B and tau C were used for the symmetric and Sommer's D statistic for the asymmetric case.[5]

Background research was carried out with the assistance of the facilities at the Board of Trade and its library in London, the offices and libraries of the High Commissioners for India and for Pakistan in London, the Dewey library and the library of the Center for International Studies at Massachusetts Institute of Technology, and the Baker Library at Harvard Business School.

In addition, several of the companies interviewed provided access to records, correspondence, and reports, while most provided financial statements and directors' reports, in some cases for the joint venture and for the local associate company as well as for the U.K. parent firm.

[4] Leo A. Goodman and William H. Kruskal, "Measures of Association for Cross-Classifications," *Journal of the American Statistical Association*, December 1954, Vol. 49, No. 268, pp. 733–764.
[5] M. Kendall, *Rank Correlation Methods*, Hafner, New York, 1955, pp. 1–48; R. H. Sommer, "A New Asymmetric Measure of Association for Ordinal Variables," *American Sociological Review*, December 1962, Vol. 27, No. 6, pp. 799–811.

Appendix A.2.
Questionnaire Form Used in the Study

The top sheet of the questionnaire form used in the study included background information regarding the study, researcher, and sponsoring organizations. It also emphasized the anonymity of the information and of the firms responding. The form was entitled *Joint Ventures in India and Pakistan.*

Details of companies and respondents were restricted to the top sheet, and the remainder of the form was the following.

Section 1—Descriptive and Financial Data
1. What are the chief products or activities of your company?
2. What was your total value of consolidated sales for the last year?
3. What is the consolidated total value of your assets?
4. What are the registered names of any joint ventures (JVs) in which your company is involved in the country of this study?
   (Please complete for each JV)
   (a) Name of JV company:
   (b) Chief products/activities:
   (c) Date of commitment agreement:
   (d) Date operations commenced:
   (e) Value of total sales: (last year)
   (f) 4(e) as % share of host country market:
   (g) Projected future share of this market:
   (h) Balance sheet value of assets and reserves: (last financial year)
       (i)   Current assets:
       (ii) Fixed assets:
       (iii) Reserves and surplus
       (iv) Other assets:
5. What is the current distribution of equity and debt holding in these JVs? (Please complete for each JV)

		% of Total Value Held by				
Total Value	Your Company	Local Associates	Local Private Investors	Host Govt.	Others

189

    (a) Equity: Voting
             Nonvoting
    (b) Debt over 3 years:
    (c) Debt 3 years or less:

6. Have there been any significant changes in the above distribution since the JV was set up? (Please describe)

7. How much of your participation in the capital of the JV was in the form of:

	Initially	Subsequently	Comments

    (a) Machinery, plant, equipment?
    (b) Technical services?
    (c) Patents, licenses, information?
    (d) Cash?
    (e) Other? (Please specify)

8. What services have been contracted with the JV by your company or by other associates? (Please indicate by whom and the basis of the contracted return)

Basis of Contracted Return				
Fixed Fee or Agreed price	% of Sales	% of Profit	Cost Plus	Other

    (a) Management:
    (b) License:
    (c) Technical assistance:
    (d) Distribution/marketing:
    (e) Contract manufacture:
    (f) Turnkey or setting up:
    (g) Sale of materials/ intermediates:
    (h) Other: (Please specify)

9. What are the names of your associates in this JV? (Please indicate after each one their % share in the JV's capital if this is not obvious from Question 5 above.)

10. Where these associates are companies, please give an estimate of their:

    (a) Total assets:
    (b) Annual turnover:
    and some indication of their chief products or activities:

11. From what source has any significant expansion of the JV been financed?

Total Value	% Coming From Each Source Below		
	Your Firm	Associ- ates	Other (Please specify)

(a) Reinvested earnings:
(b) Other equity:
(c) Other liabilities:
(d) Capitalization of
       reserves:
(e) Other sources:

12. Please provide as far as possible, the profitability figures for the JV's activities in the years listed below: (last 5 years if years below unavailable)

Financial Year	Earnings before Local Taxation	Earnings Net of Local Tax	Income Distributed	Income Repatriated to Your Company
1946				
1956				
1964				
1965				
1966				

13. Please provide as far as possible details of charges paid by the JV to your company for the reasons listed in each of the years below: (or last 5 years)

Financial Year	Interest	Royalties	Fees for Know-How or Management	Other Charges	Capital Repatriated
1946					
1956					
1964					
1965					
1966					

14. How many people of each nationality are employed in the JV at each level below?

Chief Exec.	Directors	Manager- ial	Super- visory	Other Employees

    (a) Local
        Nationals:
    (b) British:
    (c) American:
    (d) Other
        Foreign:

15. Who in your company is responsible for activities connected with this JV? (Please specify position and department or division.)
16. Is your company involved in any JVs in other countries? (Please list)

Section 2—Selection and Decision Criteria

17. Why was this particular host country chosen? (Please mark (1) for the most important reason and indicate 2nd, 3rd, 4th, etc., reason as appropriate.)
    (a) Developing new market:
    (b) To overcome tariff barriers:
    (c) Future protection for existing market:
    (d) Matching competitors: (Please name)
    (e) Geographical diversification:
    (f) To obtain raw materials:
    (g) Political stability:
    (h) Host government attitude:
    (i) Using patents/licenses:
    (j) Facilities/resources available:
    (k) Lower cost conditions:
    (l) Host government tax incentives:
    (m) Other reasons: (Please describe)
18. How was this country chosen?
    (a) After an international survey of opportunities:
    (b) After a prior survey of this country:
    (Please indicate after (a) and (b) who carried out any such survey.)
    (c) How long did any such surveys take?
    (d) Information from an external (to your company) source:
    (e) If (d) above, what was this source?
    (f) Any other method/source of information: (Please describe)
19. Who made the first approach or suggestion regarding a JV, and in what year?
    (a) Your company: (b) Year:
    (c) One of the current associates: (Please specify) (d) Year:
    (e) Some other party: (Please specify)   (f) Year:

20. Was anyone in your company familiar with: (Please describe the person(s) and the reasons for their familiarity.)
    (a) The host country?
    (b) Potential associates?
21. How long did the commitment decision take?
22. Is this longer/shorter than, or normal for such a decision in your firm?
23. If longer or shorter, please comment:
24. How did the initial contact with/consideration of your associate originate?
25. What were the reasons for your selection of your associates? (Please mark reasons (1), (2), (3), etc., in their order of importance.)
    (a) Preempted (i.e., existing government license holder):
    (b) In the same line of business as the proposed JV:
    (c) Resources/facilities complementary to those of your firm: (Please describe)
    (d) Favorable past association (i.e., agent, licensee): (Please describe)
    (e) General soundness and standing:
    (f) Other reasons: (Please discuss)
26. What other potential associates were available?
27. Why were they rejected/Why did they drop out?
28. What "vetting" was carried out, and from whom were any references received?
29. Why was the JV form chosen by you for this operation? (Please mark reasons in their order of importance.)
    (a) Host government regulations or pressure:
    (b) Spread risk:
    (c) Convenience of associates' complementary resources/facilities:
    (d) Associates' established control of resources/facilities/channels of supply or distribution made the association necessary: (Please describe)
    (e) Better access to loan funds/capital/preferential treatment by government: (Please describe)
    (f) Easier to establish identity as "local" concern:
    (g) Other reasons: (Please describe)
30. Who was the driving force in your company in favor of the commitment decision?
31. Who made the commitment decision? (Apart from final Board approval)

Section 3—Organization and Control

32. What responsibilities do your associates assume and in what areas? (Please indicate for each function whether they assume *full, joint,* or *no* responsibility, also whether they supply the executive responsible. If they have no specific responsibility under the agreement, please indicate whether they are are helpful very often, rarely, or occasionally. Please comment upon any issues which you feel are not brought out adequately by this simple framework.)

Assume Agreed Responsi- bility	Supply Exec.	Helpful		
		V. Often	Occ.	Rarely

  (a) Marketing and distribution:
  (b) Purchasing and procurement:
  (c) Technical and engineering:
  (d) Production:
  (e) Administration and control:
  (f) Financial (incl. obtaining capital):
  (g) Recruitment and personnel:
  (h) Relations with government and authorities:
  (i) Public relations:

33. Have conflicts arisen with your associates over the following issues? (Please discuss)
  (a) Reinvestment:
  (b) Increasing investment:
  (c) Growth rate of sales:
  (d) Growth rate of profits:
  (e) Transfer pricing of materials/intermediates:
  (f) Other sources of return to your company:
  (g) "Unbusinesslike" behavior:
  (h) Different criteria for evaluating performance:
  (i) Other issues:

34. Do you feel that your associates are effective participants in this JV?

35. What influence does your company actually exert and what influence would you like to exert upon this JV in the following areas of decision making and managerial policy? (Please indicate whether the JV makes major decisions in each area either independently, after consulting you for advice, or only after your specific approval. Please mark in the appropriate column (D) for what the JV actually does, and (S) for what you feel that it should do. It would also be very helpful if you would comment upon any of the criteria which you use in defining a major decision.)

JV Makes Major Decisions			Comments on Any Criteria Used
Subject to Approval	After Consultation	On Its Own	

(a) Capital expenditure:

(b) Pricing:

(c) Dividend policy:

(d) Organization:

(e) Product selection, design, or planning:

(f) Production planning of control:

(g) Quality control:

(h) Marketing and sales:

(i) Purchasing:

(j) Costing methods:

(k) Budgeting and budgetary control:

(l) Financial accounting procedures:

(m) Wage and labor policy:

(n) Selection, promotion, compensation of executives:

(o) Training:

(p) Administrative and supervisory techniques:

(q) Recording/reporting
     procedures:
36. How are any conflicts which arise between your company and your
    associates or the JV itself resolved?
37. What degree of control does your company feel to be necessary
    before participating in a JV? (Please indicate whether necessary
    (N), desirable but not necessary (D), acceptable (A), or unaccept-
    able (U). Also whether this policy applies to all JVs, only to JVs in
    the less-developed countries, or only to this JV. The following
    is a list of possible permutations, none of which may accurately
    reflect your firm's policies. If they do not, please describe this
    policy.

	JVs in	This JV
All JVs	LDCs	Only

(a) Equity majority of over 75%,
     either direct or with reliable
     fellow interests:
(b) Equity majority, direct or with
     fellow interests:
(c) Agreed Board majority:
(d) 50–50 equity holding +
     management contract:
(e) Minority equity holding +
     management contract:
(f) No fixed equity requirement,
     reliance upon: JV's need for
     (i)   Patents/licenses:
     (ii) Technical assistance:
     (iii) Future R & D results:
     (iv) Materials or equipment:
     your firm's control of
     (v)   Quality or Standard
           Operating Procedures:
     (vi) Distribution:
(g) No fixed requirements, reliance
     upon "friends in court," possibly
     obtained by your firm's willingness
     to accept a minority position in a
     "local" company:

(h) Careful selection of suitable
associates the only major
criterion:

(i) Any other permutation which is
more suitable according to your
company's needs or experiences:

Section 4—Evaluation

38. How does your company evaluate the performance of this JV?
    (a) In terms of return on investment:
    (b) What is the minimum acceptable level:
    (c) In terms of % overall profit (before or after local taxes?):
    (d) What is the minimum acceptable level:
    (e) Rate of growth of sales: (Please describe)
    (f) Achievement of other scheduled objectives: (Please describe)
39. Are the acceptable levels indicated in 38(b) or 38(d) or implied in
    38(e) or 38(f) higher/lower than, or the same as in?
    (a) Your company's parent country:
    (b) Other developed countries:
    (c) Other less-developed countries:
40. What is the cost or loss to your company, if any, of carrying out
    business in this host country through a JV, as compared with a
    subsidiary?
41. How important are local associates to the success of: (Please
    explain)
    (a) This JV?
    (b) JVs in less-developed countries in general?
42. Is your company satisfied with the manner in which this JV was set
    up and developed, and its present operations? (Please mention any
    points which you feel may not have been adequately brought out in
    this questionnaire)
43. Would your company participate in other JVs?
    (a) In the country of this study:
    (b) In other less-developed countries:
    (c) In developed countries:
44. Do you feel that JVs are a satisfactory form of enterprise for
    carrying out business in less-developed countries when the other
    associates are from: (Please comment and rank in order of pre-
    ference)
    (a) Your company's parent country?
    (b) Other developed countries?
    (c) Private sector interests in the host country?

(d) The host government or its agencies?

(e) The "general public" in the host country ("jointness" being used here in one of its widest senses)?

Section 5 — Political and Economic Environment

45. Please comment upon any effects which the host government's policies, or its actual application of those policies, have had upon the operations of the JV, its plans for expansion, and its competitive position. In particular, in the following areas:

(a) Methods of allocation of foreign exchange:

(b) Allocation of import licenses:

(c) Application of import duties:

(d) Allocation of manufacturing licenses:

(e) Regulations or pressure for exporting:

(f) Regulations or pressure against profit levels:

(g) Regulations or pressure against proposed or actual payments or returns for patents, licenses, or technical assistance:

(h) Remittance of profits or repatriation of capital:

(i) Employment or salaries of expatriates:

(j) Taxation policies:

(k) Special attitudes toward the private sector:

(l) Special attitudes toward foreign investors:

(m) Intervention on political grounds:

(n) Intervention on social or cultural grounds:

(o) Any other areas:

Appendix B.1.
Calculation of the British Stake in the Joint Ventures of This Sample

(The Indian Subsample)

Difficulty in obtaining a total figure of the U.K. stake in the joint ventures arose because details of reserves and surplus figures were not available for all cases. However, figures for issued voting equity were obtained in all but four cases. It was assumed that ratios obtained from the figures available for some joint ventures could be projected to the others that were established (i.e., more than three years old). Of the joint ventures set up before 1963, details of reserves and surplus figures were provided in 39 cases, while equity figures alone were available for 21 (all of these were ventures in India). The calculations were therefore carried out as follows:

a. For 30 pre-1963 JVs (Joint Ventures), the ratio of reserves plus surplus to equity was $38.87/59.49 = 65\%$. (Note: Total figures, not British share.)

b. As a check, this ratio was calculated for subgroups of the pre-1963 group. For pre-1950, the ratio was 90%; for 1950–1959 JVs, it was 60%; for 1960–1962 JVs, it was 100%; weighted average over percentages (rounded) came to 80%.

c. As a reasonable ratio within the range 65% to 80%, 70% was taken to represent reserves and surplus as a proportion of issued equity.

d. The U.K. share of equity in the 21 pre-1963 JVs for which equity figures only were available came to Rs. 114.9 crores and 70% of this figure was Rs. 80.44 crores.

e. The total British share of the equity plus reserves plus surplus for all the Indian JVs (i.e., all available figures) was Rs. 163.27 crores.

f. Item d plus item e = $80.44 + 163.27 = $ Rs. 243.71 crores.

Appendix B.2.
Foreign Investment in India

In order to provide a basis for testing the representative significance of the joint ventures included in this sample against data which appeared compatible at the time when the information was collected, the Reserve Bank's figures were used. These were projected forward two years, by adding to the 1965 figures, twice the average annual inflow of foreign investment in the four years preceding 1965. These estimates may have been on the high side. The increasing uncertainty over these two years, of the short-run economic prospects in India may have been a disincentive to foreign investors. There were also restraints on U.K. investment abroad during the same period. The projected figures are shown in the accompanying table.

Outstanding Foreign Investment in India (Rs. Crores)*

Source	Type	March 1965	Estimated Inflow April 1965 to March 1967	End March 1967 (estimated)
All Foreign Investment	Total	935.8	114.4	1050.2
	Direct	613.3	58.0	671.3
	Total Portfolio	322.5	56.4	378.9
	Private Portfolio	154.8	17.0	171.8
	Official Portfolio	167.7	39.4	207.1
	Total Private	768.1	75.0	843.1
United Kingdom	Total	529.3	37.2	566.5
	Direct	462.6	32.4	495.0
	Total Portfolio	66.7	4.8	71.5
	Private Portfolio	66.7	4.8	71.5
	Official Portfolio	—	—	—
	Total Private	529.3	37.2	566.5

* 1 crore = 10 million rupees (Rs.)

Appendix B.3.
Calculation of Foreign Private Direct Investment in Pakistan

State Bank of Pakistan figures, quoted in Gustav F. Papanek, *Pakistan's Development, Social Goals and Private Incentives,* p. 307, describe annual inflows of foreign private investment as follows:

(in Rs. crores) 1949–1950 = 0
1951–1952 = 2
1954–1955 = 2
1959–1960 = 9
1964–1965 = 8

(with the additional comment on p. 223, that this inflow averaged about Rs. 8 crores in the 1960s).

The arbitrary assumptions were made that (*a*) foreign investment in 1947 was zero, (*b*) annual inflows for the years since the last breakpoint would average about the same as the figure in a breakpoint. On this basis, a total was calculated for foreign investment, ignoring capital appreciation, accrued by 1966.

1948–1952 = 5 years @ Rs. 2 crores (figure for 1952) = Rs. 10 crores
1953–1955 = 3 years @ Rs. 2 crores (figure for 1955) = Rs.   6 crores
1956–1960 = 5 years @ Rs. 9 crores (figure for 1960) = Rs. 45 crores
1961–1966 = 6 years @ Rs. 8 crores (figure for 1965) = Rs. 48 crores

_____

Estimated Total   Rs. 109 crores

Appendix C.1.
Calculation of Attitude Scores between Potential Associates

Two tests of attitudes toward the five types of potential associates were carried out. In the first, respondents were asked whether each of the various types of associates were satisfactory, and their comments were placed on a five-point scale ranging: strongly positive—positive—neutral—negative—strongly negative.

Second, respondents were asked to rank the five types of associates in the order of preference of the British parent companies for the joint ventures in the sample. Responses for each type of associate were cross-tabulated with nature of business. This produced ten two-way cross-tabulations, practically all of which indicated a significant relationship between nature of business and attitudes toward, or ranking of, the type of associate in question. In terms of their significance these relationships were summarized as shown in the accompanying table.

| | Level of Significance by Chi-Square of Relationship to Nature of Business | |
Type of Associate	Attitudes toward Associates	Ranking of Associates
Fellow nationals	0.013	0.042
Other foreigners	0.009	0.012
Local private	0.250*	0.018
Host government	0.036	0.035
Local public/investors	0.026	0.137*

* Only remotely significant, included as the only less-significant subgroups.

Because of the way in which the data were collected, both sets of results from these two attitude measures could be examined at the ordinal level of measurement. A series of weighted scores was calculated from the distribution of responses in each of these two groups of tests. Responses were given a value from 1 (for a strongly positive attitude, or a first-place ranking), to 5 (for a strongly negative attitude, or a fifth-place ranking). These values were multiplied by the frequency of occurrence for each group of parent companies by nature of business, and then summed over each group. This sum was then divided by the number of responses made by the related group, to give a weighted average score which represented the group's responses to that type of associate.

Thus, for example, in their attitudes toward fellow-national associates, parent firms in the oil group gave 4 strongly positive, 6 positive, 1 neutral, 2 negative, and no strongly negative answers. This gave a weighted total of 27 over 13 responses, and an attitude score in this case of $27/13 = 2.08$. The figure of 27 was this group's contribution to the gross all-industry score for this particular type of associate.

In another form, $\overline{X}_j$, the weighted average group: associate score was calculated according to the formula

$$\overline{X}_j = \frac{\sum_i x_{ij} y_i}{N_j}$$

where $x = $ a number of parent company responses of a particular kind; $y = $ the weighting value assigned to a particular kind of response; the subscript i represented kinds of response or values as follows:

strongly positive $= 1 = $ first-place ranking
positive $\quad\quad\quad\ = 2 = $ second-place ranking
neutral $\quad\quad\quad\ = 3 = $ third-place ranking
negative $\quad\quad\quad = 4 = $ fourth-place ranking
strongly negative $= 5 = $ fifth-place ranking;

the subscript j represented different groups by nature of business; $N_j = $ sum of parent company responses in a particular group j.

An all-industry score for each type of associate was also calculated, from the weighted sums for each group, according to this formula:

All-industry score $= \sum_j X_j N_j$; or $\sum_j \sum_i x_{ij} y_i$

These scores were tabulated and a rank order defined for each type of associate, for each nature of business group, in each of the two tests in order to provide an overall basis for comparison. The results were summarized in Tables 5.3 and 5.4. In general, the lower the score, the more favorable the attitude toward that type of associate, and the higher the ranking in preferability as against other types. The actual size of the margin between scores was not strictly capable of interpretation, but the order was.

Appendix C.2.
Calculation of Structural Dependence
Scores for Joint Ventures

Executives' descriptions of the associates' functional responsibility for joint venture operations and the venture's independence from its British parent in policy matters were coded and values allocated. The values assigned in the three dependence measures, including the measure based on the parents' relative shares in equity, were as follows:

Parent Share in Joint Venture Equity

$$\begin{aligned}
\text{Under } 25\% &= 1 \\
25\% \text{ to } 49\% &= 2 \\
50\% &= 3 \\
\text{Over } 50\% &= 4
\end{aligned}$$

Associate's Responsibility for Joint Venture's Operations

$$\begin{aligned}
\text{Full responsibility} &= 1 \\
\text{Full to joint responsibility} &= 2 \\
\text{Joint to no responsibility} &= 3 \\
\text{No responsibility} &= 4
\end{aligned}$$

Joint Venture's Independence from British Parent in Policy Areas

$$\begin{aligned}
\text{Highly independent} &= 1 \\
\text{Independent} &= 2 \\
\text{Considerable control by British parent} &= 3 \\
\text{Close control by British parent} &= 4
\end{aligned}$$

The transposed values were then aggregated and averaged for each joint venture in the second and third measures. Group scores were combined and averaged for each of the three measures in much the same way as the attitude variables were treated in Appendix C.1. Frequencies of particular classes of response and allocated weights were again used to complete dependence scores. This provided a basis for comparison between groups according to the nature of business which was valid at the ordinal level of measurement. Relationships between nature of business and raw responses for the three measures were marginally significant at the 0.069, 0.069, and 0.070 levels respectively. Results of these calculations are shown in Table 6.1.

Appendix C.3.
Calculation of Associate
Effectiveness Score

Reasons given for selecting associates were examined against the importance and effectiveness which were later attributed to these partners. These reasons were significantly related to both of these variables (at the 0.025 level for importance, and the 0.004 level for effectiveness), but the high proportion of strongly favorable responses in most categories limited the sensitivity of the measurement. In order to provide an overall basis for comparison of the effectiveness of associates according to the basis for their selection, a value was assigned to each different effectiveness response. A positive statement was scored as plus one, a neutral response was valued as zero, while a negative response was given a value of minus one. A weighted effectiveness score was then calculated for each group of associates, classified by the reason for selection, according to this formula:

$$\text{Weighted effectiveness score for each group} = \frac{\sum x_i - \sum z_i}{N_i}$$

where a positive response $= x$, a neutral response $= y$, a negative response $= z$, and where the subscript i varied according to the reason for the selection of associates, and

$$N_i = \sum (x_i + y_i + z_i)$$

The effectiveness score was then plotted against each selection criterion as shown in Figure 3.2.

Appendix D.
List of Industries in Which the Government of India Would Consider the Investment of Private Foreign Capital in Joint Ventures

1. Iron and steel structurals
2. Iron and steel castings and forgings
3. Iron and steel pipes
4. Special steels
5. Nonferrous metals and alloys
6. Boilers and steam generating plants
7. Equipment for transmission and distribution of electricity
8. Furnaces
9. Marine diesel engines
10. Industrial machinery, including major items of specialized equipment used in specific industries, and general items of machinery used in several industries, such as equipment required for various unit processes
11. Ball, roller, and taper bearings
12. Speed reduction units
13. Machine tools
14. Tractors, earth-moving and construction machinery
15. Plastics
16. Industrial and scientific instruments
17. Fertilizers
18. Organic chemicals
19. Fine chemicals and intermediates
20. Industrial explosives
21. Industrial gases
22. Agricultural chemicals such as insecticides
23. Dyestuffs and drugs, including the production of basic intermediates
24. Newsprint
25. Pulp
26. Hotels

(*Source:* Government of India, Press Note, 8th May 1961.)

Appendix E.
Suggestions for Further Research

The various subjects discussed at various stages in the text as requiring further research are summarized below. The issues involved have been described in context earlier; therefore the discussion is not repeated, and the topics are merely listed, together with the appropriate chapter number (in parentheses), for convenience in reference.

1. Examination of international variations in production functions, in order to determine a scale of technological complexity that would provide an adequate basis for comparison between and within industries and across international boundaries. (Chapter 5)
2. Relationships between level of technology and size of companies investing abroad, to determine in particular the extent to which more advanced technology may tend to be a corporate asset of larger firms among such overseas investors. (Chapter 4)
3. Relative primacy, in terms of ability to attract loan capital to an overseas joint venture, of the characteristics of
   a. The foreign partner,
   b. The local associate,
   c. The project itself. (Chapter 4)
4. Definition of the procedures through which evaluation criteria are set up for overseas investments, especially in joint ventures. (Chapter 4)
5. The extent to which the issues of reinvestment and of increasing investment in joint ventures actually (as opposed to being said to) create major conflicts between partners. With particular reference to the case of 50–50 joint ventures. (Chapter 5)
6. Examination of a possible correlation between the closeness of intraindustry juxtaposition in location and strength of frictional effects and dislike among direct competitors. (Chapter 5)
7. Establishment, in definitive and preferably quantitative terms, of the relative importance of different patterns of evolution and strategies in overseas investment. With special attention to any subsets leading to joint ventures. (Chapter 5)

8. Examination of relative productivity, wage rates, living standards, levels of employment, and work force satisfaction in different areas of India and Pakistan, in order to determine whether the regional differences alleged to exist are in fact significant for foreign investors. (Chapter 6)
9. Classification of the methods through which required levels of effective control over joint ventures are achieved. Definition of possible relationships between the profitability of investment in a joint venture and
    a. The level of concern over control on the part of the foreign parent,
    b. The control actually achieved. (Chapter 7)
10. Definition of the motivations involved in selecting joint venture associates, the object being to develop an operational typology, based on the results of interdisciplinary examination of socio-cultural and psychological aspects of motivation, as well as the more apparent political and economic motivations. (Chapter 3)
11. Examination of the relative profitability for foreign investors of joint ventures, as compared with subsidiary or branch types of overseas operations. (Chapter 3)

Finally, as stressed earlier, repetition of the present study with different host countries and parent corporations of other nationalities would be useful in order to check
a. The validity of some of the generalizations put forward,
b. The wider applicability of the suggested model.
The general applicability and sensitivity of the analysis would also be rounded out and improved if a similar study could be carried out from the point of view of local associates in joint ventures.

BIBLIOGRAPHY

Books, Brochures, and Monographs

Aharoni, Yair. *The Foreign Investment Decision Process*. Boston: Division of Research, Graduate School of Business Administration, Harvard University, 1966.

Bain, Joe S. *International Differences in Industrial Structure, Eight Nations in the 1950s*. New Haven: Yale University Press, 1966.

Baranson, Jack. *Manufacturing Problems in India, The Cummins Diesel Experience*. Syracuse, N.Y.: Syracuse University Press, 1967.

Barna, Tibor. *Investment and Growth Policies in British Industrial Firms*. National Institute of Economic and Social Research, Occasional Papers No. 20. London: Cambridge University Press, 1962.

Basi, Raghbir S. *Determinants of United States Private Direct Investments in Foreign Countries*. Bureau of Economic and Business Research, Printed Series No. 3. Kent, Ohio: Kent State University, 1963.

Basu, S. K. *The Managing Agency System in Prospect and Retrospect*. Calcutta: World Press, 1958.

Bivens, Karen K., and Lovell, Enid B. *Joint Ventures With Foreign Partners, International Survey of Business Opinion and Experience*. New York: National Industrial Conference Board, 1966.

Blalock, Hubert M. *Social Statistics*. New York: McGraw-Hill, 1960.

Boeke, J. H. *Economics and Economic Policy of Dual Societies*. New York: Institute of Pacific Relations, 1963.

Bryson, George D. *Profits from Abroad—A Reveille for American Business*. New York: McGraw-Hill, 1964.

Buchanan, Daniel Houston. *The Development of Capitalistic Enterprise in India*. New York: Macmillan, 1934.

Clarke, W. M. *Private Enterprise in Developing Countries*. Oxford: Pergamon, 1966.

Coyle, John J., and Mock, Edward J., eds. *Readings in International Business*. Scranton, Pa.: International Textbook Company, 1965.

Das, Nabagopal. *The Public Sector in India*. New York: Asia Publishing House, 1961.

————, *Industrial Enterprise in India*. New York: Longmans, 1961.

Directory of Free World Enterprises and Collaborations in India, First Edition. New Delhi: Champaksons, 1966.

Farmer, Richard N. and Richman, Barry M. *Comparative Management and Economic Progress*. Homewood, Ill.: Irwin, 1965.

Fayerweather, John. *Management of International Operations*. New York: McGraw-Hill, 1960.

Fayerweather, John. *Facts and Fallacies of International Business.* New York: Holt, Rinehart and Winston, 1962.

Festinger, Leon. *A Theory of Cognitive Dissonance.* Stanford, Calif.: Stanford University Press, 1957.

Fforde, J. S. *An International Trade in Managerial Skills.* Oxford: Blackwells, 1957.

Foundation for Economic Research, University of Amsterdam. *Management of Direct Investment in Less-Developed Countries.* Leiden, 1957.

Friedmann, Wolfgang G., and Kalmanoff, George. *Joint International Business Ventures.* New York: Columbia University Press, 1961.

Gokhale Institute of Politics and Economics. *Notes on the Rise of the Business Communities in India.* New York: Institute of Pacific Relations, International Secretariat, 1951.

Hanson, A. H. *The Process of Planning—Survey of India's Five Year Plans, 1950–1964.* London: Oxford University Press, 1966.

Harbison, Frederick, and Myers, Charles A. *Education, Manpower and Economic Growth: Strategies of Human Resource Development.* New York: McGraw-Hill, 1964.

Harrison, Selig S. *India: The Most Dangerous Decades.* Princeton: Princeton University Press, 1960.

Hazari, R. K. *The Structure of the Corporate Private Sector, A Study of Concentration, Ownership and Control.* New York: Asia Publishing House, 1966.

Hirsch, Seev. *Location of Industry and International Competitiveness.* Oxford: Clarendon Press, 1967.

Hirschman, Albert O. *The Strategy of Economic Development.* New Haven: Yale University Press, 1958.

Hymer, Stephen. "The International Operations of National Firms, A Study of Direct Foreign Investment." Ph.D. dissertation in Economics, Massachusetts Institute of Technology, 1960.

Indian Investment Centre. *Investing In India.* New Delhi: Indian Investment Centre, 1962.

Jha, Shiva Chandra. *Studies in the Development of Capitalism in India.* Calcutta: Firma K.L. Mukhopadhyay, 1963.

Joshi, L. A. *The Control of Industry in India, A Study in Aspects of Combination and Concentration.* Bombay: Vora, 1965.

Katz, Daniel, and Kahn, Robert L. *The Social Psychology of Organizations.* New York: John Wiley & Sons, 1966.

Kendall, M. *Rank Correlation Methods.* New York: Hafner, 1955.

Kerr, Clark; Dunlop, John T.; Harbison, Frederick; and Myers, Charles A. *Industrialism and Industrial Man.* New York: Oxford University Press, 1960.

Kidron, Michael. *Foreign Investments in India.* London: Oxford University Press, 1965.

Kindleberger, Charles P. *International Economics.* 3rd ed. Homewood, Ill.: Irwin, 1963.

———. *Foreign Trade and the National Economy.* New Haven: Yale University Press, 1962.

Kothari, M. L. *Industrial Combinations, A Study of Managerial Integration in Indian Industries.* Allahabad: Chaitanya, 1967.

Kurian, K. M. *Impact of Foreign Capital on the Indian Economy.* New Delhi: Peoples Publishing House, 1966.

Kust, Matthew J. *Foreign Enterprise in India.* Chapel Hill: University of North Carolina Press, 1964.

————. *Supplement to Foreign Enterprise in India.* Chapel Hill: University of North Carolina Press, 1966.

Kuznets, S. *Economic Change.* New York: W. W. Norton, 1953.

Lerner, Daniel. *The Passing of Traditional Society.* New York: Free Press of Glencoe, 1958.

Levin, J. V. *The Export Economies, Their Patterns of Development in Historical Perspective.* Cambridge, Mass.: Harvard University Press, 1960.

Lewis, W. A. *The Theory of Economic Growth.* Homewood, Ill.: Irwin, 1955.

Liander, Bertil, ed. *Comparative Analysis for International Marketing.* Boston: Allyn & Bacon, 1967.

Liebenstein, Harvey. *Economic Backwardness and Economic Growth.* New York: John Wiley & Sons, 1957.

McMillan, Claude; Gonzales, R. F.; and Erickson, L. G. *International Enterprise in a Developing Economy.* East Lansing, Mich.: Michigan State University, 1964.

Malenbaum, Wilfred. *Prospects for Indian Development.* New York: Free Press of Glencoe, 1962.

March, James G., and Simon, Herbert A. *Organizations.* New York: John Wiley & Sons, 1958.

Mamoria, C. B. *Organization and Financing of Industries in India.* Allahabad: Kitab Mahal, 1960.

Martyn, Howe. *International Business, Principles and Problems.* New York: Free Press of Glenoe, 1964.

Mason, Edward. *Economic Development in India and Pakistan.* Occasional Papers in International Affairs, No. 13, September 1966, Cambridge, Mass.: Center for International Affairs, Harvard University, 1966.

Mikesell, Raymond F., ed. *U.S. Private and Government Investment Abroad.* Eugene, Ore.: University of Oregon Books, 1962.

Mill, James, and Wilson, Horace H. *The History of British India.* London: Jones & Madden, 1844.

Millikan, Max F., and Blackmer, Donald L. M. *The Emerging Nations: Their Growth and United States Policy.* Boston: Little, Brown, 1961.

————, and Rostow, W. W. *A Proposal: Key to an Effective Foreign Policy.* New York, Harper, 1957.

Myint, Hla. *The Economics of the Developing Countries.* London: Hutchinson, 1965.

National Industrial Conference Board. *Obstacles and Incentives to Private Foreign Investment, 1962–1964.* New York: National Industrial Conference Board, 1965.

Namjoshi, M. V. *Monopolies in India, Policy Proposals for a Mixed Economy.* Bombay: Lalvani, 1966.

Nigam, R. K. *Managing Agencies in India (First Round: Basic Facts).* New Delhi: Government of India, Ministry of Commerce and Industry, Department of Company Law Administration, Research and Statistics, 1958.

Nurkse, Ragnar. *Problems of Capital Formation in Under-developed Countries.* New York: Oxford University Press, 1953.

Nyhart, J. D., and Janssens, Edmond F. *A Global Director of Development Finance Institutions in Developing Countries.* Paris: The Development Centre of the Organization for Economic Co-operation and Development, 1967.

Papanek, Gustav F. *Pakistan's Development, Social Goals and Private Incentives.* Cambridge, Mass.: Harvard University Press, 1967.

Parekh, H. T. *The Future of Joint-Stock Enterprise in India.* Bombay: Jaico Publishing House, 1958.

Patnaik, K. M. *Monetary Policy and Economic Development in India.* New Delhi: Chand & Co., 1967.

Prasad, Kendernath. *Technological Choice Under Development Planning.* New York: Asia Publishing House, 1963.

Reddaway, W. B. *Effects of U.K. Direct Investment Overseas, An Interim Report* and *Effects of U.K. Direct Investment Overseas Final Report.* University of Cambridge, Occasional Papers Nos. 12 and 15, Department of Applied Economics, London: Cambridge University Press, 1967, 1968.

Reserve Bank of India. *Report on the Census of India's Foreign Liabilities and Assets, June 1948.* Bombay, 1950.

————. *Survey of India's Foreign Liabilities and Assets, 1953.* Bombay, 1955.

————. *Survey of India's Foreign Liabilities and Assets, 1955.* Bombay, 1957.

Robinson, Harry J. *The Motivation and Flow of Private Foreign Investment.* Menlo Park, Calif.: International Development Center, Stanford Research Institute, 1961.

Robinson, Richard D. *Cases in International Business.* New York: Holt, Rinehart and Winston, 1962.

————. *International Business Policy.* New York: Holt, Rinehart and Winston, 1964.

————. *International Management.* New York: Holt, Rinehart and Winston, 1967.

Rosen, George. *Industrial Change in India—Industrial Growth, Capital Requirements and Technological Change, 1937–1955.* New York: Free Press of Glencoe, 1958.

————. *Some Aspects of Industrial Finance in India.* Bombay: Asia Publishing House, 1962.

Rostow, W. W. *The Stages of Economic Growth: A Non-Communist Manifesto.* London: Cambridge University Press, 1960.

Rowan, Sir Leslie; Loudon, J. H.; Campbell, Sir Jock; Gaitskell, Arthur; and Clarke, William. *Investment and Development—The Role of Private Investment in Developing Countries.* London: Overseas Development Institute, 1965.

Schlaifer, Robert O. *Probability and Statistics for Business Decisions.* New York: McGraw-Hill, 1959.

Shearer, J. C. *High Level Manpower in Overseas Operations.* Princeton: Princeton University Press, 1960.

Shell International Petroleum Company. "Aide Memoire on Pakistan." London: Shell, 1966.

Skinner, Wickham. *American Industry in Developing Economics, The Management of International Manufacturing.* New York: John Wiley & Sons, 1968.

Srivastava, P. K. *Foreign Collaboration in Indian Industry.* Agra: Agarwala, 1967.

Theobald, R. *Profit Potential in the Developing Countries.* New York: American Management Association, 1962.

Vernon, Raymond. *Manager in the International Economy.* Englewood Cliffs, N.J.: Prentice-Hall, 1968.

von Vorys, Karl. *Political Development in Pakistan*. Princeton: Princeton University Press, 1965.

Zinkin, Taya. *Challenges in India*. London: Chatto & Windus, 1966.

———. *Foreign Capital in India*. Pamphlet No. 11. New Delhi: Eastern Economist, 1951.

Articles, Chapters, Addresses, Papers, Periodicals

Aubrey, Henry G. "Investment Decisions in Under-developed Countries." In *Capital Formation and Economic Growth*. Princeton: National Bureau of Economic Research, 1955.

Behrman, Jack H. "Foreign Associates and Their Financing." In *U.S. Private and Government Investment Abroad*, edited by Raymond F. Mikesell. Eugene, Ore.: University of Oregon Books, 1962.

Bhambri, Ranjit Singh. "Myth and Reality About Private Investment in India." *World Politics,* January 1960.

Borrmann, W. A. "The Problem of Expatriate Personnel and Their Selection in International Enterprises." *Management International Review*, Vol. 8 (1968), No. 4/5.

Burmah Group Magazine. "The March of Sui Gas" and "Sui 1966." No. 5, Spring 1966.

Business International. "India's Major Private Sector Firms." 7 May 1965.

———. "Foreign Joint Ventures Raise Formidable Barrier to Flexible Worldwide Corporate Strategy." 4 September 1965.

Chenery, Hollis B. "Comparative Advantage and Development Policy." *American Economic Review*, Vol. 51 (1961), No. 1.

Cochran, W. G. "Some Methods for Strengthening Common Chi-Square Tests." *Biometrics*, Vol. 10 (1954), No. 4.

Economic Times. Bombay. Issues cited: 27 April 1963; 21 May 1963; 10 July 1962.

The Economist. "Advance in India." 25 March 1960.

Financial Times. London. Issues cited: 10 November 1965, 19 May 1967.

Goodman, Leo A., and Kruskal, William H. "Measures of Association for Cross-Classification." *Journal of the American Statistical Association*, Vol. 49 (1954), No. 268.

Haynes, Elliott. "New Patterns for Private Investment in Developing Countries." *International Development Review*, Vol. 7 (1965), No. 2.

Hazari, R. K. "The Managing Agency System: A Case for Its Abolition." *Economic Weekly,* Bombay, Annual Number, February 1964.

Howe, Russell Warren. "Man and Myth in Political Africa." *Foreign Affairs*, Vol. 46 (1968), No. 3.

Kapoor, Ashok. "Foreign Collaborations in India." *The Oriental Economist,* Vol. 36 (1968), No. 693.

Kindleberger, Charles P. "Public Policy and the International Corporation." Statement submitted to *Hearings on "Foreign Trade and the Anti-Trust Laws,"* of the Sub-committee on Anti-trust and Monopoly of the Committee on the Judiciary, United States Senate, 27 April 1966.

Kust, Matthew J. "U.S. Aid to India—How Much is Enough." *The New Republic,* 15 December 1958.

Lewin, Kurt. "Group Decision and Social Change." In *Readings in Social Psychology,* edited by Theodore M. Newcomb and Eugene L. Hartley. New York: Holt, Rinehart and Winston, 1947.

Magee, John F. "Decision Trees for Decision Making." *Harvard Business Review*, July/August 1964.
———. "How to Use Decision Trees in Capital Investment." *Harvard Business Review*, September/October 1964.
Mani, R. S. "Strategy of Secondary Industries." *All-India Congress Committee Economic Review*, 10 November 1964.
Millikan, Max F. "India in Transition, Economic Development: Performance and Prospects." *Foreign Affairs*, Vol. 46 (1968), No. 3.
Mukerjee, Dilip. "India in Transition, Politics of Manoeuvre." *Foreign Affairs*, Vol. 46 (1968), No. 3.
Myint, Hla. "An Interpretation of Economic Backwardness." *Oxford Economic Papers*, June 1954.
Nurske, Ragnar. "Some International Aspects of the Problem of Economic Development." *American Economic Review*, Vol. 42 (1952), No. 2.
Powell, H. A. R. "Why Operate Overseas." *Planning and Managing an Overseas Business*. London: British Institute of Management, 1966.
Reserve Bank of India. "Returns on Foreign Investments in India." *Reserve Bank of India Bulletin*, May 1958.
———. "India's International Investment Position in 1963–1964 and 1964–1965." *Reserve Bank of India Bulletin*, Vol. 21 (1967), No. 1.
Robinson, Richard D. "Inter-relationship of Business Enterprise and Political Development." *The Business History Review*, Autumn 1962.
Rosen, George. "Problems of Private Investment in India by American Firms." In *American Trade With Asia and The Far East*, edited by Robert J. Barr. Milwaukee: Marquette University Press, 1959.
Rosenstein-Rodan, P. N. "Problems of Industrialization of Eastern and South-Eastern Europe." *Economic Journal*, Vol. 53 (1943), No. 210.
———. "Notes on the Theory of the Big Push," a paper submitted to the Rio Roundtable of the International Economic Association, 1957. Mimeographed.
Singh, B. K. "Incentives in the Indian Tax System." *All-India Congress Committee Economic Review*, 25 November 1964.
Sommer, R. H. "A New Asymmetric Measure of Association for Ordinal Variables." *American Sociological Review*, Vol. 27 (1962), No. 6.
Stern, Walter P. "U.S. Direct Investments Abroad." *Financial Analysts Journal*, January/February 1965.
Upadhyay, K. M. "Foreign Investments in India and New Capital Issues." *All-India Congress Committee Economic Review*, 25 July 1964.
Vernon, Raymond. "International Trade and International Investment in the Product Cycle." *Quarterly Journal of Economics*, Vol. LXXX (May 1966).
Williams, Simon. "Negotiating Investment in Emerging Countries." *Harvard Business Review*, January/February 1965.

Government Publications and Records

Government of India:

Capital Issues (Application for Consent) Rules, 1954.
Capital Issues Control Act, 1947. Section 12 cited.
Finance Act of 1966. Section 10(6) (vii) cited.
General Clauses Act. Section 3(42) cited.

Indian Companies Act 1956, as amended. Sections cited: Schedule 1, Table A; Sec. 4(7); Sec. 2(26).

Indian Constitution. Articles cited: Article 19(1) (f); Article 37.

Indian Income Tax Act, 1961.

Industrial Policy Resolution, 6 April 1948.

Industrial Policy Resolution, 30 April 1956.

An Outline of Direct Taxes in India, Ministry of Finance, 1960.

Press Note on Foreign Capital, 8 May 1961.

Prime Minister of India, *Policy Statement to Parliament on Foreign Capital,* 6 April 1949.

Report of the Managing Agency Inquiry Committee, 3 May 1966.

Tariff Commission, *Report on the Fair Prices of Rubber Tyres and Tubes,* 1955.

Government of Pakistan:

Industrial Policy Statement, 1948.

Industrial Policy Statement, 1958.

INDEX